Hope Without Hope

Rojava and Revolutionary Commitment

by
Matt Broomfield

Foreword by John Holloway

Hope Without Hope

Rojava and Revolutionary Commitment

by
Matt Broomfield

Foreword by John Holloway

AK
PRESS

Hope Without Hope: Rojava and Revolutionary Commitment

© 2025 Matt Broomfield
Foreword © 2025 John Holloway
This edition 2025 © AK Press
ISBN: 978-1-84935-566-7 (paper)
ISBN: 978-1-84935-567-4 (e-book)
Library of Congress Control Number: 2024949072

AK Press
370 Ryan Ave. #100
Chico, CA 95973
www.akpress.org
akpress@akpress.org

AK Press
33 Tower St.
Edinburgh EH6 7BN
Scotland
www.akuk.com
akuk@akpress.org

The above addresses would be delighted to provide you with the latest AK Press
distribution catalog, which features books, pamphlets, zines, and stylish apparel
published and/or distributed by AK Press. Alternatively, visit our websites for the
complete catalog, latest news, and secure ordering.

Cover design by Zachary Dean Norman
Cover image from Kurdishstruggle (https://www.flickr.com/photos/kurdishstruggle)
used with permission by CC by 2.0 license
Printed in the USA on acid-free paper

For Nazim Daştan, Cîhan Bilgin,
and all the other journalists targeted, killed, and incarcerated
for reporting on the Rojava Revolution.

When Pandora opened her box, she let loose all the evils into the world. Terrified, she slammed it shut, but hope remained inside. Rojava is like the hope that is hidden in the Pandora's box of the Middle East.
—Asya Abdullah, senior Syrian Kurdish politician, *Revolution in Rojava*, 2016

Man . . . knows not that the box which Pandora brought was a box of evils. Hence he looks upon the one evil still remaining as the greatest source of happiness—it is hope . . . in truth, the greatest of evils for it lengthens the ordeal of man.
—Friedrich Nietzsche, *Human, All Too Human*, 1876

The second version of the Pandora myth is surely the only true one; hope is the good thing that remains for men, which has in no way already ripened but which has also in no way been destroyed.
—Ernst Bloch, *The Principle of Hope*, 1954

Contents

Hope Without Hope

Foreword

by John Holloway

"In the days leading up to Turkey's first airstrikes we raced throughout Rojava," Matt Broomfield writes, "electrified by nervous energy, frantically organizing on a dozen fronts at once, knowing our efforts could never prove sufficient to resist the coming storm: and yet it was in these days we felt bound by a particular, defiant spirit of resistance, profound because it was pointless, engendering an absurd hope the enemy could never eradicate, never even understand." This book is exciting. It's an extremely knowledgeable, committed, and critical analysis of the Kurdish independence movement in Rojava and a profound, theoretically engaged meditation on the meaning of hope. Above all, it's an in-your-face challenge to those of us who want to think and do revolution today.

Matt Broomfield returns from several years volunteering as a journalist in Rojava and reflects upon his experience there. He reflects on the reality and beauty and contradictions of that revolutionary movement, reflects upon what lessons can be learnt by the anarcho-revolutionary Left in the West. He reflects, above all, on what hope can mean in a situation in which there appears to be, and probably *is*, no ground for hope at all. And that exploration takes him through the function of hope after Auschwitz, hope after death, hope and climate catastrophe. It takes him deep into *absurdist hope*, the hope of no-hope. Hope without hope. This is not just "hope in hopeless times" but something much harsher, much darker. It's not a question of desperately trying to find a way out but of accepting that there is no way out and yet still hoping.

Hope Without Hope is astute and disturbing but a great read, always engaging, always relating difficult theoretical questions to lived experience. Matt's firsthand experience is ever-present, but the book is not a narrative of his time among the militant Kurdish movement. It's more a "How do I live with what I've lived through? How do I turn what I have lived into something enriching and unsettling and stimulating for others?" His weaving of observation and contemplation makes for a very powerful and rewarding book. My own experience is very different: I sit at my desk and think about anti-capitalist hope, a hope that gropes its way forward; for me, the hope-of-no-hope is a madness that threatens all the time. But it is not a *necessary* insanity rooted in my own lived experience, as it was for Matt. Hope is inevitably an anguished hope-against-hope, but Matt takes that much further, drawing not just on Bloch but on Agamben, Camus, Kierkegaard, and many others to develop his definition of absurdist hope: "Absurdist thought is of profound relevance to our project here—a re-politicized effort to make sense of our own, ridiculous striving for a better, socialist world, even though we fear, believe, know that no such better world can be achieved."

I read *Hope Without Hope* with enormous respect and feel very greatly honored to have been asked to write a short foreword. I do not share the absurdism of a hope-of-no-hope—but I certainly feel it as a huge tsunami hanging over me, threatening to wash me and all of us away. It is a terrifying wave that has been growing and growing and growing: a wave of defeat, of meaninglessness, of lost dreams, a wave of unspeakable living and dying. Matt has the courage to take us into that world with its reduction of humanity to "bare life" and say, "And yet …"

And yet, there is something that remains, a hope that remains standing in no-hope: "The distinction here, between the fact that people have no choice but to live in the jaws of death and the fact they walk proudly into them with banners streaming, is crucial. It reinvests their excluded status with agency. Even and especially when all life is stripped away, there is something left over."

This is an important book, and it is likely to grow in importance as the world grows darker and the jaws of death come closer.

Thank you, Matt.

Introduction

An Absurd Utopia

On the eve of battle against Turkey, Kurdish fighters gather round a smartphone, tarnished AK-47s slung over skinny shoulders. These men aren't supposed to own phones, but they all have contraband Alcatels anyway, using them mostly to fill the long, dull interludes between combat by playing combat games.

The clip they are watching is popular here in Rojava, or Syrian Kurdistan. In a scene from the blood-spattered blockbuster *300*, we witness the run-up to the Spartan resistance against the Persian invasion at Thermopylae. Spartan warriors beat swords on shields, preparing for certain death. The Kurdish militants likewise stamp their feet on the earth behind the berm and chant, wordlessly, in unison.

Within a week, I think to myself, some of these men will be dead.

In the film as in the legend, the Spartans are also subsequently slaughtered. But no matter. There's a perverse optimism to the way in which dubbed Hollywood clips circulate through Syrian Kurdish WhatsApp groups, wrenched out of context and deployed in support of whatever political, military, or (perhaps more often) romantic ideal the viewer has in mind.

It's little wonder the region's Kurdish-led revolutionary forces feel an affinity with the embattled Spartans. In the face of crises set to define the coming century—proxy conflict, resource competition, state collapse, climate catastrophe—their movement has produced an unexpected and utopian response, striving to implement a unique form of direct-democratic, women-led, multiethnic governance. Yet even after liberating millions of Syrians from the brutal, misogynist, theofascist rule of the Islamic State of Iraq and the Levant (ISIS), they must perpetually battle repeated Turkish military operations aimed at extinguishing these fragile victories. Turkey has American warplanes, German tanks, the second-largest army in NATO, proxy militias packed with former ISIS fighters. The Kurdish revolutionaries have nothing save their rusty AK-47s and a handful of bleak myths, into which they read cause for hope.

These militants follow the intellectual and philosophical lead of jailed Kurdish leader Abdullah Öcalan and his Kurdistan Workers' Party (PKK). In theory and practice, in extremis and in their unexpected revolutionary triumph, the broader cluster of parties, armed groups, and civil society organizations inspired by Öcalan's PKK and collectively known as the Kurdish freedom movement has proven itself capable of finding, maintaining, and organizing hope throughout political crisis and social catastrophe. It was in response to historic defeats suffered by the PKK during the broader post-1989 collapse of state socialism that Öcalan initially developed his bold political program of grassroots democracy, women's autonomy, and minority rights. Similarly, it was the catastrophe of the Syrian Civil War (beginning in 2011) that enabled his movement to put this program into practice, following the outbreak of what is now known as the Rojava Revolution (2012).

By answering defeat with a revolutionary faith in transformation, the Kurdish movement and its foot soldiers place themselves in a particular tradition of anti-fascist and anti-colonial resistance, absurdist philosophy, and radical thought. This current of hope without hope flows unseen through the millennia to explode into the world as revolutionary fervor bound up with madness, self-delusion and self-sacrifice; as dogged resistance in the face of savage colonial violence and omnipotent, omnipresent, state-backed neoliberal hegemony; as the mystic, utopian socialist horizon that has long justified the most grueling, mundane political organization.

Though it sometimes seems otherwise, this strange, backward hope hasn't been extinguished by the dead weight of late-capitalist hegemony. During three years living and working in Rojava, I found this spirit alive and well, surviving thousands of years after the noble defeat at Thermopylae on that smartphone screen cracked like a fallen Spartan shield. And we may also follow this current down to our own diverse struggles, communities, and movements, equipping us to shoulder our own revolutionary tasks in a similar spirit of grim defiance.

The Rojava Revolution: Victory amid Defeats

Just like many of our other diverse movements across the global Left, the Kurdish movement has spent the past three decades reckoning with bloody repression, fragmentation, and above all a despairing sense that mass social transformation is no longer possible in the twenty-first century.

The Rojava Revolution is not merely a fascinating experiment or utopian outlier but directly bound up in global crises affecting us all. The Arab Spring wave of pro-democratic protests that engulfed the Middle East in 2011 is commonly seen as having resulted in widespread defeat, repression, and exploitation by both authoritarian governments and jihadist Islamists. This so-called Arab Winter brought terrible suffering to Syria, where dictator Bashar al-Assad crushed a nationwide civil uprising at the cost of up to 500,000 lives. This facilitated the rapid takeover of the opposition by state-backed jihadist groups, a shift that would ultimately culminate in Assad's 2024 deposition by an authoritarian al-Qaeda offshoot, Hay'at Tahrir al-Sham (HTS). Yet it was through these very uprisings that the Kurdish movement sought to revolutionize society throughout northern Syria, claiming to implement the unique system of grassroots, municipal governance they call democratic confederalism.

In the course of this revolution, Kurdish militants have battled not only drone strikes and ethnic cleansing, but also the same challenges faced by many of us on the global Left each day: pessimism, despair, suicide. Yet the existential nature of this struggle, the repeated losses and terrible sacrifices, enabled the Kurdish movement to unite four million Kurds, Arabs, and ethnic minority Christians and Yazidis. This tentative and unexpected multiethnic polity is formally known as the Autonomous Administration of North and East Syria, or AANES.

The Rojava Revolution can therefore arguably be understood as the most successful inheritor not only of the Arab Spring, but also the broader global movement in which popular, grassroots movements sought democratic reform from South America to the Middle East to East Asia, from Occupy Wall Street to Turkey's Gezi Park to Egypt's Tahrir Square.

To many on the anarchist, feminist, and internationalist Left, Rojava's revolution perhaps seemed a miracle, too good to be true—or else smart propaganda, masking more cynical aspirations. For as the Spartan idea has been co-opted by Jacobin republicans, militarist patriots, alt-right ethno-purists, and communist guerrillas alike (often choosing to forget the ultimate defeat at Thermopylae), various ideological forces also seek to co-opt the Rojava Revolution.

The world knows the Kurdish movement best through the stereotyped, Orientalized figure of the Kurdish female warrior, typically represented as the champion of women's rights and (liberal) democracy against the dark tide of ISIS. But this unwanted, caricatured image was thrust on Rojava after the US offered Syrian Kurdish units limited practical support during their war against ISIS, while simultaneously seeking to undermine their attempted ideological transformation of society. It diverges sharply from the Kurdish movement's own conception of an anti-fascist, anti-statist struggle against both Turkey and the genocidal Islamic "State."

More broadly, international observers understand, study, and caricature Rojava in profoundly contradictory ways. To some on the Left, the Kurds are imperialist US puppets; to others, cultish communists, ethno-nationalist separatists or grasping opportunists; to their supporters, the instigators of our century's first genuine revolution, and the first ever to achieve such large-scale and long-lasting gains while espousing anti-statist principles.

In theory, democratic confederalism consists of bottom-up municipal governance, a cooperative-based economy, autonomy for women and minorities, and a radically rejuvenated relationship to nature—not only in Rojava (Syrian-occupied Kurdistan) but throughout the Turkish-, Iraqi-, and Iranian-occupied regions of Kurdistan; the wider Middle East; and ultimately the world. Regardless of whether this ambitious political program is itself a sufficient response to regional, global, and climate catastrophe, the movement's own representatives are the first to admit that initial successes in Rojava remain imperfect and compromised. Massive social gains for women long excluded from society and the unexpected transformation of the democratic process to include social groups previously at loggerheads with the leftist Kurdish movement have yet to be matched by parallel economic and ecological developments, with the region suffering the ravages of long-term armed conflict, economic collapse, and isolation.

The reasons for this are complex, but the difficult revolutionary experience that the Kurdish movement has undergone over the past decade must challenge any crude, simplistic, utopian hope. Rojava has often been viewed in isolated terms as a sort of anarchist Paris Commune, an unexpected and fleeting irruption of revolutionary hope. But the revolutionary project deserves the seriousness of critiques that contextualize it in a complex, long-term terrain of striving between minorities and chauvinist nation-states, women and patriarchal elders, villages and centralized economies. While espousing a radical anti-statist ideology, existential military threats mean the movement has been forced into tactical yet potentially compromising relations with authoritarian and imperial national, regional, and international powers, creating further contradictions that must be analyzed as part of the revolutionary process rather than swept out of view.

The Kurdish movement's experience demonstrates that we can't wait patiently below the banner of an imagined revolution but must rather begin the messy, patient, grueling, day-to-day work of organization—without losing sight of that revolutionary horizon. And this is precisely why the Rojava Revolution can offer invaluable psychological and organizational lessons to a global Left in crisis.

World War III

The Syrian Civil War, it's becoming increasingly clear, is this century's equivalent of the Spanish Civil War. It has prefigured an emergent and still poorly understood global conflict, just as that struggle between ascendant fascist forces and a doomed yet courageous socialist opposition prefigured the slaughter of World War II. The coming international confrontation, which Öcalan has long described as World War III, is set to be defined by factors that already marked the Syrian conflict, namely proxy warfare; resource competition; state collapse; mass displacement; political shockwaves emanating from the Middle East to shake the centers of imperial power; the potential disintegration of the liberal, US-led leviathan known as the "rules-based international order"; Islamist, right-nationalist, or even Christofascist militancy as the main vector of resistance to the authoritarian state; the simultaneous statist exploitation of these reactionary forces; all of it precipitated by rising temperatures, desertification, failed harvests, and the weaponization of water resources.

This global crisis certainly demands an effective, internationalist Left, capable of organizing global resistance and exploiting the opportunities brought about by coming sociopolitical crises—as European communist movements reached their closest moment of triumph in the aftermath of World War I or socialist, nationalist, and liberal forces formed alliances capable of defeating fascism in World War II.

But no internationalist movement has yet emerged to respond to our era of pandemics, climate catastrophe, and resurgent state conflict. As recent theorists (Asef Bayat, Vincent Bevins, Rodrigro Nunes, Arthur Borriello, and Anton Jäger) have variously argued, the Arab Spring, subsequent pan-continental protest movements, and brief flourishing of social-democratic left populism were all undone by organizational and strategic shortcomings.[1] Throughout what Bevins calls the decade of the "missing revolution," a repoliticized spirit of often reckless resistance and desire for revolutionary change has not been organized into significant material victories. Millions have squandered their own hopeless hope at the ballot box (particularly in the Anglosphere and Western Europe), on barricades (particularly in South America and East Asia), or under a hail of bullets (particularly in the Middle East).

Three decades ago, many on the Left hoped the collapse of the USSR would clear the way for new, networked, horizontalist modes of political organization capable of mounting an effective, novel challenge to seemingly triumphant neoliberal capitalism. That hasn't happened. Neither anarchists, social democrats, communists, nor emergent networks of feminist or Indigenous organization have proven able to do this resurgent spirit of revolutionary commitment justice by shaping it into a force capable of shaking the centers of imperial-capitalist power.

As Israel's genocidal 2023 war in Gaza has painfully shown, the world waits in vain for a resurgent, militant internationalism genuinely capable of resisting authoritarian state violence in the Middle East and worldwide. Back in 1982, the Kurdish movement lost its first militants fighting Israel alongside leftist Palestinian guerrillas. But today, Turkey's President Erdoğan cynically exploits Palestinian suffering while enjoying backdoor trade relations with Israel. Ankara and Tel Aviv, the West's two key authoritarian allies in the region, are now striving to dominate the fragmented new Syria, simultaneously working to prevent any broader internationalist movement from developing that might counteract their growing influence throughout the Middle East.

In the spirit of clear-eyed self-criticism, a rejuvenating practice promoted by the Kurdish movement as a tonic to personal and political complacency, defeatism, and paralysis, those scattered global left movements still resisting capitalist hegemony must name our failures. Perhaps you have experienced a numbing mixture of exhaustion, grief, boredom, and anger after running into one of the following dead ends:

- The collapse of the USSR, Third World, and Non-Aligned socialism, and the subsequent absence of even an imperfect state alternative to global capitalist hegemony;
- The exhaustion of a generation's rage in fruitless street protests, from Occupy to the Arab Spring to Black Lives Matter to Extinction Rebellion;
- The failure of the diverse Corbyn (UK), Sanders (US), Mélenchon (France), Podemos (Spain), and Syriza (Greece) left populist movements toward parliamentary social democracy, all already limited and self-censored, yet rapidly crushed regardless by media hegemony and neoliberal technocracy;
- The tragic impossibility of activism, solidarity, and protest proving sufficient to halt ethnic cleansing in Palestine, Kurdistan, Sudan, and elsewhere;

- The naive utopianism that idealizes both the Rebel Zapatista Autonomous Municipalities in southern Mexico and the Rojava Revolution itself, while ignoring the impossibility of transferring these models to other (Western) geopolitical contexts;
- The revolutionary rhetoric used to mask reformist social-democratic or liberal identity politics—styling Corbyn or Sanders as communists, meeting crises we cannot solve with incongruous slogans proclaiming their imminent collapse ("Queer solidarity smashes borders," and so on);
- The endless, fatalist deferrals of Marxist organization following the collapse of mass state-socialist politics, reducing the West's Marxist-Leninist parties to tiny husks leafleting and marching for a revolution that will never come;
- The parallel, equally fatalist defeatism of anarchist retreat into a purely horizontal, prefigurative politics, content to place humanitarian band-aids on the wounds of the housing, migrant, climate, and social justice crises rather than seeking macropolitical solutions;
- The worsening displacement of suffering onto subaltern classes outside the imperial-capitalist core through resource extraction and the globalization of labor, in a crisis to which no theory of an automated, post-scarcity politics has given meaningful response;
- The ghoulish realization that this logic will continue its all-consuming creep through the slow imperialist capture of space, as the future is surrendered to Elon Musk and his ilk;
- The defeated expectation that protests, riots, squats, and occupations could themselves constitute sites of genuinely emancipatory potential;
- The Left's feeble response to the Coronavirus pandemic, and the immediate flight of nominal anti-statists into the arms of reactionary governance;
- And most of all, the imminent climate apocalypse, which both worsens all these challenges and exceeds them, posing a universal challenge to a universally unprepared Left.

Individual movements, uprisings, and communities may have achieved fleeting or local victories. But there is no point in downplaying the general failure of the international Left to pose meaningful mass opposition to state-sanctioned capitalist hegemony—not in a single state worldwide. Yet global capitalist hegemony, by its very nature, requires a global solution. Each failure reminds us of the bitter irony that *u-topia* is, etymologically, a "non-place."

No wonder so many of us feel defeated. And yet we continue to struggle for a better world, even a world we cannot believe in. How do we manage it? How is it we strive longer, harder, and more boldly than those liberal progressives who claim to hold more optimistic outlooks for the future? How is it that the hopeless still hope?

For if the Kurdish movement offers a superlative example of revolutionary commitment in hopeless circumstances, this same spirit also animates a thousand smaller land struggles, picket lines, rent strikes, and Indigenous insurgencies worldwide. Each day, admittedly weak and localized forces still somehow find the courage to withstand hegemonic capitalist powers they stand virtually no chance of overthrowing.

If there's no point in deceiving ourselves over the hitherto limited nature of our victories, therefore, neither is there any point in wallowing in an equally stultifying defeatism. Whereas the homogenizing nature of what the Kurdish movement calls capitalist modernity seeks to fragment and atomize our political struggles and social movements, this movement simultaneously believes that "the more organized society is, the stronger the struggle will be."[2] Hence Öcalan's demand for a "democratic modernity" to countermand capitalist modernity, in which "all anti-systemic forces [are] developed into a democratic-confederal organizational system at the local, regional and global levels."[3] Anything less, to the Kurdish movement, is a pessimistic abdication of duty.

The Kurdish movement has reckoned with its own defeats as part of complex strategic efforts to build up a radical alternative, learning from both the fatal internal contradictions of top-down state socialism and the proven organizational weakness of bottom-up anarchist organization. Can our movements do the same, deriving further lessons from the Kurdish movement's own historic defeats, battlefield triumphs, and ongoing struggles?

Beyond Left Melancholy

While working in Rojava as a freelance journalist and cofounder of a news and research center connecting the global media with sources on the ground, I was fortunate to travel throughout northern Syria, visiting each major city, countless villages, the military frontlines, communes, cooperatives, reconciliation committees, refugee camps, destitute neighborhoods, ISIS detention centers, diplomatic negotiations, and community meetings. I spoke with thousands of people: poets, journalists, teachers, bureaucrats, opposition figures, military commanders, rank-and-file combatants, captured ISIS fighters, international volunteers, US military personnel, students, workers, children, and mothers.

Drawing on these conversations and observations, chapter 1 will show how the Kurdish movement has drawn on the bloodshed of the horrific Syrian conflict to unite its followers. While the movement has been forced to replicate statist political logic and thus move away from its original vision of a bottom-up "commune of communes," it has responded productively to social fragmentation between communities recently at war to inspire the continued reform of its direct-democratic system. The movement has sought unexpected and often productive balances between localized dual-power projects and effective geopolitical strategy fit for World War III; between as pragmatic spirit of compromise enabling it to feed and protect millions, and a serious ideological commitment to eradicating statist hierarchy. In chapter 2, we'll further assess how the Kurdish movement has reaped the political benefits of its permanent exclusion from state power, drawing a parallel with the starkly contrasting victories won by ISIS to argue it's the Kurdish movement that models a truly radical alternative to authoritarian state governance.

These lessons are deeply relevant to the contemporary Left. Our repeated, recent worldwide failures demonstrate that our horizontalist-anarchist, verticalist-socialist, and party-populist movements are suffering from diverse species of what Walter Benjamin identified as left melancholy. This melancholy manifests as a persistent attachment to tried-and-failed forms of political organization, in order to avoid working through the consequences of the Left's historic defeat.

For the Marxist Left, this might mean indulging in the glorification of a vanished past when state socialism still presented a serious, counter-hegemonic alternative to capitalism, rather than scrutinizing the internal contradictions which contributed to state-socialist collapse. For anarchists, it might mean clinging to proven-to-fail, naively horizontalist modes of organization, rather than reckoning with their failure to turn newfound global interest in anarchistic principles, values, and methods into material victories. Historic grievances notwithstanding, there's an uncanny parallel between the decentralized, anarchist Left and its centralized, party-focused counterpart, competing with one another in their fatalistic attachment to discredited organizational tactics.

Öcalan is generally known in anarchist circles for his critique of state socialism as inevitably leading to the consolidation of power in the hands of a national elite. But as many anarchist volunteers in Rojava have found to their surprise, he's also a powerful critic of what he characterizes as Western anarchist movements' often fatal Eurocentrism and individualism. For the Kurdish movement, a radical commitment to direct-democratic ideals in fact justifies an equally radical submission to revolutionary discipline. In chapter 3, we will therefore explore the organizational crisis faced by diverse global left movements to ask whether we could learn from the Kurdish movement's example and explore our own syntheses between a utopian, horizontalist commitment and practical, disciplined, day-to-day organization.

The Socialist Faith

Philosophers have long warned of hope's narcotic effect, by definition always unfulfilled, always doomed to disappointment. From Plato down to Friedrich Nietzsche, hope has long been an ambiguous value, best avoided by the wise—and religious hope for a better world most of all. But a stubborn refusal to relinquish that hope also recurs as mythic archetype, philosophical paradox, and revolutionary ideal.

There is thus also a long revolutionary tradition that recognizes socialism as akin to, evolving from, and the only possible substitute for this faith—taken up throughout the twentieth century by unorthodox

Marxists such as Walter Benjamin, Theodor Adorno, and Ernst Bloch. Understanding the Rojava Revolution therefore means analyzing how the Kurdish movement has fashioned and implemented a new, secular, socialist faith.

Öcalan's vision of history as standing or falling on the epochal victory of democratic confederalism aims to succeed and supplant the grand Marxist concept of history as leading inevitably to state-socialist revolution. Through this startlingly bold claim, the Kurdish movement thus also offers an alternative narrative to the capitalist myth of the end of history, which asserts there is now no alternative to neoliberal hegemony.

At the same time, Öcalan critiques the positivist, materialist tradition in Marxist thought as engendering an exploitative relationship to the natural world while centralizing power in the hands of a male elite. This has led the Kurdish women's movement to refuse a pragmatic, reform-minded politics as the preserve of men, instead following a political program that willfully transcends the pragmatic, rational, and literal.[4] In chapter 4, we'll ask how we could follow their example to reimagine history and create new narratives of social transformation, adapted to our own interlinked but separate struggles, likewise capable of motivating millions to respond to social collapse and climate catastrophe with a utopian, organized alternative.

When Öcalan promises that World War III will present Middle Eastern society with a radical, kill-or-cure crisis, he locates the Kurdish movement in the radical tradition of revolutionary millenarianism. Millenarian movements have long emerged at times of social upheaval, imperialist expansion or environmental collapse, as religious prophets and anti-colonial leaders promise an imminent apocalypse, pointing to earthly turmoil as a sign that human society is about to be revolutionized through divine intervention. In chapter 5, we'll explore how these diverse religious and secular movements have proven uniquely capable of motivating resistance to seemingly overwhelming centralized power, from the radical, dissenting Protestant tradition in Europe's religious wars, through waves of anti-colonial resistance across the Global South, to China's massive proto-socialist movements. Yet many millenarian movements have been dogged by reactionary violence and ultimate retreat into quietism, isolationism, or infighting. Can we learn from their experience to equip our own movements with a similarly radical sense of historic destiny fit for the climate apocalypse?

Self-Delusion

Even beyond these useful organizational and motivational practices, Rojava has yet more fundamental lessons to offer Western left movements on the psychological level—thus demonstrating the intimate link between commitment to a utopian, horizontal political goal and the potential renewal of mass organization. This book will therefore also examine the particular ideology and the related, psychological survival tactics that have equipped Kurdish militants to endure until that mysterious point where despair becomes its reverse.

After all, we all have our personal, often unexamined forms of faith. With varying degrees of self-awareness, we deliberately set aside rationality to rebel against the absurd meaninglessness of a chaotic universe, willfully choosing to believe that the next drink is going to make us feel good, that the weather simply must be better tomorrow, that our lottery ticket might come up. Politically, too, this rebellion against the absurd is a global phenomenon—we variously convince ourselves that our votes can make a difference, that we can battle climate change by sorting our recyclables, that protest march can halt genocide. On the most fundamental level, capitalist modernity only survives through our willing participation in the mass delusion that it offers us any realistic hope of self-improvement or a decent life.

This book will therefore explore the distinct social reality of the Rojava Revolution, as it is felt, lived, and believed in by the revolutionary class, Rojava's ordinary citizens, and internationalist militants. It will also address the corresponding despair these groups experience as the years of struggle wear on. And it will thereby ask the question: If we can and do deceive ourselves in service of capitalist hegemony, why not in service of revolution? In this light, the Left's much-maligned capacity for self-delusion becomes a strength. Throughout chapters 6 and 7, we'll explore the diverse forms of self-delusion that Kurdish and internationalist revolutionaries in Rojava deploy in pursuit of their own revolutionary goals: a reclaimed aesthetic sensibility, irony and gallows humor, selective forgetfulness, political resistance as sickness or madness, a radically collective political culture. And we'll ask which of these survival tactics could be adapted to equip us for our own thankless struggles. We will therefore also explore a rich philosophical and political tradition of willful self-delusion, from Prometheus and mythic trickster figures, through Nietzsche's radical critique of truth and recent research on the placebo effect, to the meta-modern trend of oscillation between ironic skepticism and sincere commitment, which critics have identified in contemporary culture.

The Revolutionary Leap of Faith

This radical politics, responding to crisis with a renewed and utopian commitment, is what chapter 7 will define as an absurdist socialism. In the absurdist philosophy of Albert Camus and his predecessor Søren Kierkegaard, life's apparent meaninglessness does not preclude but rather creates the necessity for the continued pursuit of meaning, in full knowledge of that task's hopelessness. As with the existential quest for meaning, so too with the socialist quest for a life worth living. Marx and Engels put it simply: it's only when the workers have nothing left to lose that they are driven to shed their chains.

In Rojava I observed both Kurdish and internationalist comrades consciously and unconsciously adopt absurdist positions, arguments, and self-justifications. They survived by willfully denying the reality of shocking violence and material challenges, professing themselves believers in inevitable, global democratic confederalist revolution. Like Camus, they ultimately found that "even within the limits of nihilism it is possible to find the means to proceed beyond nihilism."[5]

If society must feel itself approaching a kill-or-cure crisis in order to accept a truly transformative politics, individual revolutionaries must surely experience the same. In the early nineteenth century, the Christian existentialist philosopher Søren Kierkegaard argued that religious salvation could only be found in a "leap of faith" beyond all rationality. We cannot reason our way toward God, he argued. Faith can only be realized when one has the courage to admit any logical belief in God is absurd: "It is great to give up one's wish, but it is greater to hold it fast after having given it up."[6] Again, hope must begin from hopelessness.

There are lessons to be learned from both the Kurdish movement's naive new recruits and the occasional disaffected, sneering veteran. But the most effective militants are therefore those we'll identify as the "cynical idealists," capable of living out a similarly absurd commitment to revolutionary transformation each day, in simultaneous knowledge of the limited and contingent nature of their hopes.

Kierkegaard was writing in a Christian age, urging a moral devotion to godly ethics against the lure of individualism and aestheticism: yet as we'll see in chapter 8, a strikingly similar transformative sentiment is alive two centuries later among Rojava's secular revolutionary class. The Kurdish movement requires its militants to abandon personal possessions, family ties, and individual values to devote their lives wholly to the struggle, in a single, radical act that closely recalls Kierkegaard's notion of an instant of choice forever defining the life of any true religious believer.

Kierkegaard declared he would search the world to find someone capable of truly making this notional, philosophical "leap of faith."[7] We can only wonder what the philosopher would have made of Kurdish militants like Botan, who saw Turkey kill thirty-eight out of the forty comrades with whom she first underwent her training during decades of guerrilla war, only to descend from the mountains to find Öcalan's long-promised social revolution finally underway in Rojava. Having made her own desperate leap of faith and joined the revolutionary movement as a teenager, here she was finally landing, all those terrible sacrifices finally justified.

Just like the millenarian concept of history approaching imminent apocalypse, this intoxicating, all-or-nothing concept of revolutionary commitment is so powerful it must be handled with extreme care. This radical form of political commitment equipped a small band of Kurdish revolutionaries to stage a heroic resistance to ISIS in the city of Kobane. But it has likewise surely encouraged many would-be revolutionaries to shut their eyes to abuses, self-destructive tendencies, internal violence, and the counterproductive centralization of power, as indeed it has at points in the Kurdish movement's own history. We will therefore ask what it would take to engender such a radical spirit of commitment in our own social movements—while avoiding the pitfalls of a crude utopianism that justifies any and all suffering today on the basis of nominal revolution tomorrow. The Kurdish movement's own learning journey, concept of resistance, militant discipline, practice of criticism and self-criticism, and politicized concept of death and martyrdom can all help moderate these potential excesses.

Auschwitz and Apocalypse

The socialist leap of faith may help us endure the darkest days we face in our own contexts, lives, and struggles. But any contemporary attempt to find cause for hope must reckon with two catastrophes: the twentieth-century history of totalitarian, fascist, and anti-Semitic violence culminating in the Holocaust and the twenty-first-century future appearing to culminate in climate apocalypse. In chapters 9 and 10, we will explore how a dubious self-help industry emerged out of the ashes at Auschwitz, promising a simplistic, optimistic vision of hope as accessible to all. Repudiating this cynical appropriation of the Holocaust as moral exemplar, Jewish writers in the mystic-utopian socialist tradition have conversely struggled to find an absurdist hope-in-extremis even following the genocide their people suffered. They hold out socialist transformation as the only possible response, even as they doubt the very possibility of any such revolution under capitalist modernity. Through its conscious embrace of the Middle Eastern conflict as life-and-death existential struggle, the Kurdish movement similarly represents the genocide it faces as justification for its pursuit of a utopian alternative.

Handled with care, these examples can equip us to politicize our own response to interlinked contemporary and potential catastrophes, including the Western suicide epidemic, pandemics, mass global displacement, and genocides from Kurdistan to Palestine. In chapter 11, we will particularly ask what newfound forms of absurdist political commitment might emerge in response to the coming climate catastrophe. Climate disaster both opens a final possibility for and further imperils the hopes of revolutionary, global transformation—as in Syria, where Turkey is pumping the Euphrates River dry, imperiling millions of people living under the

AANES. The shock of climate catastrophe may well tear apart centers of statist power hitherto untroubled by decades of protest, but it's currently violent paramilitary nativism that seems poised to emerge from and exploit these crises, rather than any socialist or democratic confederalist alternative. By adopting an organized, absurdist, millenarian approach to the climate apocalypse, we can avoid the dead end of climate doom and defeatism and prepare our movements to meet this universal crisis.

The Revolutionary Commitment

The Kurdish movement's oft-repeated slogan that "resistance is life" and their insistence that "hope is more worthy than victory" do indeed mark an open confession of military, political, and material weakness.[8] But through this confession, the movement proves itself the inheritor of a particular spirit of melancholy resistance, one that has motivated socialist, anti-colonial and liberation movements throughout history. When there is nothing to fight for, we may as well fight for everything.

This is a movement whose jailed leader Öcalan has been formally denied what international law calls the universal "right to hope" for early release from his life sentence on an isolated prison island, even as he proves capable of inspiring hope in millions of people worldwide.[9] This is a movement whose militants claim to "love life so much they are willing to die for it," who through their understanding of revolutionary sacrifice derive hope from the very deaths of their dearest comrades.[10] There's a utopian spirit here that can only be reached in extremis, after passing through the darkest hours of repression.

The search for a cause worth believing in, a burning desire to meet revolutionaries still capable of truly radical political commitment, has already brought thousands of anarchist, communist, and internationalist volunteers to Rojava. Watching horribly wounded Kurdish comrades marching proudly at the head of mass demonstrations, meeting mothers holding aloft pictures of their slain children as they dared Turkish soldiers to gun them down, speaking with the young female survivors of ISIS's brutal violence who nonetheless managed to treat captured ISIS members with extraordinary compassion, Rojava's international friends and supporters understood this revolutionary commitment could only have emerged from conditions of true despair.

Or so it felt on the good days. More often, those struggling to defend Rojava's revolutionary gains were faced with the harsh reality that hopelessness does not necessarily alchemize into absurdist hope. Bitter ironies abounded. As soon as ISIS was defeated in 2019, the West turned its back on its nominal allies, denying the Kurdish "terrorists" any space in formal negotiations over Syria's future and giving the Turkish Armed Forces the green light for ethnic cleansing, in an operation Turkey perversely dubbed Peace Spring. Civilians pelted the withdrawing US military convoys with stones, hating these unwanted colonizers yet knowing their departure would pave the way for still worse atrocities. Kurdish fighters on the frontline sought to draw airstrikes onto their own positions, aiming to prove to a disinterested international community that Turkey *was* lying about the ceasefire it claimed to have implemented. Each day, the movement's partisans were reminded how cruel it is to hope in spite of admitted hopelessness.

But sometimes, spite is enough. The leap of faith is made from a zero point, a paradoxically freeing volte-face made in the dark, what Kierkegaard called the moment of "absolute resignation" which paves the way for our release into revolutionary conviction. This is why the Kurdish movement draws on the revolutionary theorist Frantz Fanon to celebrate the emancipating power of the first violent blow struck or bullet fired against the seemingly omnipotent colonial master, suddenly revealing his mortality. If we are able to experience the moment of seeming political or personal defeat as an opportunity for total renewal, we can turn the tables on our seemingly omnipotent oppressors.

To this end, the Kurdish movement's partisans offer a parable, part of the PKK's creation myth. As the PKK began its long struggle for self-determination in the 1980s, two of its militants—one male and one female—were captured, detained, tortured, and raped in Turkey's notorious Amed (Diyarbakır) prison. These two militants were thrust naked into a cell together, with the intent to humiliate them still further. But rather than looking at one another's nakedness, they held one another's gaze. The captured militants found the hope that can be won only when there is nowhere lower to sink. Their refusal to submit, their pride won through shame, made all the difference. This is hope without hope, and I caught glimpses of it in Rojava just as we can throughout the history of human struggle, against both political authoritarianism and the blind cruelty of existence itself.

Rojava is no ideal utopia. It's a concrete place, full of real people, true stories—and myths equally worth hearing. Global left movements can learn from its disappointments, contradictions, setbacks, and betrayals, just as we can from its idealistic vision. As the sky darkens not only over the Middle East but our whole world, as we seek ways to support revolutionary movements on the front lines of existential struggle against imperial power while equipping our own movements for the final fight ahead, these hard lessons are more relevant than ever. Just as in the dungeons of Amed prison, or in Kobane when ISIS encircled the city, hope without hope is not cheaply found. It remains to be won, at grave cost.

Of course, writing this book is itself an exercise in hope without hope, a wild attempt to speak out, as though there were any realistic chance of influencing the world beyond its covers. Yet whatever happens next as the Syrian conflict enters its latest iteration, the Middle East crisis worsens, and World War III continues to unfold, Rojava's revolutionaries have already won their place in the deep philosophical history of struggle against an absurd universe, and in the Left's history of struggle against totalitarian power. They deserve to be considered as more than anarchist outliers, idealized and sexed-up female fighters, or partisans in a half-forgotten ethnic spat. And our organizations and movements deserve the opportunity to enter into conversation with Rojava's rich, contradictory, provocative perspective on what it will take to launch an effective challenge to capitalist modernity. Beginning (as the Kurdish movement did) with basic tasks in our local communities, we can nonetheless always keep the utopian, internationalist horizon of democratic modernity in view.

My own hope is therefore that Rojava's curious and unexpected example will help you to keep hoping, whatever dungeon you find yourself struggling in today, however far from the light.

Chapter 1

The Rojava Revolution

Finding Hope in Crisis

Rojava's political representatives see their unique political model as treading a third way beyond assumed ideological polarizations.[1] Beyond naive, utopian hope and cynical, materialist despair; beyond capitalist hegemony and tried-and-failed state socialism; beyond liberal reformism and anarchist idealism; beyond ineffective horizontalist organization and paralyzing, top-down control; beyond acquiescence to either the brutal Assad regime or the authoritarian, murderous Islamists and criminal militias who overran the Syrian opposition; beyond the US- and Russian-backed blocs in the Middle Eastern conflict; and ultimately, beyond presently existing modes of social organization altogether, there exists what the revolutionary Kurdish movement regards as the truly democratic plane of political engagement.

To Abdullah Öcalan, the jailed Kurdish revolutionary leader and theorist, any successful twenty-first-century politics must likewise take place in what he calls the "third domain" of "democratic modernity," a newly constructed civil society superseding both traditional, conservative village life and the capitalist nation-state.[2] These plural third ways are not simple compromises, synthesizing a little verticalist discipline with a little horizontalist democracy, a little capitalism with a little communism. Rather, they aim to forge a new revolutionary leap forward, transcending these assumed oppositions altogether.

This history of the Rojava Revolution will therefore also follow a third way. Supportive writers have generally been content to platform

23

Rojava's ideologues, idealistically framing bottom-up, multiethnic democratic confederalism as a panacea to Middle Eastern crisis or representing the region as a utopia fit to inspire the global Left. Conversely, mainstream academics typically analyze democratic confederalism in realist, geopolitical terms, downplaying the Kurdish movement's genuine belief in women's autonomy, direct democracy, and global revolutionary transformation to represent the movement as seizing and wielding quasi-state power in pursuit of oil wealth, regional dominance, and Kurdish nationalist objectives.

Each approach can prove productive, illuminating either the revolution's self-conception or the material and ideological challenges it faces. As disillusioned comrades seeking newfound cause for hope, we might be tempted to follow the first course, idealizing Rojava and downplaying its shortcomings. As cynics doubtful that revolutionary change is possible in an era of left melancholy and capitalist hegemony, we might be tempted to follow the latter.

But this history will rather attempt to explain the contradiction through which Rojava is popularly represented as an anarchist utopia, even as others see democratic confederalism's utopian ideals as contradicted by the Kurdish movement's Leninist, authoritarian tendencies. We will look beyond Rojava's initial moment of revolutionary triumph, assessing the movement's equally unexpected ability to endure existential warfare and engage in unprecedented collaboration with conservative, antidemocratic social forces. In this way, we can understand the Kurdish movement's productive navigation between pragmatic, centralized practice and an idealized, democratic vision as revolutionary in its own right.

In later chapters, we'll also see how the Kurdish movement treads a *psychological* third way, situated in a cultural, philosophical, and latterly revolutionary tradition that leaps beyond both blind utopianism and realistic despair. Western movements' general loss of a clearly envisaged socialist future in which to invest our political hopes can lead us to reformism or to a hapless and disorganized horizontalism. To challenge these tendencies, we can first consider how the Kurdish movement's militant commitment and absurdist hope have emerged through the crises it has faced.

The Rojava Revolution has evolved in response to inhospitable conditions facing the Kurds, the militant Kurdish movement, Öcalan himself, and millions of Syrians: violent repression by Assad, ethnic warfare by Turkey, attempted genocide by ISIS, the collapse of the Syrian pound, economic embargo, and near-total geopolitical isolation. Throughout this grueling revolutionary process, the Kurdish movement's necessarily pragmatic and responsive politics is always justified with reference to its utopian, democratic confederalist horizon. The next two chapters will tell the story of the Rojava Revolution as a victory won through repeated setbacks, challenges, and losses—suggesting ways we can reckon with our own defeats.

Kurdish Statelessness: "Negative Utopianism"

The historical record is politically contested, but the ancestors of the present-day Kurds have been present in the Middle East for millennia. Throughout the centuries, various Kurdish principalities and dynasties achieved varying degrees of autonomy or prominence within the Middle East's various dominant polities. But the tribal nature of Kurdish society helped prevent any modern sense of Kurdish nationalism developing until after World War I, too late to win even exploitative support from the European powers.

Rather, the Middle East was carved up through treaty by the imperial powers, culminating as the Armenian genocide laid the ground for the establishment of the modern, ethnocentric Turkish Republic. The Kurds' traditional, mountainous homeland was left divided between what would become four diverse, repressive regimes. That's why we now speak of Turkish (Northern) Kurdistan, Iraqi (Southern) Kurdistan, Iranian (Eastern) Kurdistan, and the smallest of all these regions, Syrian (Western) Kurdistan—or Rojava. You can picture modern-day Kurdistan as a compass formed by intersecting borders, with each quarter therefore occupied by a different foreign power. Ever since the Treaty of Lausanne (1923), the Kurds have been forced to live in the borderlands, the extreme limits where state power is put to the test.

A long-term resistance to centralized authority, partially rooted in patriarchal tribal culture and even in Islamic opposition to the secular Turkish Republic, predates the leftist Kurdish movement's latter-day organization of this tradition. From the Sheikh Said and Ararat rebellions in Turkey (1926, 1927–1930) to the short-lived, Soviet-backed Republic of Mahabad in Iran (1946), successive Kurdish bids for quasi-state autonomy have been systematically eradicated by regional state powers backed by international guarantors. Even the so-called Kurdish national anthem, "Ey Reqîb," was written in an Iranian jail cell and expressed as a negative lament: its title means "O Enemy!" This long-term opposition to central authority has since been politically reclaimed by Öcalan and his followers, who view it as engendering a Kurdish spirit of anti-authoritarianism.

The concept of a negative utopia is useful here. Writing after World War II, the critical theorist Theodor Adorno felt utopia could exist only insofar as it could be imagined through the negation of the horrors of the recent past and what he perceived as the nightmarish logic resurgent throughout capitalist modernity. In his words: "We may not know what absolute good is. . . . We may not even know what man is or the human or humanity—but what the inhuman is we know very well indeed."[3] Any (socialist) utopia could only be understood as the opposite of present reality, with suffering therefore the precondition of truth, and universal, transcendent meaning forever unobtainable. In a similar fashion, the Kurdish culture of anti-authoritarianism has emerged on the very basis of the Kurds' long-term statelessness.[4] If Öcalan's democratic confederalism does hold out the promise of a utopia, it's a negative one, developed on the basis of centuries of repression and exclusion from the nation-state order.

The New Paradigm: Learning from Defeat

It was in this unpromising context of repression and repeated defeat that Öcalan's militant Kurdistan Workers' Party (PKK) first took up arms in 1984 to fight against Turkey's ultranationalist regime. The PKK emerged from a Marxist-Leninist underground that sought to overthrow Turkey's repressive, Western-aligned government and establish state socialism. In distinction, Öcalan and his PKK came to see the country's many millions of Kurds as an "internal colony" who had to be liberated not only from Turkey's centralized, extractive capitalist economy, but also from brutal, authoritarian rule which denied their very existence.[5]

From the outset, and unlike most other now-marginalized Marxist-Leninist movements throughout the postcolonial world, the PKK has engaged in long-term processes of what has been termed "learning from defeat," evolving in pragmatic response to internal dissent and external pressure.[6] Notably, Öcalan's own intellectual evolution was determined by material circumstance as much as utopian ideal. Historic and contemporary state violence against the Kurds; the collapse of the USSR as a potential sponsor of Kurdish aspirations to socialist statehood; the PKK's ultimate inability to shake the foundations of Turkish state power; and Öcalan's 1999 capture by Turkish intelligence services all contributed to the gradual evolution of the Kurdish leader's revolutionary new perspective.

Öcalan has been held in virtually total isolation on the prison island İmralı ever since his arrest. There, he gradually determined that no state, no matter how communist, liberal, or revolutionary in its self-conception, could ever truly liberate the Kurds—or any of its subjects.

Under further internal pressure from the vocal, militant Kurdish women's movement and influenced by his study of political philosophy and longue durée Middle Eastern history, from behind bars Öcalan developed what is now called his revolutionary "new paradigm," maintaining that all historic, social, organizational, and personal hierarchies have to be undone as the precursor to true freedom. In particular, women's autonomy has to precede national liberation.[7] This led Öcalan to his proposed program of decentralized, bottom-up, municipal democratic confederalism.

As Öcalan has written: "The supposed defeat of the PKK that the Turkish authorities believed they had accomplished by my abduction to Turkey was eventually reason enough to critically and openly look into the reasons that had prevented us from making better progress with our liberation movement. . . . The ideological and political [change] undergone by the PKK made the seeming defeat a gateway to new horizons."[8]

A relatively obscure figure on the international stage while at liberty, Öcalan's global influence paradoxically grows the more he remains isolated on İmralı. For years, the Kurdish leader was held totally incommunicado in what his supporters call a "deafening silence"—another paradoxical term, suggestive of the thunderous implications of his detention. In a moment of historic defeat for Marxism-Leninism in general and the PKK in particular, Öcalan proved able to derive an idealistic vision from the crisis he faced, through his pragmatic self-critique of Marxism-Leninist theory and practice, the USSR, and the PKK's own organizational approach.

Prior to the 2012 outbreak of the Rojava Revolution, this novel ideology was disseminated among the PKK's own militants, trialed in a remote refugee camp loyal to Öcalan, and partially implemented through dual-power organizing in Turkey's Kurdish-majority cities. But for the most part, it remained a noble idea. It would take another unexpected catastrophe—the outbreak of the Syrian Civil War—for Öcalan's vision to become reality.

Outside the State

July 19, 2012, is now celebrated as the anniversary of the Rojava Revolution. Yet there were few bullets fired as the dictator Bashar al-Assad's Syrian Arab Army units withdrew and the Syrian Kurdish wing of Öcalan's movement took control of Kurdish cities in the country's largely rural north.[9] At this time, the Syrian regime was embattled. Following a 2011 pro-democratic, anti-government uprising forming part of the Arab Spring, Syria's brave but under-resourced and disorganized grassroots opposition was rapidly overtaken by more-organized, armed Islamist groups sponsored by Turkey, Qatar, and the Muslim Brotherhood. Assad's cynical depiction of the opposition as nothing but violent jihadists soon became an effective reality, as regime atrocities drove ordinary Syrians to arms and Assad released thousands of veteran Salafi jihadists from jail.[10]

In the 1980s and 1990s, Assad had generally offered a safe haven to Öcalan and his PKK, on the understanding that the latter would concentrate their attacks on Turkey. But in the post–Cold War era, Turkey and Syria reached an agreement that resulted in Öcalan's 1999 expulsion from Syria and eventual capture, followed by years of especially violent repression targeting his movement. Large numbers of local affiliates were subjected to detention, torture, or deportation by Assad's forces, including most of the party's senior leadership in Syria.[11] Though the 2012 outbreak of civil war meant the Assad regime was now forced to liaise with the movement it had spent a decade repressing, its coordinated withdrawal from northern Syria was nonetheless cynically planned to abandon the Kurds to their fate, creating a buffer against Turkish military incursions and the Islamist opposition. And yet this withdrawal allowed Öcalan's followers the opportunity to move into the open and begin the seemingly paradoxical process of implementing their grassroots, bottom-up ideology as the region's newly dominant political and military force.

There would be a price to pay later, as the Syrian Kurdish People's Protection Units (YPG) and all-female Women's Protection Units (YPJ) engaged in sporadic running battles against the Assad regime; their famously bitter campaign against ISIS and the jihadist opposition; and a still ongoing struggle against Turkish occupation. But from those first hours onward, as the major Syrian Kurdish cities fell without a fight into the Kurdish movement's control, Rojava's revolution survived in an ambiguous, productive zone between competing state powers. The confrontation between Syria and Turkey, two of the state powers that benefited from the colonial division of Kurdistan, created room for an autonomous and anti-statist alternative to emerge.

Philosopher Giorgio Agamben has famously argued that the capitalist nation-state achieves hegemony through the necessary, permanent exclusion of certain populations, voiding them of political agency and leaving them to live what he terms a barren existence outside society—Kurds in the Middle East, Jews in the Holocaust, migrants in Europe. The state proscribes certain limits to its violence, only to suspend them in these exceptional cases, licensing violence against these barren populations, which then becomes the new ordinary for the whole of society. "The rule, suspending itself, gives rise to the exception," and whole populations suffer under a permanent and increasingly global "state of exception."[12] Agamben thus politicizes those lives excluded from politics as traditionally understood, by representing their exclusion as fundamental to the power of the contemporary state.

Öcalan, too, theorizes that a state of crisis has become perpetual across the globe. Yet this concept rather serves to repoliticize the Kurds' supposedly "bare" life. The stateless Kurdish nation is restored to the center of Öcalan's global political analysis, granted a world-historical role precisely thanks to their centuries-long exclusion from nation-state politics. The moment Öcalan determined the nation-state had to be surpassed as a political category, the Kurds' permanent exclusion from this supposedly history-ending political form was suddenly and alchemically transformed, making the stateless Kurds the founding subjects of a new political order.

We in the West likely find ourselves struggling in some different zone of the global state of exception. But could we imagine theorizing the world-historic role of gig workers, climate refugees, or other potential subjects of contemporary anti-capitalist struggle with the same transformative force Öcalan has achieved for his own Kurdish people?

Gassed and subjected to genocide in Iraq, executed in Iran, tortured in Syria, driven from burning villages in Turkey, systematically denied their language, identity, and legal existence—like other subjects of the state of exception, the Kurdish people know full well what it means to be excluded from the state. In Syria, the Kurds were written out of state politics to the point that hundreds of thousands of them were literally denied identity papers, following a deeply racist 1960s policy intended to "Arabize" the country's north by displacing the Kurds, described as a "malignant tumor . . . in the body of the Arab nation."[13] To this extent, Rojava prior to its revolutionary organization by the Kurdish movement was a case study of the desperate, excluded, barren life.

This explains what happened when the Syrian state took the logical next step of withdrawing from those unwanted border cities filled with easily expendable Kurds, abandoning them as a buffer against Turkish incursions, mere meat, bare life. During the Syrian conflict, the country tellingly known as the Syrian *Arab* Republic spilled incredible amounts of blood to keep Arab-majority cities in its grasp: that it withdrew its forces to hand control to a ragtag Kurdish militia shows how little value it placed on the lives of its nominal Kurdish citizens. In the regime's view, Rojava was indeed a *utopia*, but in the original, etymological sense—a *non-place*.

What happens when the state of exception consumes itself, and the barren, excluded population is literally abandoned altogether? Following

Agamben, we might expect total death, obliteration, the permanent silencing of the excluded population.

But the Kurdish movement, lean, hard, and organized from long years of struggle, and deeply rooted in Rojava's villages and working-class neighborhoods, could offer a political alternative.

Organizing the State of Exception

The Rojava Revolution does indeed demonstrate that self-directed, state-free autonomy is a viable possibility—but only since the revolutionary Kurdish movement had by then been operating clandestinely in these communities for decades, building support for a seemingly distant revolutionary future beyond state authority. The movement could take out exploitative landlords, resolve community blood feuds, and do what the state could not. In this novel synthesis, a militant, vertical organization empowers a communal, horizontal politics. This paradoxical yet effective approach has important implications for other left movements seeking to learn the lessons of the decade of missing revolutions worldwide and temper horizontalist ideals with verticalist pragmatism.

Thus there is little individualistic, Western-style lifestyle anarchism on display in Rojava. Where the old hierarchies of family, tribe, and state are being challenged, it is rather through the establishment of what one Kurdish expert has called a "communal autonomy" seeking self-determination as Kurds, as women, as a given village or neighborhood—not as individuals.[14] While this might appear less autonomous than more individualist traditions, from the Kurdish perspective it allows for a more community-minded approach to undermining repressive hierarchies.

Most importantly, the Kurdish movement spent decades cementing unshakable community support through the blood shed by many thousands of Syrian Kurdish youths as they joined the guerrilla war against the Turkish army in remote mountain ranges. This recruitment process inspired many fraught conversations with patriotic but careworn mothers, but also an unbreakable spirit of intergenerational commitment forged through sacrifice. "The guerrillas are all our children," the mothers of these "martyrs" often avow.

These *welatparêz* or "homeland-loving" families, the gray concrete walls of their houses covered with vibrant photos of generations of martyrs, are a living testament to the depth of the Kurdish movement's imbrication in local communities. Rojava's successful revolution is the result of many years' clandestine organizing, of coded messages hidden in babies' cribs and the kissing mouths of prisoners' wives, of housewives clambering over backyard fences to attend underground meetings while evading Assad's secret police.

Better accounts of the revolution stress this process, what other recent scholarship on hope-in-crisis calls "revolutionary legwork," in contradistinction to the "fetishism of violence, confrontation and spectacle" through which Rojava has so often been popularly perceived.[15] Organization of grief and pain into effective action is not the preserve of an exclusionary revolutionary class but rather spread by that class throughout the whole of its society, among millions of people, over decades. In a complex process, the Kurdish movement's original vision of a grassroots network of village- and neighborhood-level communes has evolved into a diverse system of municipal, administrative, civil society, and even tribal bodies all united as part of what is now formally known as the Autonomous Administration of North and East Syria, or AANES. Absent their decades of armed struggle in defense of a violently repressed national identity and the existential war they waged against ISIS, the Kurdish movement could never have succeeded in mobilizing the mass movement that it has, still less in forging a tentative trans-ethnic consensus between both Kurdish and Arab victims of both ISIS and Assad.

For example, during a public meeting in ISIS's former capital Raqqa, I witnessed Syrian Kurdish leader Ilham Ahmed issue a powerful rebuttal to allied Arab sheikhs who criticized the Kurdish movement's pragmatic, diplomatic negotiations with Assad. Ahmed responded that the Syrian Kurds knew the brutality of the Assad regime better than anyone—she had lost comrades to torture in Assad's dungeons. Nonetheless, she asserted, to keep their political vision alive the Kurdish movement was ready to negotiate with any Syrian force short of ISIS. Here a utopian sensibility undergirds the most pragmatic politics imaginable. It justifies the banal, the long-term, and the ugly.

With these organizational realities in mind, we can avoid any simplistic, idealistic analyses that treat Rojava as a straightforward, "positive" utopia, rendering it a sort of anarcho-feminist Potemkin village or adventurist experiment, doomed to fail.

Here's a representative example. While I was working in Rojava, Black Lives Matter protesters in Seattle took temporary "control" of a few streets, declaring the small strip of asphalt a cop-free Capitol Hill Autonomous Zone (CHAZ). At the behest of a US newspaper, I was dispatched to interview a Kurdish political organizer on potential parallels between the AANES (area: 50,000 square kilometers; population: ca. 4 million; dates active, 2012–present), and the CHAZ (area: six city blocks and a park; population: low thousands; dates active: three weeks in June 2020). She responded with the typical stern maternalism of an experienced Kurdish militant: "I don't think that will work. The time is clearly not right. They need to go home and begin conversations in their own communities, with those around them."

It wasn't the revolutionary zeal of the would-be insurrectionists in Seattle the Kurdish organizer found lacking so much as their structural inability to organize that hopeless anger. And indeed, the CHAZ soon degenerated, following a series of protester-on-protester shootings, to a rapid restoration of police control—just as many other would-be utopian communes or flash-in-the-pan horizontalist movements have rapidly descended into chaos and internal violence.

Certainly, we should not fall into the opposite trap and dismiss the Kurdish movement as operating purely on pragmatic realpolitik, its success in taking power the result of contingent factors and geopolitical happenstance, talk of democratic revolution mere propaganda to mask a statist power grab. Such cynical, narrow-minded analyses, which depoliticize the revolution and deny the determinant role of the Kurdish movement's unique ideology, are as flawed as those that mindlessly valorize Rojava from afar.

Instead, we can eschew both realist cynicism and idealistic utopianism to understand it's precisely this dynamic interface between utopian ideals and bitter reality that has enabled the revolution to endure. As exemplified in Öcalan's pursuit of new horizons through his imprisonment, and in the Kurdish movement's long-standing preparation of local society for revolutionary transformation on the very basis of its historical repression, we can identify political crises as *negative-utopian openings*, sites for the transfiguration of hopelessness into its opposite. In an era of severe political crisis reaching throughout and beyond the Middle East, yet largely devoid of transformative organizing ideologies capable of offering a potential alternative to statist repression, the Kurdish movement's negative-utopian response to catastrophe offers strategic lessons worth taking seriously.

Surviving in the Crisis

In his manifesto *The Sociology of Freedom*, Öcalan writes that society is experiencing a civilizational crisis that will result in either the destruction of society or the resolution of overwhelming social tensions into new systems, contingent upon the ability of "anti-system forces" in society to organize resistance to the hegemonic powers tearing society apart.[16]

Here as elsewhere, Öcalan's terms recall Lenin, who viewed revolutionary transformation as requiring the rupture of a revolutionary crisis, instigated by irreconcilable contradictions between oppressed and oppressing classes. But crucially, the Kurdish movement is surviving *in* its own crisis, the dialectic of history not necessarily propelling the revolution onward to either proletarian dictatorship or bloody defeat but rather towering over Rojava like a great, frozen wave.

This tension was long made tangible in the complex, interlocking geography of Rojava's de facto capital, Qamishlo, where the Assad regime controlled some street intersections and the Kurdish movement others, until the dictator's overthrow. Anarchist internationalists passed off-duty Syrian regime soldiers, each ignoring the other—unless an internationalist should accidentally approach a regime checkpoint, collapsing the fantasy of security as both instantly become horribly present in the same place.

For the Rojava Revolution was, through necessity, a revolution quite unlike previous statist revolutions. Following Öcalan's pragmatic-idealistic critique of the nation-state, Syria's Kurds refused the obvious paths before them. Neither return to the prewar status quo under Assad, nor acquiesce to Syria's dominant Islamist opposition forces.

Neither bloody smash-and-grab expropriations in pursuit of centralized socialism, nor the establishment of an oil-rich capitalist client state like that across the border in the semi-autonomous Kurdistan Region of Iraq (KRI). Kurdish nationalist in name, in practice the KRI's rulers are willing collaborators with Turkey.

Temporary alliances and pragmatic relationships with both the Syrian opposition and the Assad regime notwithstanding, from 2012 on the Kurdish movement demanded a third way out of the Syrian crisis. This decision was surely proven correct by the rapid Islamification of the broader Syrian opposition, culminating in ISIS's 2014 rise to power.[17] Reactionary, well-funded, state-backed forces determined to repress women's and minority rights achieved dominance at the expense of the disorganized and isolated local committees that had initially attempted to direct the broader resistance against Assad.

This is perhaps the greatest political tragedy of the Syrian revolution. In theory, there was a clear ideological affinity between these ad hoc local councils and the Kurdish movement's vision for a municipal and devolved Syria, and in cities like Manbij and Raqqa, Arab opposition figures who had suffered under and resisted ISIS could and did take up the opportunity to play a leading role in governing their cities through the AANES's own local councils. But the opposition's Islamification and forced reliance on Turkish sponsorship, coupled with the AANES's own negotiated truce with Assad, prohibited the rise of any broader federation capable of spreading secular and democratic governance nationwide. Instead, it was al-Qaeda offshoot Hayat Tahrir al-Sham (HTS) who ultimately managed to depose Assad, in pursuit of their own authoritarian agenda.

From the outset, the AANES's representatives repeatedly emphasized their desire to organize regional society in a different way, refusing separatist or statist aspirations in favor of democratic confederalism.[18] The imperialist powers that variously besiege, invade, and pressure the autonomous region have refused to recognize this process. Yet, it's precisely these tensions that not only enabled the AANES to survive but forced it to continue pursuing a necessarily federal, non-statist, compromised (and therefore democratic) politics. It evolved a mode of stateless democracy that could exist only in the zone of indistinction, excluded from and yet defined in opposition to state power.

The Western press, academics, and policymakers insist on understanding the AANES through a reductive, militaristic lens, Orientalizing the polity as a patch of bloodstained desert fought over by warring ethnic groups. In so doing, they dismiss the AANES's complex internal politics as irrelevant to black-box "realist" analyses based on the assumption that all political actors must solely seek statist hegemony.

For example, the neighboring KRI is trapped in a neo-feudal relation to state power, striving in vain to become a new Dubai where Turkey and the US can project military power and extract oil wealth as they please, untouchable colonial overlords.[19] The US has long sought a similar policy in the AANES, pressuring its military and civilian leadership to forge closer bonds with its ideological nemesis, even as the KRI has aided and abetted Turkish war crimes against the revolutionary Kurdish movement. The US thus operates in striking parallel to the erstwhile Assad regime, which at the beginning of the Syrian uprising and throughout years of off-and-on conflict likewise attempted to win back the Kurds on the cheap, promising to recognize their long-denied language and cultural rights but without offering any true political or military autonomy. The AANES's political and diplomatic representatives steadfastly refused. Despite its stated opposition to Assad, Washington has similarly pressured the Kurdish movement to abandon its vision of multiethnic confederation, reducing Rojava to just another ethno-nationalist project —pressures that are only intensifying following the Islamist takeover in Damascus.

In line with these geostrategic efforts, Western journalists and academics constantly attempt to rewrite the Kurdish movement's aims in terms more palatable to the West. For example, millions living under the AANES are still typically referred to as "the Kurds." This lazy shorthand elides the crucial distinction between the Kurdish nationalist KRI and the AANES's multiethnic, democratic confederalist alternative. These distinctions are existential in nature. Notably, it was the Kurdish freedom movement's PKK that liberated the Yazidi minority from ongoing genocide at ISIS's hands as the militant Salafist group swept through Iraq in 2014. Conversely, the Kurdish nationalist forces fled before ISIS's advance.

More importantly, this synecdoche illustrates how hegemonic global powers are constantly seeking to press the AANES into recognizable statist form, not only suitable for manipulation as military proxies but also enabling Western powers to flatter their own self-image. In this stereotypical conception, the Kurds are good guys; they are secular; their men are brave and their women sexy. This reductive image helps the US war machine to sell its own imperial policy to a suspicious domestic public, putting a novel spin on the war on terror conceit of heroic struggle against a wicked, Muslim other through the false yet hegemonic representation of the Kurds as pro-Western freedom fighters.

From the Kurdish perspective, nothing is so clear. For one, Kurdish residents of the AANES, and Kurdish YPG and YPJ fighters, are now well outnumbered by the region's Arab population and Arab defenders, united with the Kurds in a military coalition known as the Syrian Democratic Forces (SDF). It's this multiethnic coalition that won temporary and transactional support from the US-led coalition formed to defeat ISIS, beginning with 2014 airstrikes, continuing through the 2017 liberation of Raqqa and culminating in ISIS's 2019 defeat. This operation aimed to achieve the US's own foreign policy objectives in the region at a minimal cost to US lives by profiting from the sacrifices of Syrian Kurds and Arabs in their life-and-death struggles to free their own communities from theocratic fascism, all masked by the familiar interventionist rhetoric of women's rights.

If anarchists sometimes overinvest hope in Rojava as a direct-democratic utopia, US military strategists want Rojava to become just another obedient, clientelist ethno-state, while the liberal press and politicians seek to rewrite the revolution as a triumphant example of "democratic" US intervention abroad. They cannot understand what is happening there otherwise. And if it's to survive in the new Syria, the AANES may well be pushed into yet more compromising relationships with its Kurdish-nationalist rivals or imperialist states, testing its revolutionary commitments to the limit.

And yet. In spite of the obvious material and geopolitical advantages the assumption of a Kurdish nationalist quasi-state form would bring, the AANES has continued stubbornly to insist on its third way, even following Assad's demise and the Islamist takeover of the remainder of Syrian territory. Again, this is pragmatism-as-idealism: AANES leaders know they would face violent existential opposition from Ankara and Damascus if they assumed state form.

Crucially, though, the AANES makes a virtue of its exclusion from state politics. Its leaders know they rely on continued tensions between hegemonic states to survive. The AANES has played Turkey against the US, the US against Russia and Iran, Russia against Turkey—playing and being played, of course, but playing as best it can. This ability to derive the means of survival from the potential causes of destruction is a revolutionary necessity, particularly for those of us interested in thinking through viable, mass, non-state alternatives in an era of resurgent state reaction.

It's easy for international observers to understand the Syrian crisis as a matter of international horse-trading between imperialist powers, the AANES's continued autonomy the result of mere contingency. But it's precisely the four million inconvenient "bare" lives being lived in Rojava's state of exception that mean these powers have been unable to find a mutually beneficial accord, even pushing NATO's two largest armies (Turkey and the US) into confrontation. At points during Syria's miniature, reheated Cold War, the SDF even literally mediated between competing Russian and American patrols when they clashed on border roads in AANES territory. These interventions offer a striking depiction of the precarious dance between imperialist powers that enabled the region to retain its revolutionary agency throughout years of war.

The AANES thus repoliticizes Agamben's "zone of indistinction," in which the "very distinction between peace and war (and between foreign and civil war) becomes impossible."[20] Certainly, in this state of exception, any attempt at statehood is doomed to failure. But the Kurdish movement rather claimed the zone of indistinction itself as the Kurds' national territory, taking up arms in its defense. The opposition between state and exception is short-circuited. Exclusion becomes a paradoxical source of political agency.

To this end, the US–SDF anti-ISIS alliance can be usefully understood through analogy with capitalist, imperialist powers' inconstant sponsorship of communist partisans during World War II and the concomitant unbalanced but two-way relationship this implies. In order to placate Turkey's concerns over the potential for permanent Kurdish autonomy, the US disparages its relationship with the SDF as "tactical, transactional, and temporary."[21] While the US is attempting to exploit the SDF, this transaction cuts both ways: the SDF has long resisted US pressure to become its proxy in an unwanted war against Iran, instead profiting from its tactical relationship with the US to pursue its own agenda.

As senior PKK commander Cemil Bayik has announced, "We are on the side neither of Russia nor the [US] . . . no one can make a merely tactical alliance with the Kurds anymore. Those days are over. . . . The Kurds are not the same as yesterday. The Kurds have now taken their destiny into their own hands."[22] This policy has enabled the Kurdish movement to benefit from the clashes of hegemonic states in order to implement a non-statist politics.

Could our Western, horizontalist organizations, which typically run a mile from verticalist state power even when it's far from trying to ethnically cleanse us, manage an analogously strategic relationship with state power? Where are the zones of indistinction that we, too, can reclaim and strategically organize? What would it take to organize excluded populations (Black people in US prisons, refugees at the EU border, the destitute urban street vendors who were a core constituency of the Arab Spring) in such a way that we not only provide humanitarian care or solidarity but also reap strategic capital from their location at the nexus of state power?

As the Middle East has fragmented into a chessboard of proxy wars pitting one autocratic state against another, Rojava has demonstrated that it is possible for communities torn apart by war to unite rather than divide for survival; that anti-imperialist resistance in the Middle East need not take Islamist form, easily co-opted by other imperialist state actors; that through long-term organization, communities that appear permanently excluded from power can prepare for the unexpected revolutionary crisis.

Statism Outside the State

Through its pragmatic-idealistic refusal of statist form, the AANES defiantly places itself outside the statist consensus, its people choosing to continue living bare lives without protection under international law. Eleven thousand locals lost their lives in the defeat of ISIS, and the Kurdish movement is often not even named—denied their identity once again, just like their forebears under Assad. US spokespeople instead allude glibly to "our partners" in the Middle East when trumpeting ISIS's defeat. Among the 150 delegates invited to official, UN-backed opposition negotiations over Syria's future, there was not a single AANES representative, while Turkey is now working hard to prevent the AANES from negotiating with Syria's new rulers.[23]

As Agamben has argued, those who live a "bare life" are easily killed but never commemorated as a sacrifice. In Rojava, their names are emblazoned on every wall; as far as the rest of the world is concerned, all those 11,000 fallen fighters are buried in the tomb of the unknown soldier.

It's no wonder people in the AANES experience a sense of political lack, craving the unobtainable security and comfort that statehood would bring. The statist system is ordered to pressure their hopes into recognizable political categories. Some locals passively ignore the AANES's ongoing efforts to reorganize society, keeping their distance because participation would leave them exposed, outside the law of the Syrian and Turkish states. For example, despite the slaughter of the Syrian conflict, most middle-class Kurdish locals chose to keep sending their children to Assad-regime-controlled universities rather than the more progressive institutions opened by the AANES. An Assad-stamped qualification was internationally legitimate and so, too, will be the qualifications issued by HTS, while those signed off by the AANES remain worthless outside the autonomous regions.

The pressure to conform to statehood operates on all levels, from the concerned mother wanting what's best for her children to the AANES's geopolitical strategy. In order to defend its people, the revolutionary movement is regularly forced to compromise, mimicking or adopting statist practices and policies.

The necessities of dealing with conservative tribal actors and authoritarian neighboring states; a reliance on black-market oil revenues to keep millions from starvation and maintain national defense against genocidal violence; parochialism, anti-Arab chauvinism, and patriarchy among the non-vanguard population; Leninist, authoritarian tendencies among the Kurdish vanguard; an ongoing ISIS insurgency; pressure from international guarantor powers—in various constellations, all these obstacles stand in the way of democratic confederalism's utopian, decentralized vision of a bottom-up "commune of communes." Any left movement hoping to actually change society must be prepared to meet similar contradictions, even if not yet on such a massive, national scale.

In such circumstances, the AANES must necessarily operate a centrally directed defense policy; maintain a standing army with conscripted recruits; provide subsidized, centrally funded bread, diesel, and other necessities; engage in pragmatic trade, security, and diplomatic relations with the authoritarian neighbors simultaneously working for the AANES's overthrow; operate prisons for thousands of radicalized ISIS members; and maintain its own tenuous legitimacy via sundry, quasi-state ideological apparatuses such as the media, the school curriculum, religious messaging, and cultural events.

These actions are born of necessity but potentially in conflict with the AANES's stated program. They are often described with the Turkish loan word *mêcbur*, meaning forced, compelled—as in a chess game where there is only one possible move to make.

For example, given the embargo, smugglers must be allowed to operate so the AANES can access medicine, cooking oil, bullets, and other vital supplies: *mêcbur*. Therefore the economy remains capitalized, prices driven up by black-market Turkish goods. The bootleg "Abibas" tracksuits being peddled in regional markets illustrate a larger point. This revolution is at its weakest in its moments of *dewletbûn*, or becoming-a-state, when conditions compel it to take on the form of the state it can never be. Instances of *dewletbûn* range from the faintly comic (knock-off YPG-liveried iPhone cases) to the potentially troubling (US-trained personnel operating detention centers for ISIS captives). These efforts, too, inspire a sense of lack, an unfulfillable desire for the security of statehood.

During protests in Rojava, it was always painful to hear people repeat the familiar refrain "*Ka mafên mirovahiyê? Ka netewên yekbûyî?*" (Where are our human rights? Where is the United Nations?). Appeals to these values inherently bound up with the state form were repeated almost as an invocation: not in any real expectation of intervention, but as a rhetorical device to demonstrate how far outside these protections Rojava remains. The language of international norms is deployed precisely to demonstrate these norms can never protect the stateless.

Agamben mournfully notes that "the only thought adequate to the task" of overcoming a global statist hegemony that endures even in the twilight of the nation-state "would be [a form of thought] capable of both thinking the end of the State and the end of history together and mobilizing the one against the other."[24] With typical if legitimate pessimism, he detects no such emergent form. Yet, as Öcalan's followers necessarily negotiate the paradoxical reality of existence in a post-state zone of indistinction still defined by statist power, this is precisely the ideological task they assume.

The extent to which the AANES is pressured into state form confirms Agamben's grim vision of an end of history in which the husks of state power shamble on amid the malaise of permanent global capitalist hegemony. But conversely, when it reclaims its precarious non-state status as an ideological triumph, the AANES also reclaims the "state of exception" as a site of legitimate political identity.

A friend who worked in Rojava's filmmaking cooperative observed that his young colleagues found it difficult to create new ideas, to dream, to hope—how can you start to really picture another world when the one around you might be wiped out tomorrow? At the same time, he said, many of these young Kurdish women had to fight their families for years to be allowed out of the home to join the cooperative. Their participation in the cooperative, in a city right on the Turkish border, was itself a victory. To be alive, free, and Kurdish in such circumstances was by its nature a challenge to state hegemony.

On the one hand, the filmmakers' exclusion from the state form did indeed inspire malaise, hopelessness, and the muffling of their political voice. But this same exclusion served to reinvest their very existence outside the state with political significance.

Devolution Under the AANES: Hope from Crisis

With any serious study of the Rojava Revolution or any time spent working in the AANES, the revolution's shortcomings become readily apparent. The Kurdish movement calls these shortcomings "contradictions" (*nakokiyan*), to be recognized, analyzed, and overcome.

Fields from education to warfare to civil society have faced pressure to conform to state form—but they also see the dialectic production of diverse new forms, tactics, and social relations. Denied access to international funds and placed under a trade embargo, Rojava's revolutionaries are forced to live out its promise of rebuilding society literally from the ground up, concocting political solutions as ad hoc and improvised as the rusty homemade tanks with which they defeated ISIS or the hand-constructed ventilators with which they took on the Coronavirus. This jury-rigged aesthetic is emblematic of the revolution's paradoxical strength in weakness.

The most important manifestation of this paradoxical process, wherein the worst crisis dialectically produces the most unexpected, hopeful, revolutionary results, lies in the most significant challenge that has faced Rojava in the years between ISIS's defeat and Assad's fall—managing relations with the conservative, impoverished Arab regions that were ISIS strongholds until their 2016–2018 liberations by the SDF. Rather than merely constituting an obstacle for the Kurds to overcome, their fractious relation with neighboring Arab communities has created genuine, if imperfect, moments of democratization, prohibiting any potential dictatorship of the Kurdish subaltern from acquiring too much power.

The anti-ISIS campaign illustrates the opportunities brought about by the unlooked-for Kurdish-Arab "popular front," to draw another useful comparison with the World War II policy of diverse socialist, reformist, and nationalist forces uniting against a common fascist threat. The AANES's defense of women, Kurds, Christians, and Yazidis in the face of genocidal threats, coupled with its progressive and pro-Kurdish agenda, certainly brought it into direct or indirect conflict with sections of the Arab population. Yet most of ISIS's victims were themselves Sunni Arabs. Thus the reality of existential warfare against a genocidal opponent forced unprecedented inter-community cooperation. Thousands of Kurds, Arabs, and minorities left their homes to live and work together on a dynamic, rolling front line that provided a microcosm of the future AANES: pluralistic and partially devolved, while nonetheless underwritten by centralized oil revenues and centrally directed by senior Kurdish militants in matters of geostrategic and military significance.[25] Thanks in large part to the Leninist discipline and ideological anti-fascist commitment instilled by the militant Kurdish movement, highly trained and highly motivated Kurdish units did prove decisive in winning 2016–2018 battlefield victories. But they could not have been won without the constant simultaneous sacrifices of Arab communities.

This inter-ethnic collaboration has faced challenges from the outset. From their ultimate 2019 defeat to the present day, ISIS sleeper cells have continued to stage a deadly insurgency, killing hundreds to date, while Turkey and the Assad government tirelessly fanned the flames of inter-ethnic grievance. In 2023, the Arab leader of one of the SDF's own military councils plotted a failed uprising in collaboration with Assad, in a complex crisis where legitimate protests followed in the wake of armed clashes and counterrevolutionary intrigue. Meanwhile, locals have long resented the slow pace of reconstruction and the imposition of a Kurdish-led project seen as advancing Kurdish interests, women's autonomy, and liberal-secular values at the cost of conservative Arab culture.

Yet there has never been a simple split between democratic, progressive Kurdish regions and backward, ungovernable Arabs. Kurdish communities are also riven by patriarchal gender norms, honor killings, and conservative, clan-based social organization, immediately troubling any such binary. From the outset, the AANES was forced to seek multiple, complex accommodations with conservative elements in its own Kurdish constituency. More unexpectedly, it's arguably in Arab regions where the movement's stated commitment to devolutionary, bottom-up politics has been most concretely realized in practice. For example, male conscription into the SDF is universal in Kurdish regions but not always in Arab regions; polygamy is banned in Kurdish regions but only frowned upon (though prohibited for AANES personnel) in Arab regions; and the AANES curriculum, which emphasizes progressive values, women's rights, and religious diversity, was rolled back in Arab regions following heated protest.[26] All these flashpoints represent genuine moments of democratization—a reality that is often missed in the simplistic narratives of Arab-Kurdish tensions that are advanced by the AANES's supporters and detractors alike.

Crucially, these devolutionary moments have occurred even and especially when conservative Arab demands contradict the AANES's broader progressive vision. When Arab protesters mingle both legitimate demands for greater devolution and unacceptable calls for the release of detained ISIS militants, when devolution to a regional minority results in a rollback of women's autonomy, it's clear there are no easy answers. Today, Sunni Arab communities that long suffered under Assad might well prefer the dictator's vanquisher in HTS to the AANES's secular alternative, particularly given these communities' own likely disposition toward a strict interpretation of Islam. This creates fresh challenges for the AANES as it seeks to protect women's and minority rights in the new Syria while preserving communities' stated right to self-determination. Yet these challenging processes themselves mitigate against any simple retreat into isolationist Kurdish nativism, forcing the AANES to continue reckoning with what its utopian ideology means in practice.

For example, an autonomous women's village called "Jinwar" regularly appears in the media as a working microcosm of democratic confederalism under the AANES. This project hosts dozens of women—Kurds, Arabs, widows, divorcées, abuse survivors—living together with their children according to the Kurdish movement's communitarian, holistic, ecological principles. It's a remarkable endeavor. But it's relatively unique in the extent to which the Kurdish movement's ideology serves as a guiding principle of civilian life.

A more representative model of what the Rojava Revolution looks like day to day might perhaps be an AANES-administered refugee camp like that at Tel Samen. Here Arabs, Kurds, and members of the Turkmen minority—some displaced three times by war—must live side by side, solving grievances via the local reconciliation committee. It's in camps like this, and not in the still impoverished but comparatively well-off Kurdish heartlands, that the large and growing agricultural cooperative is a genuine lifeline for destitute families.[27]

Rather than an unfortunate failing to be explained away by the revolution's apologists, it's the tension between utopian ideals and material compromises that generates the movement's most revolutionary moments. Local commune meetings in Kurdish regions might witness complaints over (for example) road quality or price gouging, but these communities broadly align behind the AANES's geopolitical and strategic vision. It's rather in recently liberated Arab territories that the AANES has been repeatedly forced to rethink, revise, or defend its positions—whether through its formal political channels, pressure from conservative tribal federations, or street protest.

For example, from 2020 through to 2023 the AANES held a series of public consultations in response to Arab unrest. These admirably open-minded discussions demonstrate the AANES's imperfect but genuine commitment to the continued working out of democratic politics in response to social, ethnic, and community differences—in contradistinction to the authoritarian, exclusionary state politics that previously typified Syrian political life.

At one such consultation I attended in Raqqa, discussions took place in the AANES's lingua franca, Arabic, in a standard but still significant gesture toward inter-community cooperation. Secular AANES representatives undergirded their speeches with Quranic references in an effort to conciliate more traditional, conservative communities. And crucially, AANES representatives openly solicited dissenting opinion: when an Arab AANES employee voiced an impassioned defense of the AANES's efforts in the face of extremely adverse circumstances, emphasizing the AANES was "not like Allah" and could not achieve miracles, the chair interrupted, encouraging participants to offer free, open, constructive criticism.[28]

It's precisely these internal tensions that have pushed the AANES to commit in practice to its stated vision of decentralized, bottom-up governance. Doubtless, Öcalan never envisaged tribal sheikhs quarreling with Kurdish women's activists over the primary school curriculum, but these thorny controversies are the lifeblood of this unique democracy. In Syria as in our own communities, a non-purist politics open to compromise and collaboration is not merely a practical necessity. In and of itself, it produces democratization.

Similar arguments could be advanced with regard to democratic confederalism's other ideological pillars: self-determination for women and minorities, radical environmentalism, the cooperative economy. For example, Kurdish economist Azize Aslan correctly notes that community-level cooperatives that Öcalan mooted as an alternative to monopoly capitalism have failed to supersede a war economy, capitalist markets, and small-to-medium agriculture in the region. Ironically enough, the very movement that urges a revolutionized relationship to the natural world is forced to rely on crude oil produced through leaky infrastructure in order to feed millions of civilians and protect them from genocidal violence.

Yet, as Aslan argues, this ongoing political crisis has driven a broader cooperativization, an ongoing social, personal, and economic realignment to communitarian ends.[29] By using its oil resources in order to fund the distribution of subsidized bread, diesel, and other necessities and to enable local communities to pursue reconstruction projects, the AANES has unexpectedly ended up operating in rather more socialist fashion than its own advocates sometimes realize.

In all these instances, the fact of exclusion from the state form opens up rather than forecloses the possibility of novel political thought and mass participation. The zone of indistinction becomes the Kurds' long-sought homeland.

Powerlessness as Resistance

The claim that permanent exclusion from state form can dialectically produce revolutionary results has been proven by these moments of unlooked-for collaboration and democratization. But it's also true in the purely negative moment of despair. By articulating the unavoidable *mêcbur* moves they are forced to make as though they were a choice, the people of Rojava have found a way to compensate for their lack of statehood. More than a mere psychological defense mechanism, this militant organization of weakness constitutes a reclamation of selfhood, a politicization of bare life. When ISIS closed in on the Syrian Kurdish border city of Kobane in 2014, Turkey lined up its tanks on the border to block the only possible escape. There was no choice save a seemingly hopeless resistance. But the YPG and YPJ fought as though there *were* still hope, proudly, freely, in a resistance that won them global support and turned the tide of that war.

Or, as leading Syrian Kurdish politician Saleh Muslim stated when Donald Trump first announced his intention to withdraw US troops from the AANES, exposing the region to a deadly Turkish invasion: "We did not call the Americans here, and we are not sending them away. We won't beg anyone not to attack us or beg to be protected. We are here. We can handle our own defense."[30]

As it would transpire, the region could *not* handle its own defense, with the total lack of geographic cover along the pancake-flat border region making rapid defeat by Turkey's infinitely more advanced military an inevitability. Yet, crucially, this total lack of control over the material forces pressing in on all sides itself becomes a point of pride, the people greeting their bare, excluded status with arms spread wide. At this point zero, a paradoxical space of resistance is opened in which humanity may be reclaimed.

Agamben struggles to imagine the active, organized resistance of bare life. When he says he "politicizes" bare life, he means he demonstrates its indispensability to state politics, at which point its political agency is utterly voided. But through a more radical concept of politicization, bare life can be restored to the center of political organization.

For example, Agamben's theory treats Guantánamo Bay inmates kept in permanent isolation as paradigmatic examples of bare life, wholly excluded from the statist order.[31] Yet through hunger strikes conducted as a terminal act of protest, consuming their own mortified bodies as the only resource remaining to them, these inmates proved able to reclaim their bare status as a site of political contention.

Jailed members of the Kurdish freedom movement have frequently used the same method to win political concessions. From the Kurdish movement's revolutionary perspective, partial or total self-sacrifice can enable mere death to become martyrdom, laying claim to and reversing the processes through which state power produces and excludes bare life.[32]

As in the case of the young Kurdish filmmakers, the AANES's insistent presence outside the (Turkish) state is necessarily an act of resistance. When Turkey invaded the AANES in 2019, people willingly put their bodies on the line. Civilians flooded in their thousands to what they themselves called "human shield" protest camps on the border, linking arms before Turkey's tanks and warplanes. The distinction here, between the fact that people have no choice but to live in the jaws of death and the fact they walk proudly into them with banners streaming, is crucial. It reinvests their excluded status with agency. Even and especially when all life is stripped away, there is something left over.

Agamben notes the etymological link between "witness" and "martyr," a link that also exists in the Kurdish/Arabic/Turkish word *şehîd/shahid/şehit*. He argues that people consigned to bare life and totally denuded of political agency by state violence cannot bear witness to their suffering, thus becoming mere victims.[33] But death, loss, and exclusion can themselves become organized. When the Kurdish movement repeats their slogan "*şehîd namirin*" (martyrs never die), they restore agency to their thousands of slaughtered comrades. When these victims are redefined as martyrs, that is to say as witnesses, the fact of their violent depoliticization itself becomes a point of political struggle and pride.

If the revolution had been followed by the establishment of a liberal, capitalist Kurdish nation-state, as many Kurds hoped it would, perhaps Rojava would have faced a threat even more existential than its present crisis. Certainly, the region urgently needs weapons, market access, and an end to Turkey's systematic destruction of its infrastructure. And as HTS's rapid institutionalization suggests, the decision to exclude the AANES from formal diplomatic recognition has always been a political choice on behalf of the neo-imperialist powers. But perhaps the political support Rojava's representatives long unsuccessfully sought from indifferent Western powers would not be such a panacea after all, international capital rushing in before the ideas being rooted in the democratic confederalist academies truly have time to grow.

The difficult years ahead will see these profoundly contradictory pressures reach new heights, potentially risking the democratic confederalist revolution's very survival. The US has long used a network of NGOs to establish soft counterpower to the AANES and undermine its determinant social and political role, aiming to reduce the region to another gray blur in the global zone of indistinction.[34] As Syria opens up to international markets and the AANES seeks further protection as it faces further bouts of ethnic cleansing at the hands of key Western ally Turkey and a profoundly uncertain future in a HTS-dominated Syria, the AANES's political representatives are likely to continue seeking an ill-defined diplomatic recognition from those same Western powers. While acknowledging these geopolitical contingencies and the existential threats faced by women, Kurds, and minorities living under the AANES, it's important to interrogate the risks and benefits any such Western engagement might bring.

Today, the narrow path between destruction and exploitative co-option appears more razor-thin than ever before. Yet by excluding those four million lives inhabiting the AANES's zone of indistinction from their power plays for so long, the imperialist powers have granted them a paradoxical power of their own. It was precisely because they were excluded from state power, fighting without a choice as though there were a choice, that the Kurdish movement won the international solidarity that has enabled their revolution to endure thus far.

The State of Emergency

An Arab organizer in the AANES's youth movement once told me a story, illustrating his take on the revolution's unexpected survival: A king happened to witness a shepherd endure a scorpion's sting without a whimper. Impressed, he fired his lazy vizier, replacing him with the shepherd. But the crafty vizier argued the peasant should serve a year's probation, all the while plying him with fine food, silks, and other luxuries. After a year and a day had passed, the vizier prodded the shepherd with a simple thorn— and elicited a terrible scream.

His point was that constant crisis has equipped the revolutionary vanguard for struggle and civil society for continued hardship. There is a dialectic sense in which hopeless circumstances produce necessarily utopian results.

To recap: taken together, the Kurds' permanent exclusion from the statist political order, the PKK's historic defeat, and Öcalan's incarceration are constitutive of Öcalan's subsequent negative-utopian proposal. The collapse of Syrian state power and subsequent intrastate conflict provided the revolutionary crisis necessary for this revolutionary proposal to be implemented. Rojava's exclusion in a permanent state of exception has prevented it from assuming statist form, enabling the AANES to reclaim this exclusion as a political victory. And the extreme internal and external pressures constantly operating on Rojava have forced the region to retain and renew its revolutionary ideals.

In the safe zone where nothing is safe; in the deconfliction zone where war is a constant reality; in its permanent state of emergency, the Kurdish movement found victory in defeat. Homeland in exclusion. Strength in fragility. Hope in crisis.

Chapter 2

ISIS, Rojava, and the Non-State Alternative

The Rojava Revolution has made a virtue of the supremely challenging objective circumstances it faces. But crisis does not necessarily produce any such utopian response. Rather, the Kurdish movement's ideology has played a determinant, subjective role in this process, repoliticizing the state of exception by organizing the Kurdish people's suffering and losses.

Before we ask how our own movements in the West could build on these lessons to reckon with the distinct yet related setbacks we have suffered throughout the past decades, it is important to acknowledge that harsh circumstances and material defeats can equally lead to nihilistic despair or authoritarian reaction. To this end, we can draw a useful comparison with another non-state actor that effectively responded to Middle Eastern crisis to implement a radically counterhegemonic ideology, thereby attracting support from around the globe: the Islamic State of Iraq and the Levant, or ISIS.

What Makes a State

ISIS is the Kurdish freedom movement's dark double. It's hard to resist the Manichean, heroic image of the two nemeses locked in deadly battle, women against men, light against dark.

ISIS's political program entailed the "erosion of formal borders between Iraq and Syria . . . challeng[ing] a world order based on sovereign territories and the permanency of the post–First World War regional order."[1] This aim recalls the Kurdish movement's own geopolitical agenda, which explicitly aims to undermine regional state borders laid down in the post-WWI Treaty of Lausanne. The militant Salafist group similarly recognized that a true critique of hegemonic global forces can only emerge from that barren, excluded, scorched space outside the state's flickering circle of firelight.

ISIS sought to restore an extremist interpretation of "original" Islam, predicated on the subjugation of women and nonbelievers and total submission to theocratic rule. As scarcely needs restating, this vision was the total inverse of the Kurdish movement's progressive, women-led social revolution. There are few greater instances of hope emerging through utter hopelessness than existential war against ISIS's theofascism proving the basis for the trans-ethnic women's revolution under the AANES.

But there is another crucial difference, one often overlooked in the West, though emphasized in the Kurdish movement's own analyses: ISIS styled themselves a new state, in fact *the* state (*al-Dawlah*), the only legitimate state.[2] In practice, rhetoric, and strategy, there is a sense in which the Islamic State itself represents the extreme limit of the statist, post-Westphalian Western order—whereas the West's Kurdish allies in the fight against ISIS in fact model a truly radical alternative.

To be clear, the Kurdish movement has no interest whatsoever in terrorist attacks against the West, or in enforcing domestic rule through corporal punishment. Rather, democratic confederalism is conceived of as (peacefully) transcending state boundaries and, ultimately, the state form altogether. The question is rather which mode of social organization—authoritarian reaction or a defiant, utopian leap toward decentralized self-determination—will characterize those future polities that emerge as the cracks in the state system, already visible in Kurdistan, widen and spread worldwide.

Liberals and ISIS: A Faustian Pact

Agamben uses "the camp" as a simple shorthand for "the concentration camp." He follows Michel Foucault in representing the (concentration) camp as the ultimate site of twentieth-century biopower, where the contemporary state establishes its omnipotence through the total and permanent exclusion of disciplined, bare human lives.[3]

Agamben's analysis remains relevant in the twenty-first century as states increasingly define their existence in opposition to rapidly growing excluded refugee populations confined in camps within and without their borders. Yet there is also room for resistance here. As the Kurdish movement knows full well, metaphorical and literal camps can also be highly politicized sites ("He was in the pro-Western camp," "She attended a terrorist training camp," and so on). As with the broader state of exception, it's possible for the camp to be repoliticized as this seemingly paradigmatic site for the production of bare life is reclaimed by its inmates.

And in Rojava we're immediately confronted by a curious paradox. Following ISIS's ultimate defeat, the fate of most captured ISIS members is to remain held in prisons and camps guarded by the Kurdish-led, multiethnic SDF. The AANES once boasted a lower rate of detention than any state (save San Marino) due to its stated principles of restorative and community-led justice. Today, it detains around ten thousand Syrian and Iraqi ISIS fighters and commanders, alongside another thousand combatants from all over the world.

Meanwhile, tens of thousands of ISIS-affiliated women and their children are held in a site called Hol Camp, a vast tent complex surrounded by tall fences and administered by the AANES. Despite regular security operations, highly radicalized female ISIS members manage to run a clandestine mini-caliphate within the camp, governing other residents through a campaign of beatings, arson, and murder, even continuing to hold Yazidi women in secret slavery. Hol Camp is therefore commonly described as a "ticking time bomb" or breeding-ground where ISIS can recruit and rebuild.[4] There's a cruel irony here. Perhaps the largest space on earth populated only by women and children is not an autonomous women's village or commune forming part of the AANES, but rather the prison camp it's forced to operate to hold foreign-national ISIS members.

At the same time, the AANES also shelters up to a million internally displaced people (IDPs); most of them are ordinary Arabs and Kurds with no or limited connection to ISIS, and some of them also reside in Hol. The Kurdish-led administration thus shoulders a vast humanitarian, political, and security burden, caring for tens of thousands of radicalized ISIS affiliates alongside countless ordinary civilians, all on what would be one of the smallest state budgets worldwide and with little external support. Meanwhile, Turkish airstrikes and deliberate destruction of water and power facilities immiserate millions and enable ISIS members to escape, regroup, rebuild, and slaughter hundreds during an insurgency ongoing since their 2019 defeat.

These structural challenges notwithstanding, liberal commentators and institutional, US-linked NGOs have regularly castigated the AANES for the conditions in which these vanquished militants are detained. As a result, many casual observers are more familiar with the plight of the West's bête noire in ISIS than they are with the broader humanitarian crisis faced by the AANES, which struggles to care for not only captured ISIS members but also countless other civilians who have suffered death, brutality, and displacement under ISIS's rule.[5]

Hol Camp is formally recognized as a refugee camp by the UN, with its inmates offered extensive official support by Western NGOs. Conversely, the AANES itself has not been granted diplomatic recognition as a UN member state, observer, or even legitimate political actor within Syria. As a result, it's relatively easier for the West to deliver aid to Hol Camp than to other refugee camps elsewhere in AANES territory, including those set up to shelter the *victims* of ISIS. These geopolitical contingencies have created a perverse situation where the very locals who survived ISIS's genocidal violence now minister to them in health clinics and camps. International NGOs working in Hol offer far higher salaries than the AANES can, meaning skilled locals are more likely to work for the UN caring for ISIS than they are in the political task of remaking Syrian society. As a Kurdish colleague observed, this contributes to a severe brain drain from the AANES, worsening the loss of so many bright young people in the war.

As the head of the AANES's Foreign Affairs Bureau recently lamented, "All these humanitarian organizations come to Hol Camp. At the same time, close by, there are camps . . . for people who fled the Turkish occupation leaving their homes, and yet there's no interest in these camps from the international community."[6] (Conversely, it should be noted these "unseen" camp residents at least are free to leave if they find work or shelter elsewhere, unlike Hol's inmates, and need not live in perpetual fear of ISIS violence within their own camps.)

There's a paradox here. The supposed victors, the Kurdish-led forces that operate the ISIS holding camps, are placed outside the law. The supposedly "bare" camp inhabitants, the foreign ISIS militants, are granted media attention, humanitarian concern, and both formal and informal legitimacy. As we saw with reference to the AANES's political program, those excluded from state politics can nonetheless find ways to make their exclusion a source of strength.

It's clear that ISIS still plays a particular role in the West's cultural imagination and disciplinary politics. Even in defeat, ISIS styles itself the nightmarish executor of an impending, dystopian judgment on the West—to powerful effect. And yet the Kurdish movement, maligned and overlooked, continues working on a utopian political project no less radical in its stated goals.

The prison camp therefore serves ISIS's ends perfectly. The West agonizes endlessly over the fate of the "ISIS brides" in Hol and other AANES-operated camps. Perhaps half the inquiries my media NGO in the AANES received from foreign press were concerned solely with the relative handful of foreign ISIS members detained there.

The furor around one infamous "ISIS bride"—Shamima Begum—offers a paradigmatic example. This young, British-born woman traveled (or was trafficked) to Syria in 2015 when she was just fifteen years old. She enthusiastically participated in ISIS's rule, including the enslavement and rape of equally young Yazidi girls. Following her eventual capture by the SDF, she made a series of ill-judged media appearances in which she initially appeared unrepentant before belatedly begging to be brought back to the UK. The British public reviled her, and in 2019 the British government stripped her of her citizenship.

In the UK, a liberal-conservative culture war has developed around Begum. Liberal commentators plead for clemency, representing Begum as both a victim groomed by ISIS members and now, as a brown, Muslim woman, suffering her own exclusion from the protections the British state offers its other citizens. Conservatives would prefer Begum be perpetually condemned to a Syrian detention camp. Yet neither side is interested in the perspectives of the equally young Kurdish women who fought and died in the struggle against ISIS or in the even younger Yazidi girls ISIS raped, tortured, and murdered by the thousands.[7] Although motivated by legitimate concerns over Islamophobia in the US or Europe, the Western liberal discourse over foreign ISIS members inadvertently silences their Syrian and Iraqi victims—who are of course also brown, Muslim women excluded from Western citizenship. As Leila Al-Shami and Robin Yassin-Kassab write in their heartbreaking survey of the broader Syrian revolution and its rapid capture by Islamist armed groups, "It's one of postcolonialism's saddest ironies that some of the new colonists are the grandchildren of colonized people."[8]

Lurid accounts of the suffering endured by ISIS's Western recruits offer a key flow of capital to the ailing terror group. If the decision by a small number of relatively privileged Western citizens to join ISIS constitutes the upper limit of alienation from Western society, so too does the spectacle of ISIS in defeat scratch a certain itch for the liberal order ISIS sought to destroy.

In this way, the women of Hol short-circuit the refugee camp's intended technology of punishment. Foucault theorizes that post-Enlightenment society aims to create a "totally useful time" for its citizen-inmates, disciplining them to play their respective roles in a fiercely regulated social order.[9] It could correspondingly be argued that the refugee camp is intended to embody society's reverse, a totally useless time. But as in the Kurdish movement's determined repoliticization of their own state of exception, in Hol Camp ISIS too has reclaimed and repoliticized the state of exception. The spectacle of the camp becomes grist for the ISIS propaganda mill. Suffering, ISIS-linked women and children are represented as the victims of Western cruelty against the *Ummah*, or international community of Muslims, thus rallying global support.

The Kurdish movement problematizes overly simplistic representations of Western ISIS fighters as alienated subjects of a hegemonic, white, Christian society. For one, although the Kurdish movement is ideologically secular, the vast majority of those who died fighting ISIS were themselves from impoverished Sunni Muslim families—a fact often lost on Western observers as the Muslim Kurds are reimagined as Christian, Western proxies.

From the perspective of the Western foreign policy establishment, the war against ISIS was the culmination of the war on terror's project of eliminating a "terrorist" non-state actor. Some on the Left, therefore, concluded the war on ISIS must be opposed in all its forms as part of a broader opposition to American neo-imperialism. Hundreds of leftist organizations in the US demanded "US out of Syria!" with little sense of the complex distinctions on the ground and the conflicting ways in which the US has simultaneously propped up and undermined Assad, ISIS, the Syrian opposition, and the AANES.[10] Ignoring these complexities, sections of the Western Left reflexively supported Assad against "the West" despite his authoritarian, neoliberal regime's long-term imbrication with Western interests. This approach, which has been called the "anti-imperialism of fools," rapidly collapses under any "closer examination of the [Assad] regime's neoliberal policies and security collaboration with the West, and of American willingness to tolerate the regime's destabilisations."[11] Yet as in Begum's case, domestic US politics has often been simplistically projected onto the Middle East in general and Syria in particular, regardless of the actual implications for millions of ordinary Syrians.

To the Kurdish movement, ISIS's wickedness had nothing to do with its non-state, "terrorist" political identity or nominal opposition to the West per se. That ISIS gained such global notoriety was rather because it presumed to act like a state without being one, practicing unmasked the unspoken, unspeakable cruelty of theofascism.[12] For its part, the SDF is perfectly willing to oppose Islamist violence in both its non-state and statist forms, whether in the person of ISIS, Turkish, or Qatari-backed Sunni-Arab-supremacist militias, or the Islamist authoritarians who now rule Damascus. A principled position that recognizes and opposes ISIS as a state should be uncontroversial. So should the AANES policy of militarily eradicating ISIS as a fundamentally fascist entity while also working positively through political education, community programs, and pragmatic reconstruction in order to counter the appalling material conditions, sectarian and religious divisions, and deep-rooted patriarchal mentality that have facilitated ISIS's explosive rise. Yet Rojava's representatives often seem to stand alone in proposing a third-way alternative to both neo-imperialist Western intervention and the virulently misogynistic Islamism that imperialism helped birth.

The standard liberal conception views ISIS as mere primitives refusing progress and liberal modernity. A countervailing anti-imperialist analysis prefers to depict the terror organization's rise as a catastrophic but inevitable response to neo-imperialist interventionism in the Middle East, the invasion of Iraq, and repressive technologies brought to bear against dissident, subaltern Arabs by the occupying US forces. But it's possible to move beyond this opposition, recognizing these liberal and anti-imperialist analyses as two sides of the same coin.

To Foucault, the Enlightenment inevitably brought with it technologies of repression that "have their technical matrix in the petty, malicious minutiae of the disciplines and their investigations."[13] Disciplinary technologies were developed precisely in order to further rationalist, positivist ideologies of progress, like that used by neocons to justify US intervention in the Middle East. Following this logic, if ISIS opposes post-Enlightenment liberal values, it must inevitably oppose the post-Westphalian regime of broad, disciplinary control through technology, state, and social institutions as well. The two are inseparable. Yet rather than seeking to supplant the repressive liberal state order with any kind of progressive alternative, ISIS of course sought to dominate society through just the kind of spectacular medieval violence that has largely been superseded by the emergence of these new regimes of disciplinary control.

Given that ISIS's project opposes liberal modernity from the theocratic extreme Right, the punishment technologies of the camp therefore fail to constrain ISIS. In Hol, ISIS has its own morality police, its own hierarchy, its own monopoly on violence. The camp is intended to hold up ISIS as an abject example of bare, excluded life, to extol the inevitable victory of the post-Westphalian liberal order. But it signally fails in this task.

Foucault famously used the panopticon—a notional prison system wherein each individual prisoner never knows if they are currently under observation and thereby feels compelled to conform to discipline—as his model of a modern surveillance society in which direct, violent discipline and restraint are no longer needed and we effectively police ourselves.[14] But in Hol Camp and the prisons throughout northern Syria in which ISIS affiliates have repeatedly launched uprisings in which hundreds are left dead, the terror group in fact operates its own panopticon. Avoiding their jailers' gaze, ISIS loyalists operate as a self-observing cell, holding one another to an alien moral code, stoking their own admittedly radical commitment.

In another parallel to their Kurdish vanquishers, ISIS's militants have managed to maintain or even increase their strength, organization, and legitimacy while in formal detention, using the very fact of their detention in Hol to demonstrate the historical justification of their mission to international sympathizers and funders.[15] In the classic formulation of statist biopower, these should be disorderly, abject, excluded bodies, but they are ordered, organized, refusing to be cowed by the world's gaze. Through this continued "remaining and expanding" (*baqiya wa tatamadad*), as a famous ISIS slogan has it, the terror-state retains its power.[16]

As with all bare subjects of state politics, ISIS militants reside in an ambiguous zone, fulfilling a role in the statist order defined by their very exclusion from the state.[17] More precisely, they are what Foucault calls "delinquents"—outlaws produced by a disciplinary, carceral system in order to illustrate its continued necessity, locked in a mutually parasitic relation.[18] A carceral society needs these "bad guys," who can never actually challenge its foundations, living in an endless cycle of crime-punishment-recidivism. ISIS cannot help but be plugged into circuits of moral outrage and sublimated violence that serve only to feed the system they are supposed to be subverting.

And so from the perspective of a Western state, ISIS needs to be punished, left in a desert to rot—never mind the fact that "desert" is also home to millions of civilians who have suffered under ISIS's rule. If we view permanent exclusion from the liberal state order in the Syrian desert as a fitting punishment for ISIS, what does that say about the West's perspective on the AANES's millions of ordinary residents, who have endured these exact conditions all along?

The liberal West needs ISIS to be punished, but it also wants to expiate its guilt over the cruelty of this punishment, and it knows any repatriation program will be costly, legally fraught, and domestically unpopular. And so responsibility is transferred to the AANES. With extraordinarily limited resources, the AANES struggles to care for members of the same terror organization that sought to eradicate them from the face of the earth. It would surely be reasonable to expect the infinitely richer US, and its partner states in the coalition assembled to fight ISIS, to shoulder the vast burden of feeding and sheltering thousands of recalcitrant ISIS loyalists. The global anti-ISIS coalition spent billions to bomb the caliphate into ruins only to turn their backs as soon as the bombs stopped falling, refusing to properly support the AANES in the infinitely more challenging task of rebuilding Syrian society and infrastructure in such a way as to permanently frustrate ISIS's ability to exploit Sunni Arab discontentment. In the West, there is little political appetite for this sort of long-lasting support for the AANES—only for building more prisons on its territory. It seems no lessons have been learned from the similarly brutal atmosphere of the detention centers established by the US during the Iraq War, which fostered ISIS's original leaders.

Whether clutching its pearls over ISIS's treatment or calling jingoistically for their perpetual detention or even execution, what's important is that the West focus its gaze solely on ISIS and ignore the alternative political, juridical, and social solutions that the AANES proposes in the same terrain. Instead, the punishment of ISIS affiliates plays out before cameras that will never stop rolling. Hol Camp's inmates suffer what Agamben termed a living death, a permanent and mutually beneficial exclusion that enables ISIS to continue "remaining and expanding" until its next opportunity to escape and resume its state-building project.

A Non-Statist Solution for the Islamic State

The blood shed defeating ISIS cements together the AANES's diverse political and ethnic constituencies. There nonetheless remains a risk of legitimate anger over ISIS's crimes deepening fissures between the Kurdish and Arab communities now attempting to form a united polity in the AANES, producing further cycles of violence.

In private conversations with Kurds who suffered at ISIS's hands, though never in public politics, it's relatively common to hear ugly sentiments directed at Arab neighbors cast as complicit in ISIS's crimes. Here lurks that inevitable danger that Agamben, like Öcalan, foresees in the "end of history": statist violence constituting itself against an excluded enemy group who admittedly did everything possible to put themselves outside the law.[19] Under severe pressure from the ISIS insurgency and Turkish- and Assad-sponsored destabilization, the SDF has been heavy-handed when policing Arab regions liberated from ISIS, reproducing violent, statist logic as it strives to maintain basic security, and thereby jeopardizing the AANES's efforts at intercommunal federation. To this extent, the SDF fails to escape its own capture within the statist juridical order.

But as we saw above, the crisis the AANES faces simultaneously produces an alternate, non-statist politics. Kurdish veterans, civilians, and officials simultaneously express pride in how well the captured ISIS fighters are treated, in distinction to both ISIS's own practices and those of the Kurds' erstwhile nation-state allies. Even during the war, ISIS members went to great lengths to surrender to the Kurds rather than to Iraq or Assad, knowing it was only here they'd receive reasonable treatment.

Along with most female ISIS members from Western nations, Begum is held at another internationally recognized site called Roj Camp. It's a closed detention facility, yet women here enjoy twenty-four-hour electricity, ready access to clean water, and TV. When I lived close to Roj with Syrian colleagues, we envied these luxuries, unavailable to most ordinary locals. Conditions in Hol Camp are certainly harsh, but thousands of Kurdish and Arab AANES employees risk life and limb to ameliorate them each day. The AANES has set up women's houses and rehabilitation programs in ISIS refugee camps, cares for hundreds of orphans and children born to jailed ISIS fighters, and (perhaps most significantly) offered managed amnesties for convicted ISIS members and affiliates, enabling them to return home and begin rebuilding their lives—even to begin working for the AANES.[20]

The AANES's bold, imperfect, underfunded, vital efforts to do things differently have largely been ignored by the Western public. Rather, that public clamors bloodthirstily for ISIS fighters to suffer, with one survey showing 82 percent of respondents approved of Iraq's plans to execute European ISIS fighters. Most governments refuse to repatriate their own nationals, viewing any such move as political suicide.[21] In 2020, Norway's governing coalition collapsed over the potential repatriation of a single "ISIS bride," in a stark demonstration of ISIS's outsized hold on the

Western imagination. Meanwhile, the AANES has systematically refused to enact revenge, though with 11,000 dead that right would surely belong to the AANES if it were anyone's.

I vividly recall visiting Roj Camp, the more hospitable detention center for female ISIS detainees. It was then administered by a twenty-year-old Kurdish woman. She was clearly loved by some of the ISIS women, and she loved them in return, even though three members of her family had been slaughtered by the terror group. At such points, it was possible to see that even the terrible burden of accommodating ISIS on the very soil they sought to rule can dialectically produce unexpected, hopeful resolutions.

By refusing to exercise violence against captured ISIS members, the AANES refuses to wield the monopoly on violence that is a marker of statehood. During bitter urban campaigns against ISIS, SDF commanders resisted international pressure to carpet-bomb ISIS into nonexistence—measures intended to protect civilian lives, but for which they were roundly criticized by the Western press.[22] The SDF even allowed ISIS to indulge in repeated fake surrenders, sending suicide bombers and gunmen with white flags to attack their ranks, sooner than risk the lives of civilians or surrendering ISIS members. This restraint and self-sacrifice should be commended, not condemned.

Similarly, while the AANES has outlawed capital punishment, the collapsing Iraqi state to Syria's east remains state enough to exercise the death penalty. Many Western powers would secretly be glad to see the AANES follow suit in executing ISIS members, ridding themselves of an inconvenient problem while distancing themselves from guilt by condemning the AANES for inevitable shortcomings in their judicial proceedings.

Instead, though, the AANES has spent years desperately appealing for foreign states to repatriate their ISIS-linked nationals; for the anti-ISIS coalition, the UN, or the International Criminal Court to come to Syria and put ISIS on trial; or, latterly, for the AANES to be allowed to try foreign ISIS members themselves in their own courts. The AANES's courts are imperfect and hampered by that same sense of *dewletbûn*, becoming-a-state, hopelessly striving to become the state organs they cannot ever be and naturally falling short when measured by normative Western standards. Yet the AANES courts remain the region's fairest juridical bodies. Around 10 percent of locals put on trial for ISIS membership are found innocent, in sharp contrast to Iraq's kangaroo courts for ISIS captives or the gulags operated by Assad's fearsome security apparatus. Many more have served out sentences in AANES prisons and been released via semi-regular amnesty programs intended to promote clemency and community reconciliation.[23]

These amnesty programs, like the AANES's broader response to the ISIS crisis, are pragmatism-as-idealism in action. Here as elsewhere, a juridical form recognizable to the West would be impossible to achieve. But crucially, the AANES has often proven willing to relinquish the pursuit of statist forms of justice, creating the space for a novel and alternative politics to emerge. Dystopian hopelessness once again proves the necessary precursor to hope.

The True Alternative

It's Rojava, not ISIS, that represents the unseen subject, the truly countersystemic alternative to the statist order's global juridical regime. Yet Rojava's model is wholly ignored as the Islamic and post-Westphalian states feed off each other's hatred, enabling Western governments to maintain disciplinary regimes founded on anti-terrorist paranoia and enabling ISIS to continue rebuilding and winning Islamic sympathy in camps and prisons. Recent developments in Syria prove the point once again. HTS (which, like ISIS, evolved out of the decentralized al-Qaeda network) embodies this close affinity between the authoritarian state and radical Islam. After capturing central government from Assad, HTS is rapidly being recognized as Syria's legitimate sovereign power, while the AANES is left devoid of international recognition, far outside the circle of firelight in which Turkey, Russia, Iran, the US, and Israel circle with drawn knives, as ISIS prowls round the perimeter.

As in the revolutionary parable of the two naked Kurdish revolutionaries staring into one another's eyes, at its most defiant the Kurdish movement refuses to meet the global liberal order on its terms. In the heart of the Turkish prison's panopticon, those two revolutionaries short-circuited its expectations, finding freedom where it was least expected. By upending geopolitical expectations of ISIS's treatment, the AANES once again demonstrates its ability to relinquish the assumed dyad of a) authoritarian state and b) excluded other, in pursuit of a revolutionary third way.

Like ISIS, the Kurdish movement necessarily developed a strategic response to imperialist intervention, the disenfranchisement of minority populations, and broader social atomization under exploitative states. But in contrast to the would-be Islamic State, Rojava's very exclusion from the statist order drove it to avoid replicating that politics in microcosm. As the Middle East fractures further along fissures already apparent as ISIS first surged through the Levant, and Syria itself cries out for a federal path beyond authoritarian state governance and Islamist reaction in line with the principles of its original revolution, the Kurdish movement seems to stand alone in proposing any such alternative.

As we consider how we might better organize ourselves in response to forthcoming breaches in the statist, capitalist order, we will therefore be closely concerned with the Kurdish freedom movement's ideology, organizational concepts, internal practices, and psychological playbook.

Chapter 3

Revitalizing and Reorganizing the Left

The Kurdish movement particularly hopes to disseminate its radical, utopian proposal in Kurdistan; to unite Syrian communities; to challenge state power in Turkey, Iraq, and Iran through the mobilization of those countries' Kurdish populations; and thus, ultimately, to implement democratic confederalism as a progressive political alternative in the current and future battlegrounds of "World War III."

But the ideological and organizational alternatives it proposes have relevance beyond Kurdistan and the Middle East. The Kurdish movement formulated its own democratic confederalist alternative in response to the historic collapse of state socialism in the 1990s, the Left's epochal fragmentation in the 1990s, and the PKK's experience of repression and partial collapse in the post–Cold War era. The Rojava Revolution is just one outcome of an ongoing global quest for alternative modes of organization capable of learning the lessons of this defeat and reckoning with global neoliberal hegemony backed by resurgent authoritarian state power.

Rather than rejecting the organizational lessons of the twentieth century outright, the Kurdish movement has therefore synthesized a continued commitment to Leninist organizational principles with a horizontalist, bottom-up approach to community organization. The past two chapters began to suggest some of the lessons we could learn from its highly effective revolutionary and organizational strategies.

At the same time, it's readily apparent that the present situation in the US, UK, and Europe radically differs from the Syrian Civil War. The scale of the immediate threat and prospect of imminent collapse of central state power is rather less, while social individualism and alienation are rather more advanced. As an organizer who worked in Rojava and is now trying help dual-power alternatives take root in Western Europe has written, "Rojava . . . is certainly not a blueprint that can be transplanted from one country to another. . . . We will need to come up with our own system of democratic governance, [formed] by our historical, cultural, social, economic context."[1]

In conversation with international comrades, the Kurdish movement doesn't propose the wholesale export of either democratic confederalism's utopian ideal nor yet the pragmatic Rojava model sketched in chapter 1. Instead, it poses a series of questions to the global Left in general and to Western comrades in particular. These challenges emerge both explicitly through the Kurdish movement's rhetoric and implicitly through its practice. How can we, too, think in terms of decades and cross-generational sacrifice not brief victories? How can we re-engage with communities that are conditioned to fear and disregard leftist solutions, even where these might be able to lessen their suffering or transform their lives, today or in three generations' time?

Or, as Öcalan once challenged the anarchist Left:

The dissolution of [state] socialism, the development of ecological and feminist movements, and a general surge in civil society sentiment have no doubt had a positive impact on anarchists. But sitting around talking about having been right is pointless. The question they need to answer is why they were unable to develop or build an ambitious system that reflected their goals, a question that draws attention to the chasm between their theory and their lives. Have they really overcome the modern life they criticize so much? More precisely, how consistent are they in this regard? Can they leave behind a Eurocentric way of life and truly step into global democratic modernity?[2]

In fact, a Kurdish militant once put a related challenge to me in yet more striking terms: "ISIS was able to bring thousands of people to fight in Syria. Why do Western activists struggle to bring a few dozen people to join our resistance or even to a protest in their own cities?"

To answer these challenges, we can review the state of the contemporary Western Left; how our movements have evolved since 1989; and the extent to which we've been able to learn the lessons of twentieth-century communist defeat, perpetual anarchist marginalization, and the failures of recent protest movements to achieve meaningful systemic change.

This assessment marks the first step in pursuit of our own negative utopias. Long ago, Marx laid the theoretical framework for global, twentieth-century revolution by assessing crushed uprisings, reaction, and repression in his contemporary nineteenth-century world.[3] Rather than naively predicting what a communist society would look like, he ruthlessly criticized contemporary socialist, economic, and philosophical theory and practice in order to identify the path a truly internationalist socialist movement had to tread. Likewise, we have a duty to assess the continued failures of global left movements and thus establish a more constructive mode of politics fit for the twenty-first century, World War III, and global climate catastrophe.

The "Missing Revolution"

As Öcalan observes, the collapse of state socialism gave a shot in the arm to anarchist and horizontalist movements advocating for a localist, decentralized approach to political organization. The anti-globalization movements that proliferated as the most powerful expression of (Western) anti-capitalist sentiment in the late 1990s generally relied on street protest, direct action, and spectacle aimed at grabbing media attention to get their point across. Decentralized affinity groups of activists swarmed conferences uniting the G8 countries, the International Monetary Fund, the World Bank, and other architects of the new neoliberal hegemony.

Simultaneously, these activists drew on a horizontalist, anti-hierarchical set of organizational principles. Within the protest camps and the nominally leaderless movements, this prefigurative politics sought to model the dismantling of global inequality in microcosm, with various movements hoping their own leaderless, grassroots nature would prefigure the society they hoped to help create. This approach offered a welcome tonic to the inflexible hierarchies of creaky party-political structures. But it also risked reinforcing informal social hierarchies; fostering a spirit of competitive individualism inimical to effective organization, discipline, and training; inspiring a vague politics always at risk of defaulting to mere reform; and distancing activists from ordinary people through ritualistic, performative purity politics.

From the watershed 2008 financial crisis on, movements seeking to challenge seemingly triumphant globalist, state-backed capitalism and its corresponding austerity measures began to seek governmental change. This logic was taken up in the Middle East, where the 2011 Arab Spring of street-level uprisings and public occupations was marked by a suspicion of revolutionary ideology; horizontalist, bottom-up organization; and vague but passionate demands for economic relief and the fall of the regime. In Syria as elsewhere, local committees initially sought to organize civil resistance, justice, aid, media activism, and grassroots forums for local democracy, sometimes even in forms that closely recalled Öcalan's ideal vision of a nationwide commune of communes.

These massive protests resulted in occasional reforms and the fall of several governments but also reaction and repression by authoritarian regimes, capture by more organized and increasingly reactionary Islamist forces, and collapse into post-ideological civil war. For example, Syria's grassroots local committees lacked a unifying ideology, local legitimacy, deep organizational experience, and international funds. Within the year, internationally bankrolled jihadist militias were exploiting the conflict to suit their own agenda, persecuting and driving the original revolutionaries into exile. Assad could easily present his brutal rule as the only alternative to chaos.

In form and content, the Arab Spring provided direct inspiration to the Occupy movement first in the US and then worldwide, in a political moment that catalyzed grassroots movements likewise seeking to topple, take over, or force reform upon national governments amid global austerity measures. In his book *If We Burn*, journalist Vincent Bevins traces linked uprisings diversely motivated by economic and political disenfranchisement, spiraling from Tunisia to Egypt's Tahrir Square to Bahrain, Yemen, Turkey, Brazil, Ukraine, Hong Kong, South Korea, and Chile.

All these diverse movements drew on the same tactical playbook: temporary occupation, spectacular street protest aimed at achieving national visibility via new and traditional media, and nonviolent, leaderless, anti-hierarchical organization. None managed to achieve lasting political power or reshape national politics along more democratic lines.

In Bevins's analysis, only Chile's protest movement can be counted as anything other than a failure for the country's Left, since it was only there that the protesters actually managed to "win power and get to work."[4] And even though the Chilean activist-turned-politician Gabriel Boric did manage to take top office, a reforming, leftist constitution in fact partially inspired by Rojava's own Social Contract was recently roundly rejected by Chilean voters. Likewise, as of 2024, none of the Arab Spring countries has seen successful, pro-democratic regime change at state level. Tunisia, previously often described as the Arab Spring's sole success, regressed into authoritarianism following a 2021 power grab. Though Syrians were rightly delighted to see Assad fall, his ousting by deeply authoritarian Islamists only proves the point once more.

Throughout the past decade, the US's Black Lives Matter protests have deployed a similar set of tactics, pursuing more specific goals of judicial and carceral reform. Once again, BLM failed to achieve these objectives as media interest dissipated and an elite activist coterie gained control of the movement, in a further demonstration that nominally horizontal grassroots movements are open to the fatal spread of informal hierarchy and often struggle to turn media headlines into material outcomes.[5] Similar arguments could readily be applied to the contemporary Extinction Rebellion and Just Stop Oil movements, whose thus-far-unsuccessful attempts to urge climate policy reform on disinterested national governments rely on spectacular public stunts aimed at grabbing media attention.

Asking "How is it possible that so many mass protests apparently led to the opposite of what they asked for?" Bevins draws on hundreds of interviews with activists in these diverse international movements to diagnose a failure of organization, an inability to translate nights of decentralized rage into concrete change.[6] Statist reaction and resurgent nativism or Islamism allied with the hegemonic guarantors of international financial capital to snuff out disorganized and decentralized movements' efforts at democratic and economic reform.

Hence Bevins's characterization of 2011 to the present as the era of the "missing revolution." These massive global protests were not led by any revolutionary ideology or strategic organization, and thus they were incapable of achieving systemic change. Though he's more optimistic about certain reformist outcomes, sociologist Asef Bayat has similarly described the Arab Spring as a series of revolutions without revolutionaries, its protest movements doomed to defeat and repression through their neoliberal, postmodern suspicion of ideology and strategic organization.[7]

As Boric's struggles after taking office suggest, it isn't only the grassroots, protest-focused Left that has failed to translate widespread global anger at austerity politics, neoliberalism, and "the bankers" into material change. In their recent *The Populist Moment*, Arthur Borriello and Anton Jäger similarly assess how the US's Bernie Sanders, the UK's Jeremy Corbyn, France's Jean-Luc Mélenchon, Greece's Syriza, and Spain's Podemos variously failed to accrete populist coalitions of workers, the disaffected middle-class, and students strong enough to take over or displace the chewed-out husks of social-democratic parties and translate grand promises made while in opposition to actual, governmental rule.[8] Only Syriza took office, but they infamously capitulated in the face of severe pressure from European financial institutions to accept the very austerity measures they were elected to defy. (More recently elected left populist leaders in Latin America perhaps model a more effective strategic alternative bound to their regional political context).

In different ways, these would-be party-political movements have drawn on the same tactical tradition sketched above, relying on protests, rallies, new media, and mass political participation to construct attempted alternatives to decaying social-democratic party structures. Here, too, these tactics proved insufficient to resist international finance capital and its state guarantors.

Hopeless Disorganization

We might well consider the past decade of protest—including protest votes for left populist candidates and/or against EU-imposed austerity—in the light of that word's simpler connotation. These were howls of protest, emphatic shrieks let out under the weight of capitalist hegemony, often achieving little more than fleeting media attention.

The decade of the missing revolution has therefore also been a decade of utopian political investment. Comrades worldwide placed their hope in projects that could never bring that hope to fruition—whether in parliamentary or protest movements, or even through joining the Rojava Revolution itself. The collapse of state socialism denuded the world of a "communist horizon," or a material, organized global alternative to state-backed capitalism.[9] But this has not prevented millions from sacrificing years and lives in the desperate pursuit of revolutionary change. On the contrary, younger generations show renewed commitment to revolutionary transformation—to hope in hope's absence.

There are many examples of this overinvestment in ineffectual or less-than-revolutionary struggles with revolutionary significance. I think of anarchist comrades fighting a grim war of national defense in Ukraine, desperately assuring me that the medical support networks there are a site of decentralized post-capitalist economy to assuage their own doubts over the political company they're forced to keep, fighting side by side with ultranationalist militias. Or of the way in which utopian rhetoric found itself shackled to rather ordinary social-democratic movements in the Anglosphere, with Sanders and Corbyn becoming the awkward outlet for socialists who spoke of "fully automated luxury communism" without any real idea how to get there beyond the ballot box. Of endless street protests that either devolve into ritualized antifa-vs.-police violence or are simply ignored by calm, content, business-as-usual capital. There's an excess of hope in the air, lacking form and direction, coalescing temporarily around protest movements and politicians only to dissipate into the ether of capitalist realism.

We're used to hearing that Gen Z is a despairing, directionless, hopeless generation. In 2017, only 13 percent of the global population thought the world was getting better; as of 2023, global optimism was at a ten-year low.[10] Yet this same bleak political moment has produced a newfound wave of left populist political commitment. Polls encouragingly show that Gen Z is the most pro-socialist and pro-union generation in the US.[11] But this survey asked young people whether they *supported* unions, not whether they were actually in one. It's the language of liberal performance rather than material imbrication in class struggle. Gen Z's aesthetic, rhetorical, and emotive commitment to leftist ideals is encouraging, but this genuine commitment is commonly frustrated by the lack of material, organizational possibility. It's not Gen Z's fault that, absent prospects for effective union organization in a gig economy, they often default to a more performative mode of politics. Sometimes, performance is the only available option.

When we engage in political firefighting, rushing to prevent an eviction or shut down a highway intersection while lacking the power and conviction of an organized mass movement behind us, it's easy to feel each defeat as terminal. As with the Syrian Kurdish protests demanding universal rights they know full well they can never access, the popular protest chant "Whose streets? Our streets!" betrays a repressed sense of lack. These are not and never were the protesters' streets, as the grim spectacle of US police officers shouting the slogan so painfully shows.[12]

As with the UK's "Kill the Bill" protests against anti-protest legislation, we're often necessarily pushed back into protesting *for* protest, forced to consider activism in identity politics terms as a discrete political category that must be defended against authoritarian repression, rather than working productively to advance the interests of a wider class. The NGO-ification of the international Left carries related costs. Comrades in Eastern Europe, the Middle East, and elsewhere often rely on European Union resources or on liberal, transnational funding bodies to fund important community work—and even political organization amid the Arab Spring. This further separates the activist class from the ordinary people, confining their activities to a ritualized, sanitized sphere.

These organizational shortcomings, and the global lack of revolutionary transformation throughout the past fifteen years, don't mean we have nothing to learn from one another's organizational experiences. As the tragedies of the Arab Spring remind us, revolutionary crises cannot be readily predicted or anticipated. Even within the hyper-disciplined and self-confident Kurdish movement itself, most people thought Rojava was the least likely of Kurdistan's four divided parts to witness a revolution. When the revolution did break out in 2011–12, the very name "Rojava" was still unfamiliar to many Syrian Kurds, carrying revolutionary-nationalist implications they would subsequently learn on their feet.

And so we must also find ways to respond to crises we signally failed to anticipate; to react, learn, and respond rapidly should our small, disorganized movement suddenly find itself at the head of an inchoate national movement, like those that raced around the world in 2008–12 and in the rebellious years thereafter; and to reckon with the fallout of a failed revolutionary crisis, carrying forward whatever medium- or small-scale victories and lessons we can recoup from the carnage. On all these points, the Arab Spring and post-Occupy uprisings offer rich learning experiences, individual moments of triumph, instances of policy reform, and inspiration for political organizations which in some cases continue their activity until today.

But none achieved their stated goals. In the case of the Arab Spring countries, the economic and political situation is generally far worse than it was prior to the uprisings, the original activists all dead, silenced, or exiled, and the surviving young people leaving in droves. Although we can't know how or when the revolutionary crisis will emerge, we can surely predict that as long as the Left remains so disorganized, we will continue to relive the tragic history of the missing revolution time and again.

This reality has been proven once again through the Coronavirus crisis. As with the 2008 economic crash, the pandemic unexpectedly provided a breach in business-as-usual capitalism, where an organized Left might have harnessed the mass discontent registered throughout the prior decade. But this time around, we did even worse. Our failure to find safe, effective, transformative alternatives to a panicked retreat into insularity in line with government directives once again demonstrated that global despair has yet to be organized into effective leftist hope. With climate catastrophe fast approaching, we may not get a third chance to hear the cock crow its warning before we are left to rue our repeated denials, our inability to commit to truly revolutionary change.

Left Melancholy

Often, the Left appears to be in love with its losses, resigned to a ritualistic politics that exculpates us from the need to reckon with the defeats of the twentieth century or the failures of contemporary mass protest movements.

This is what's called "left melancholy." A century ago, Walter Benjamin was the first to represent the Left's defensive attachment to a vanished past as a Freudian defense mechanism, helping us avoid being forced to confront the slow death of an actual left alternative. This process is marked by "the metamorphosis of the political struggle from a drive to make a political commitment into an object of contemplative pleasure."[13]

In the twenty-first century, left melancholy has been theorized as: a) an aesthetic attachment to the forms, rhetoric, and imagery of twentieth-century state socialism as a way to avoid reckoning with these states' historic failure; and b) an attachment to the performative politics of prefiguration and protest as a way to avoid contending with the loss of an organized, effective socialist alternative.[14] Communists might cling to the imagery of state socialism, perhaps even to apologia for contemporary, authoritarian, client-capitalist regimes from Putin's Russia to Assad's Syria for their nominal opposition to the US or NATO; anarchists, to pastoral fantasies that remain an impractical pipe dream; and all of us, most relevantly, to direct-democratic organizational practices and protest tactics that have failed to achieve lasting material change. Multiple recent analyses of the Left's failures over the decade of missing revolutions conclude by pointing to the continued structural role of left melancholy in conditioning our relationship to both street protest and the cyclical boom-and-bust of populist movements.[15]

As we'll see, the Kurdish movement's valorization of an idealized natural society can itself fall into the trap of left melancholy, preventing Kurdish militants from reckoning with the real-world challenges of remodeling contemporary Middle Eastern society and instead retreating into navel-gazing fetishism of a nonexistent, idealized past—sometimes with an ethno-nationalist tinge. Meanwhile, a simplified vision of Rojava as anarchist-paradise has latterly served as a catalyst in perpetuating some leftists' melancholic attachment to an imagined or vanished past where violent struggle leading to genuine political change in Western states was a material possibility, rather than adventurist fantasy.

During political education in Rojava, would-be militants from Western countries are encouraged to scrutinize their unexamined attachments to protest tactics, acclimatization to ritualized violence, fetishization of spectacle, and reflexive valorization of pure horizontalism. Similarly, I once heard a Kurdish organizer cite the spectacle of masked insurrectionists in Greece smashing ATMs with hammers during a run on the banks at the start of the country's debt crisis, thereby preventing workers from accessing their dwindling savings, as demonstrating the anarchist Left's inability to alleviate the material causes of people's suffering.

As Freud theorized it, melancholy must be worked through to create a productive path forward beyond endless repetition of an unreconcilable past. Whether we cling dogmatically to the forms and imagery of top-down state socialism or else to the horizontalist, decentralized methodology that rose to dominance after state socialism's collapse, we deny any possibility of working through the historic defeats of these movements and thus establishing any third-way alternative. Street protest not backed up by serious, long-term, and sustained organization is inherently melancholic in nature, a repeated externalization saving us from facing our actual losses. The organizational failures of the past decade, developed by a Left that "didn't fundamentally care if they won," demand just such a reckoning if we're to overcome the "ritualistic nature" of strategies that remain "laden with a heavy dose of fatalism."[16] As contemporary theorists of political hope in times of crisis have suggested, when this work is not done, disorganization directly engenders hopelessness: "The more spontaneous, horizontal, and leaderless social movements which have mostly overtaken communist . . . parties over the past half-century do not have the institutional capacity to ground their disappointment in a longer vision unmoved by momentary defeats."[17]

Writing at the onset of the decade of lost revolutions, T. J. Clark pessimistically urged the embrace of "a Left with no future" to reconcile ourselves to a non-revolutionary, non-utopian mode of organization that recognizes there can be no possible repeat of the great twentieth-century socialist victories.[18] Conversely, Enzo Traverso has argued that our melancholy has cut us off from an accurate appreciation of revolutionary socialist movements' past achievements, with the eventual defeat of communism making us perceive twentieth-century history as though communism was *always* doomed to fail. "Deprived of its horizon of expectation, the twentieth century appears to our retrospective gaze as an age of wars and genocides" culminating in the Holocaust, with the genuine revolutionary triumphs of twentieth-century history erased from view—a Left with no past, either.[19] As Clark notes, the very term "Left" denotes an absence: left behind, left out, floating in the doldrums of a perpetual present, concentrating on firefighting, prefigurative politics, and scattered protests in a malaise that we will assess as part of a broader individualization of hope.

In the twentieth century, socialist revolution proved itself the only political ideology truly capable of instigating a totalizing, global new order, with colossal Leninist and Maoist victories certainly justifying Marxism's ideological claims to world-historical significance, whatever their subsequent cost. In our present era, socialism is rather increasingly unique as a political dogma whose own proselytizers doubt its very possibility. We are not only severed from our past and thus unable to think the future but stuck in an endless, melancholic repetition that prevents us from effectively responding to contemporary crisis—a Left with no past, future, *or* present.

The Hope Industry

Rethinking our relationship to both the collapsed state-socialist entity and the subsequent, ineffective horizontalist alternative is therefore an urgent task—not least because the contemporary liberal center and far Right have their own highly effective brands of hope in hopeless times, which they peddle to people desperate for a personal and political future worth living. We must therefore also ask how hope is used, appropriated, and exploited by these hegemonic and counterhegemonic political forces.

The demise of state socialism was the apparent victory of market liberalism, emerging triumphant to present itself as the only viable socioeconomic system, in the stasis that cultural critic Mark Fisher has termed "capitalist realism." A pop-psychology ideology of hope blossomed in the perpetual twilight of the liberal end of history and seemingly ineluctable capitalist hegemony.[20] To facilitate this new, hegemonic consensus, hope had to be depoliticized and marketed as available to all participants in the permanently open global market.

In the climate of the 1990s and early 2000s, therefore, hope became ideologically decoupled from concrete circumstance. Post-communist, globalist liberalism asserted that we were all world citizens, free to sell our labor in an increasingly digitized labor market, just as we could hope to escape our diverse material contexts through emergent online communities. The route to emancipation passes through individual achievement and capitalist advancement, we were told, not through mass organization or class struggle.

Left movements' turn toward prefigurative, localized politics and liberal identity politics followed in the wake of this broader ideological shift, as social movements internalized the logic of individualization. In the Middle East, neoliberal interventions have similarly destroyed the ideological basis of leftist, nationalist, and socialist movements. This transition has therefore taken the form of a turn to a culturalist, post-ideological, individualist Islamism, operating in an ideological affinity with the neoliberal fetishization of individual wealth and personal enhancement.[21] Syria's new rulers are a case in point, coupling an authoritarian and identitarian Islamism with a technocratic flavor of crony capitalism.[22]

More broadly, the neoliberal consensus found tacit justification through the flourishing self-help, self-care, and therapy industries —what we might collectively term the "hope industry." This hope industry writes off any sense that hope might be correlated to material conditions, instead marshaling hope in order to placate and discipline workers and subaltern classes. (As we'll see in chapter 9, this industry partially grew out of dubious efforts to place the Jewish experience in the Holocaust in the service of depoliticized, liberal self-help ideology.) Older generations batter the young with the message that they never had it so good, that the "boomers" were able to will themselves into an easy life with a can-do attitude, and that anyone able to work themselves toward a better future will find it magically unfurling below their feet.

Hope researchers and experts champion the claim that hope is "an equal opportunity resource," divorced from income or social class, a claim that thereby forecloses any actual impetus for systemic change.[23] Comprehensive meta-research delivers the inspiring news that a hopeful attitude can enable a person to give their bosses an additional day's work each week in comparison to their despairing peers.[24] Sundry studies demonstrate that hope can help businessmen, athletes, the mentally ill, and even cancer patients to better achieve their goals, building on a neoliberal ideology of nominal equality in the marketplace to suggest that each of us is equally warranted a better future if we would but try. In one representative survey, participants were asked how hopeful they were before being shown a funny video, after which they reported increased levels of hope.[25] Such claims trivialize and dematerialize the notion of hope by reducing it to a mere squirt of endorphins.

Accompanying this popular "science" of hope, the broader hope industry deploys a range of lucrative strategies. The booming astrology industry, soon projected to pass $30 billion in annual profits, currently fulfills a similar social role to that played in the twentieth century by simplified and Orientalized philosophies of karma, reincarnation, and individual submission to a transcendent will. Astrology's pop fatalism tutors its acolytes in the belief that while anything positive that befalls them is proof of their special status, any difficulties they may encounter are the result of pre-determined, unalterable laws. The result—apolitical deference to a divine, omnipotent order—perfectly conditions people for life under neoliberal capitalist hegemony.

Critical theorist Theodor Adorno famously condemned what he called the "health unto death," the attempt to reconcile oneself to a fundamentally diseased society, whether through psychotherapy, philosophical sophistry, or neo-occult mysticism. The sprawling self-care industry has not only taken up this task with aplomb, it has even gone a step further by repackaging the deathly act of reconciling ourselves to capitalism's rule as political activism *in its own right*. (Naturally, this industry typically distances itself from the radical self-care-as-survival practiced by Audre Lorde, Angela Davis, and the Black Panthers.)

Where young women are marketed astrology apps, young men are peddled reheated Stoic philosophy. With book sales of Stoic classics and greatest-hits compilations similarly soaring, a watered-down neo-Stoicism has become "arguably America's leading nonreligious doctrine."[26] To the Stoics, hope is dangerous, even the root of evil, responsible for the desires, appetites, and yearning that must be overcome if we're to achieve personal tranquility. Yet when quotes from

Marcus Aurelius's *Meditations* are circulated on social media, reframed as "life hacks" and deployed to promote a highly masculinist, tradition- alist, pick-yourself-up-by-the-bootstraps ideology, they serve to advance a rather more palatable interpretation of Stoicism as a self-help ideol- ogy of hope. As with neo-occult astrology, this contemporary Stoicism often finds itself uncomfortably shackled to a vaguely spiritual sense of destiny, typically manifesting as the petit bourgeois expectation of busi- ness success.

On the political stage, the hope industry reached its apogee when it took over the White House in 2008. Barack Obama brilliantly marketed hope as an endpoint in and of itself, encapsulated in the famous Shepard Fairey poster emblazoned with that single, loaded word. Tellingly, Obama was lauded as "Marketer of the Year."[27] As the activist Left has been driven to protest for protest, so too Obama offered us a post-ideological, ill-defined "change we can believe in." This is what we could call "hope for hope," a second-order hope for hope's return to politics.

For example, Obama's bestseller *The Audacity of Hope* places itself in a revolutionary, anti-imperialist tradition that it immediately betrays.[28] The title is derived from a sermon by firebrand radical preacher Jer- emiah Wright, a onetime confidant of Obama's. But en route to the White House, Obama was naturally forced to recant and distance him- self from any association with Wright's radical anti-colonial screeds and Black-nationalist depiction of the US as a terrorist entity; instead, Obama carefully and deliberately scrubbed his agenda of any "partisan and ideo- logical strategy."[29]

Obama was lauded for, and received a significant electoral boost because of, an artful speech repudiating Wright's claims that the US was irrevocably racist and prone to slaughter innocents in its pursuit of its foreign policy objectives. Unsurprisingly, therefore, Obama assiduously avoided any major reforms over crucial domestic issues like criminal justice or affirmative action, paving the way for the subsequent rage of the Black Lives Matter protests; failed to hold the bankers to account or reform financial markets in the aftermath of the 2008 crash, paving the way for Occupy; and ensured the US's global bombing campaigns con- tinued unimpeded through his covert drone wars in the Muslim world, paving the way for Islamist reaction in the Middle East.

Like the broader hope industry, Obama's rhetorical hope for hope offered no substitute for a systematic, material politics. Indeed, it has been convincingly argued that the immaterial lie of vacuous liberal hope for the future peddled by Obama opened the door to the subsequent resurgence of a bitter, cynical, alt-right countermovement, culminating in Donald Trump's rise to office.[30]

Right Populism: Hope for Hopelessness

It's little wonder that many young people are turning to the ultra-cynical alt-right and populist nativism. From Donald Trump's US to Jair Bolsonaro's Brazil, these ideologies offer an alternative, grimly compelling narrative to the liberal hope industry's vague promises of hope as equal-access resource.

Across the board, the contemporary Right's discourse is marked by a jaded "negative solidarity"—the logic of *if I can't have it, they can't either*.[31] This plays out as a self-defeating and self-pitying politics that invests hope solely in excluding the other from a nation-state, rather than the more traditional conservative goal of preserving the good life for a nation's subjects. This is what we could characterize as an alt-right hope *for* hopelessness, conditioning people to make a political virtue of their own suffering and the marginalization of the other, rather than seeking actual transformation in their own lives.

Trump, Bolsonaro, Hungary's Viktor Orbán, Argentina's Javier Milei, and indeed Turkey's Recep Tayyip Erdoğan are among the Right-populist heads of state to have peddled variants of this negative solidarity and hope for hopelessness, expanding alt-right tactics onto the global stage by repackaging a reactionary nativism as somehow transgressive and countercultural. Anger against neoliberal elites is channeled into electoral politics and sporadic street violence, while those elites secure themselves a seat at the governmental table under the false premise that they will overturn it. Meanwhile, the Left struggles to articulate a historic alternative capable of drawing these frustrated, alienated populations away from the lure of nativist vitriol blaming immigrants, ethnic scapegoats, and LGBTQI+ people for their socioeconomic plight.

The Right-populists' isolationist, protectionist, America First–style rhetoric belies their comfortable accommodation with the neoliberal order. Though they might talk of protectionism or isolationism, none of them would ever disentangle their nations from the global market or global debt relations. Rather, their authoritarian regimes typically serve as the local guarantors of unfettered free market access.

On this point, it's worth revisiting the work of neoliberal ideologue Francis Fukuyama, who infamously heralded the "end of history" and the permanent victory of liberal-capitalist hegemony. His critics variously point to the surge in Right-populist nativism, 9/11, the recent waves of global protest, Russia's war on Ukraine, and Israel's war on Gaza as evidence that historical crises and upheavals continue. But Fukuyama never claimed there would be no more global conflict, only that after the decline of communism and fascism, regional, ethnic, or religious disputes would no longer trouble the historically destined forms of liberal democracy and the market economy.[32] While liberal democracy may tremble, on the point of market capitalism's continued hegemony, Fukuyama is yet to be disproven.

Andrew Tate, ISIS, and the Hopelessness Industry

Again, a broader industry has followed on the coattails of the new Right and its negative solidarity. Acolytes of far-right masculinist influencer Andrew Tate and a thousand "grindset" podcasters are conditioned to expect labor and suffering without immediate reward, summed up in the "rise and grind" slogan that has been disseminated on Instagram from the world of business self-help books. "Your pain has a purpose," Tate's mantra runs. That is, your suffering under capitalism demonstrates that you're really striving. This hustler mindset requires that each individual personally accept economic hardship as penury, thereby differentiating themselves in some numinous way from the remainder of their struggling, casually employed class.

Ideologically, this movement has an affinity with the neo-Stoic, pop-mystic psychobabble of the liberal hope industry. Each holds out the promise of personal advancement on the basis of a mystic, psychic readjustment to one's miserable station under global capitalism.

The masculinist Right affects to oppose the liberal hope industry—Tate exhorts his followers that the world "doesn't owe you anything" and so forth. But he also conditions his disciples to expect no true alternative. The "red pill" he offers as a way out of "the Matrix" of contemporary society is another edgy repackaging of a miserable, conventional existence, radicalizing a generation of young men worldwide into the profoundly conservative, misogynistic assumption that they will spend their lives in precarious work alleviated only by female subservience and unpaid domestic labor.

Whether it's Tate targeting young white males or ISIS recruitment videos targeting young Muslims, a global crisis of masculinity has given fresh impetus to narratives falsely claiming to offer young men agency on the basis of an age-old bargain: accept a society conditioning you to useless, anonymous atomization, and become the alpha male in your own sorry bedroom (or, failing that, explode into public violence via a school shooting or suicide bombing). Professing to challenge liberal-capitalist modernity through a reactionary appeal to past values, Tate and ISIS both in fact valorize the most ordinary, hegemonic, petit bourgeois ways of life, repackaged as counterculture. It's a political vision reaching millions of young men—not only in the US but also in the Middle East, where Tate's claim that his misogynistic vitriol in fact forms part of an Islamic worldview contra Western liberal hegemony is paying dividends. In fact, both Tate and ISIS fit comfortably within the logic of individualistic, self-serving neoliberal culture.

In Rojava, the Kurdish movement has attempted to counteract this trend through a radical reconceptualization of masculinity. In an educational process the Kurdish women's movement calls "*kuştina zilam*" (killing the [dominant] male), young men are encouraged to critique their patriarchal socialization and enter into a freely chosen life defined by an equal, communal, liberated relationship to women and society, in another third-way alternative.[33] But the smartphones that rank-and-file Kurdish fighters carefully keep hidden from their commanders are often filled with Tate videos, offering a compelling alternative. An international volunteer involved in *kuştina zilam* workshops for military personnel says these programs often failed to prevent the masculinist Right's cynical exploitation of younger generations' despair, with young Syrian men all too readily picking up on Tate's claim of a way out from their admittedly bleak existence.

ISIS's highly effective global recruitment, Tate's wild popularity, and Right-populist electoral victories are all proof of the same fact: young generations' willingness to make a political commitment in the face of seemingly impossible odds can easily be manipulated for hegemonic purposes. The Right is working tirelessly around the world to exploit young people's ability to willfully refuse the evidence of their eyes and their legitimate yearning for dignity, discipline, and sacrifice, conditioning them to their subservient, precarious economic role.

Many young people who recognize the lies of the liberal hope industry become captivated by the equally false promises of a radical Right that claims to deliver red-pilled liberation through hard work and a "return" to patriarchal social values, promises that leave them suffering the same old isolation and impoverishment but newly empowered to blame women and migrants for their plight. The individualistic logic implicit in the liberal hope industry's false promises of advancement is laid bare in the new Right's naked cruelty.

Networked Leninism: Organizing against Melancholy

The liberal center and nativist back-to-the-soil Right are each able to lay claim to a sense of historic political destiny, respectively advancing through market capitalism's end-of-history triumph and battling against epochal civilizational decay. If the Left is to stand any chance of countering these powerful world-historical claims, we must reassess our melancholic relation to the past, through a thoughtful critique of both our victories and defeats.

In *If We Burn*, Bevins closes his assessment of the Left's recent organizational failures with an intriguing call for "networked Leninism." The term implies some novel mode of political organization able to derive lessons from the proven organizational effectiveness of the traditional, highly disciplined Marxist-Leninist party, while also benefiting from decades' subsequent critique of that organizational structure and experiments in building more horizontal, bottom-up forms of internal democracy.[34]

The term is borrowed from Rodrigo Nunes, who, in *Neither Vertical nor Horizontal,* draws on network theory to provide a taxonomy of contemporary left-wing organizational structures, principles, and tactics that are "not meant as a blueprint for a future movement but as a description of what is always already the case to a greater or lesser extent."[35] Nunes follows Jo Freeman's well-known essay "The Tyranny of Structurelessness" in the claim that nominally bottom-up and decentralized movements like Occupy inevitably see the emergence of informal hierarchies. There can be no network or organization without a center of some sort, he argues; any structure at all necessarily has a "vanguard" where it interacts with other systems. We accept this principle in practice, even if we might deny it in political debates. Rather than restaging the tired debate between bottom-up anarchists and top-down communists, Nunes proposes we recognize that all our organizational approaches already necessarily lie somewhere between the two, on the spectrum between "horizontality and verticality, diversity and unity, centralization and decentralization, micropolitics and macropolitics."[36]

For both Bevins and Nunes, "networked Leninism" is perhaps more a provocative claim than a material reality. Nunes worries the term will drive away anarchist and other organizers to whom the very term "Leninism" is anathema. Yet as we saw in chapter 1, there's a strong sense in which networked Leninism is already underway in Rojava, where a strict, disciplined, hierarchical organization is attempting to implement a direct-democratic commune of communes—verticalist organization toward what we could call a "horizontalist horizon." This model offers a novel vertical-horizontal synthesis fit for the twenty-first century crisis, of proven effectiveness on a mass scale.

Bevins neglects to mention Rojava altogether, though the region offers a rare model of success in the era of otherwise missing revolutions. Nunes briefly refers to the revolution, but there is no room in his theoretical analysis for an exploration of how the AANES's model might differ from other horizontalist-leaning movements or offer a case study of networked Leninism in practice. Meanwhile, throughout his masterful survey of the organizational and revolutionary shortcomings of the Arab Spring, sociologist Asef Bayat repeatedly refers to the Mexican Zapatista movement's fusion of organic local struggle with a broader anti-globalist agenda as an admirable model of renewed ideological commitment in the twenty-first century. Yet he fails to mention the similar political transformations the revolutionary Kurdish movement has instigated on a much wider scale in the Middle East itself. We might therefore productively build on these analyses to ask what revolutionary conditions were missing in Istanbul, Oakland, and Homs yet present in the AANES's scattered market towns.

The Rojava Revolution cannot provide a blueprint to the global Left, but it can help us think through the consequences of our own missing revolutions. By identifying the continued verticalist tendency of the Kurdish movement's political practice amid the more usually lauded horizontalist aspect of its organizational approach, we can better analyze Rojava's relative successes and our own relative failures. Over the course of decades, the movement has steadily critiqued itself and abandoned aspects of its strict hierarchical organization while retaining its militant commitment, broad social support, and ability to defend territory, as well as its ability to build serious counter-state power and rapidly construct non-statist political, military, and administrative bodies once Syria's revolutionary crisis broke out.

The Kurdish movement does make use of street protest aimed at attracting media attention and influencing government policy, after the fashion of Occupy or the Arab Spring. But their occasional resort to dramatic confrontation with state authorities is justified by a broader, deeper range of strategies including the construction of dual-power community organizations, cooperative economic alternatives, community justice mechanisms, and women's programs in Kurdish cities; electoral and diplomatic politics; strategic alliances with social, state, tribal, and other regional actors, plus international anti-state, feminist, and leftist organizations; and armed struggle.

Nunes calls for us to recognize our political movements as made up of "distributed leaders," a diverse, multifaceted vanguard straining ever outward like an amoeba's pseudopodia.[37] It's an apt description of the Kurdish movement's complex model of leadership, through which each wing of the broader Kurdish freedom movement (the autonomous women's movement, the militant PKK, Öcalan himself, Kurdish civil society) has variously played a vanguard role in pushing for internal reform and external action at various crucial junctures in its history. The movement sees no contradiction in relying on its central committee to maintain cohesive discipline while simultaneously allowing young street activists to instigate civil uprisings, or autonomous women's bodies to insist on radical structural reform.

Similarly, rather than following Öcalan's critique of state socialism to reject all hierarchy outright, the movement continues to respect seniority, experience, and organizational ability while striving to countermand the detrimental effects of internal hierarchy. Among other measures, it fills all leadership positions with one male and one female co-chair, rotates all but the most senior organizational figures through different positions, and often requires seasoned militants to rejoin basic political training in order to remain close to the organization's grassroots.

The same principle holds true on the broader organizational level. The Kurdish movement's own prefigurative efforts to model an ideal society by demanding its militants submit to a totally communal mode of existence can appear extreme to Western eyes. Yet through its long-term work in conservative rural communities, the movement has proven itself capable of meeting local populations halfway, softening its militant practices and revolutionary language while also tending to these communities' basic needs by offering tangible support rather than retreating into purist insularity. The movement is thus simultaneously more vertical and organized than most Western movements (due to its Leninist culture of sacrifice, ethics, and discipline) and yet more horizontal and democratic (due to its broad base of social support and determined construction of anti-state counterpower).

Each aspect of this hybrid approach has naturally faced its various challenges—power is far from universally disseminated throughout Rojava's civil society, while state repression constantly seeks to drive wedges between the movement's diverse military, parliamentary, regional, and civil society structures. This doesn't mean these measures are flawless or that the Kurdish movement has avoided all the pitfalls of Stalinist verticalism and anarchist disorganization: far from it. Committed anarchists and communists would doubtless critique one or another aspect of the Kurdish movement's practice. But by the same token, the movement's attempt to instigate bottom-up democracy through top-down control illuminates shortcomings in both anarchist and party-political organization. Whether we prefer to think of it as networked Leninism or vanguard anarchism, we can surely stand to learn from their example.

If the Kurdish movement still tends to an excess of verticalist hierarchy, in our own movements the danger likely emerges from the opposite end of the spectrum. Arriving from the chaotic, fragmented, horizontalist Western Left to be confronted with the Kurdish movement's strict organizational framework, Rojava's internationalist volunteers had ample cause to recall Lenin's proclamation: "Have no fear, gentlemen! Remember that we stand so low on the plane of organization that the very idea that we could rise too high is absurd!"[38]

The New Internationalism

The AANES's unique organizational synthesis evolved in a specific cultural and political context. At times, the Kurdish movement's self-conception can tend to an essentialist, nationalist chauvinism, valorizing the Kurdish struggle as uniquely effective and existentially justified. By setting up a relatively black-and-white binary between its own practices and a Western Left portrayed as ultraliberal, libertine, and hopelessly divided, the movement can downplay contributions made by other global political movements throughout their three decades' quest for organizational alternatives.

But the Kurdish movement also seeks to reanimate a spirit of internationalist socialist solidarity, remade for our era of grassroots, decentralized struggle. Absent the sponsorship of communist powers, Kurdish movement representatives have portrayed themselves as a sort of grassroots International, successors to the Communist International, the Third-Worldist Non-Aligned Movement, and the 1966 Tricontinental Conference in Havana, Cuba.[39]

This is another reason why the Syrian conflict is framed as the new Spanish Civil War and Rojava as a twenty-first-century Paris Commune: they, too, can be understood as militarized crises capable of providing training to thousands and inspiration to millions of leftists worldwide, even as deepening domestic divisions set a staging ground for reactionary violence. Non-military volunteers in Rojava arrive to an "internationalist commune," to be exhorted via the dicta of internationalist icon Che Guevara to bring their ideological training back to their own countries and build grassroots counterpower there, in conversation with the Kurdish movement's perspectives.[40] Accordingly, while the AANES might focus on fostering pragmatic ties with Syrian and Middle Eastern communities, the Kurdish movement's youth, women's, diplomatic, and internationalist wings are at work around the globe, building links to groups such as the Black-led solidarity economy network Cooperation Jackson in Mississippi, to South Africa's Landless People's Movement, to movements organizing among India's landless Dalits and in Kenyan slums. In 2023 and 2024, for example, the movement held conferences in Paris and Beirut uniting the youth wings of national liberation, women's, ecological, Indigenous, Marxist-Leninist, and anarchist movements from over sixty countries.

In the West, a resurgent spirit of internationalism is witnessing currents of unorganized leftist hope flow toward renewed political investment in (armed) struggles in the Global South, from Rojava to Palestine. This palpable turn toward internationalist solidarity is often symptomatic of a desire to break away from localized politics and re-engage with mass, disciplined political organization, in reaction to the melancholic hopelessness of the decade of missing revolutions. This sentiment finds one extreme manifestation in the Western "martyrs" who gave their lives in defense of Rojava's revolutionary ideal—embodying a noble, internationalist hope for *another's* hope.

Mass protests couldn't prevent Israel's genocide in Gaza, any more than they could halt the US's 2003 invasion of Iraq. In the coming years, a growing skepticism over the protest form may therefore catalyze a further turn away from the protester and back to the internationalist, as left movements learn political, practical, and organizational skills abroad they apply at home—whether in pursuit of their own specific agendas or to strike more effectively at the centers of imperial power in acts of internationalist solidarity. At the least, by enabling theoretical and practical engagement with real-world organizational models beyond street protest, direct action, and leaderless decentralization, the internationalist idea can inspire critical reassessment of our own political practice. The ultimate significance of the Kurdish movement's knowledge-sharing is less the potential construction of any formal, global counterpower to capitalist hegemony than in allowing the diversification and rejuvenation of strategic perspectives. Rather than fondly expecting Syrian-style revolution in Madrid or London or conversely rejecting revolution outright in favor of purely local reformism, we can work through our melancholy in practice and conversation with the Kurdish movement and others with experience of actually achieving revolutionary change.

Through this process, we can gain insight on our own fleeting moments of triumph to cement more lasting change. For example, what might it have taken for Black Lives Matter to achieve the total overthrow of the US justice system in a single state or city, replacing it with a truly grassroots alternative? At the least, any such victory would require decades of organization and preparation in diverse Black communities throughout (for example) Ferguson or Louisville; steadily accumulating money, property, and expert personnel; emboldening thousands of young people to risk lives and livelihoods in pursuit of a common goal; and fostering ties with experienced international comrades with real-world experience of establishing effective counterpower to the state. The fraught yet functional examples of Rojava's reconciliation committees or (for example) Mexico's self-governed Chéran community could help a rejuvenated BLM movement further grasp and work through the limitations of their attachment to reactive street protest aimed at winning media attention.

At present, even this thought experiment feels naively utopian. But internationalism provides a conduit for the two-way exchange of material support, political education, and ideological inspiration, between Western movements and global militants. It offers us that crucial utopian "horizontalist horizon," which in turn can equip activists for the messy, repetitive tasks of day-to-day organization.

Self-Criticism as Negative Utopianism

As part of this process, the Kurdish movement offers a potentially useful tool to help the global Left break old attachments in pursuit of new organizational alternatives: its unique model of criticism and self-criticism.[41]

During daily or weekly sessions of what's called *"tekmil,"* comrades in a given collective or commune systematically identify selfish, patriarchal, destructive, or unhelpful behavior patterns in themselves and their comrades.

Unlike the bitter haranguing associated with a Maoist struggle session, criticism in the Kurdish movement is seen as useful only if it leads to generative change. Tekmil is intended to be calm, productive, and therapeutic. Militants are not supposed to criticize the actions of individuals in isolation but rather refer to the aspects of their upbringing and socialization that have engendered the counterproductive behavior in question. For example, they might note a university-educated male comrade's patriarchal replication of intellectual hierarchies, a city-dweller's disrespect for the natural world, a Western internationalist's Orientalizing fetishization of violence. At the same time, the individual being criticized has the responsibility to take the criticism seriously and implement concrete steps toward its resolution—for example, that patriarchal male comrade might step back from leading group study-sessions, volunteer for extra kitchen duty, and ask other male comrades to monitor his behavior in conversations.

In a sense, tekmil is marked by the same spirit as Adorno's "negative utopianism," expressing hopes for the new only through a radical assessment of the failures of the old. It seeks to cultivate revolutionary new personalities and collectives through a critique of what is capitalistic, patriarchal, and individualistic in the old. And this radical, negative, constructive process can help us not only on the individual but also on the organizational scale. As Nunes writes, "Perhaps we should start from the assumption that everything has failed."[42] Recognizing state socialism's ultimate defeat by imperialist capitalism and the bloody suppression of would-be anarchist revolutions is not an excuse to wallow in melancholy for what could have been; it is an urgent reason to rethink both sets of tactics.

Can we follow the Kurdish movement's historic reassessment of its organizational practice to engage in a similar self-critique, rather than moving reflexively from the horizontal toward the vertical? Could organized, vertical-yet-horizontal, mass-scale movements built around other stateless, subaltern, or Indigenous causes have enabled the post-Occupy/Arab Spring wave of global protest movements to succeed elsewhere? What concrete steps can we take to begin organizing now, with the intention of one day achieving revolutionary change in response to emergent crises currently set to be exploited by resurgent state authoritarianism?

This type of productive interrogation of both the Western psyche and our political movements formed a core component of political education for internationalist volunteers in Rojava—a majority of whom, it should be noted, hail from richer Western nations in general and Germany in particular. As in their message to the would-be insurrectionaries of the Capitol Hill Autonomous Zone, Kurdish organizers did not critique internationalist revolutionaries' enthusiasm for change but rather their haste and disorganization. They enjoined their internationalist comrades not to give up on political struggle in the heart of empire but return to their communities to listen, learn, and begin the long, slow process of dual-power organization.

For example, German comrades were challenged to reckon with their squeamishness around words like *volk* (people) or *heimatschutz* (akin to the Kurdish movement's crucial ideological concept of *welatparêzî*, "love of the homeland"). These are core constructions in the Kurdish movement's political analysis, yet when directly translated into German, they're tainted by their past association with Nazism. German comrades were therefore charged to articulate a functional alternative capable of speaking to their nation as a whole rather than ceding this vital political terrain to the nativist Right. Similarly, British and US comrades were pushed to overcome their tendency for knee-jerk disavowal of their own country's history in toto, and to instead explore the radical emancipatory current buried in their long histories of class struggle and defeat.

If we have no way of drawing on a deep historical tradition to inspire a broad political base to long-term, dedicated action, we're doomed to the melancholic repetition of what has already failed. The reclamation and reassessment of history are thus understood by the Kurdish movement as the crucial first steps toward reanimating an epochal revolutionary politics. The next chapter will explore this daunting task.

Chapter 4
"Could It Be?"
The Myth of History

The contemporary Left is terrified of grand, totalizing political narratives—Marxism in particular but also nationalism, essentialist feminism, and liberal democracy. We not only struggle to believe in any one story explaining the disjointed and infinitely varied nature of modern existence but also fear that any such simplification would do active harm to those who don't fit within its terms—a trend particularly catalyzed by the collapse of the USSR. This postmodern dearth of viable myths, which post-anarchist philosophy has termed a crisis of metanarrative, is a contemporary manifestation of what Friedrich Nietzsche famously called the death of God.[1] In the Middle East, young generations' turn to a reactionary and individualist Islamism, marked by a fanatical belief in divine destiny, is another symptom of this general malaise. Yet if we're to find hope in hopeless times, we must find ways of working through and making sense of a decade of left failures; a twentieth century similarly marked by the Left's historic defeats; millennia of worsening oppression; and perhaps even the fact of predation and competition in the natural world.

Öcalan offers one novel response to this crisis. By synthesizing utopian, universal rhetoric and the pragmatic, nationalist organization of the Kurdish people, he places all of human history and struggle in the service of the Kurdish freedom movement's political agenda—and vice versa. By asking how the Kurdish movement understands the construction history, its historical precedents, and its own historic role, we can consider how to place our own dilapidated national and leftist histories in the service of a revolutionary, transformative tomorrow. Claiming hope from a seemingly hopeless past is the first step toward refashioning it today.

Mythmaking: Öcalan and Bookchin's Historical Metanarratives

Particularly following the 1989–91 collapse of state socialism, historic defeats inflicted on the PKK, and his own 1999 capture, Abdullah Öcalan embarked on a reassessment of the basic tenets of Marxist-Leninist nationalist struggle. As is relatively well known, American libertarian socialist and ecologist Murray Bookchin (1921–2006) exerted crucial influence on Öcalan's developing thought in the course of this paradigm change.

As thoughtful scholarship has demonstrated, it is insufficient if not actively Orientalist to view Öcalan as merely reheating Bookchin's theories. The Kurdish thinker's critiques of state socialism, patriarchy, and standard liberal and Marxist accounts of history all predate his imprisonment, while he also draws on a broader range of influences including Fernand Braudel and Immanuel Wallerstein's *longue durée* histories of capitalist expansion, Maria Mies's theory of patriarchal primitive accumulation at the expense of women, and Michel Foucault's concept of discursive "regimes of truth."[2]

That said, Öcalan's version of how modern capitalist society ineluctably evolved from prehistory is certainly indebted to Bookchin, with whom he corresponded toward the end of the American political philosopher's life. Like Marx, Öcalan and Bookchin both offer us political teleologies: that is, they explain history as progressing toward a particular set of political outcomes. Both thinkers represent their political programs as the natural conclusion of a longue durée historical analysis dating back to prehistory—or even further. They reach into the murky eons of evolutionary biology, right down to the molecular, atomic, and quantum levels of analysis, from which they conjure essentialist proofs that cooperation and harmony are "natural."[3]

To Bookchin, gerontocracy (or the subjugation of the young by the old) instigated the first hierarchies in primeval human societies. This was followed by male subjugation of women, with the institutionalization of repression through clan, city, and state soon following. In a crucial distinction, the Kurdish leader instead follows Mies to describe womankind as the "first colony" exploited by man. Following these initial points of departure, both thinkers trace the development of social and political hierarchy as it metastasizes into our present-day system of state-backed, exploitative, extractive, and environmentally destructive capitalism marked by extreme social atomization. Both argue it is hierarchy that must first be deconstructed, beginning with its roots in male exploitation of women and human exploitation of nature, before capitalism can be overturned.

Succinctly put, Bookchin's chosen metanarrative to describe our existence is the dispersed ecosystem as opposed to the linear food chain. What he calls "social ecology" therefore seeks to deconstruct all biological and social hierarchies, initiating a renewed role for humankind as the highest expression of nature's organic, mutual interdependency. (To an extent, this social ecology prefigures Rodrigo Nunes's call to think of our political action ecologically as the complex interplay of systems.)

There's a certain mysticism to Öcalan's writings, the more apparent when set against Bookchin's arguments. The Kurdish leader's works were written from memory, without access to books, and reputedly transmitted to the outside world from his prison island in lieu of defense submissions at court. The subsequent lack of footnoted references can certainly make Öcalan's arguments hard to parse. His works are peppered with rhetorical questions and gnomic historical and metaphysical speculations, often bracketed by disclaimers. What should we make of musings like the following:

> Could the universe be composed just of the dual antagonism of a humongous black hole and matter? Is matter non-matter that makes itself visible? Does this mean that we can see the universe, which has made itself visible, as a big, living being? Can it be that all dual antagonisms in life are reminiscent of this universal dual antagonism? Can love and hate, good and bad, beauty and ugliness, right and wrong all be the reflections of this universe?[4]

The late anarchist and anthropologist David Graeber seeks to reclaim this anti-academic ambiguity as inherent to Öcalan's critique of deterministic, positivist history. In a characteristically deft analysis, he addresses Öcalan's ambiguous role as "the intellectual leader who advises his followers to reject all the certainties that ordinarily flow from the role of an intellectual leader, the patriarch who calls on men to kill the patriarch within them." As Öcalan is engaged in a paradoxical struggle to critique authoritarian centrist political organization while leading a democratic-centralist Leninist party, it is in fact wholly appropriate that he writes in "suggestions, disruptions, confessions, and narratives that resist being read in any biblical or ex cathedra form."[5]

This offers a useful way to understand Öcalan's unique style. But as Graeber seeks to burnish the Kurdish militant's horizontalist, anarchist credentials, he perhaps goes too far. Graeber claims Öcalan is "not a totalizing thinker" and that his political voice deliberately eschews the typical tenor of a Marxist "prophet" issuing solemn prescriptions to his followers.[6] But contrary to Graeber's attempt to redeem the Kurdish leader from charges of vanguardism, Öcalan's intellectual significance only makes sense when he's read as a prophet, preaching to his followers rather than speaking to the academy.

Öcalan's brilliance lies precisely in translating and transfiguring Bookchin's ideas for the Middle Eastern context, distilling them into prophetic maxims capable of motivating and organizing the Kurdish people, and granting them a world-historic mission. He achieves this by adapting a Bookchinite account of history unfolding through the epochal extension of hierarchies from the Mesopotamian city-state to the contemporary capitalist system and thus reminding the Kurdish people that ancient history's Fertile Crescent is modern-day, occupied Kurdistan. The Kurds are therefore marshaled as the inheritors of an idyllic "natural society" long vanquished by the expansion of centralized, hierarchical power from priest-infested Sumerian ziggurats to the modern authoritarian state. (And as Rojava gained its autonomy in 2012, Kurdish militants did indeed position their heavy weapons among the storied ruins of these same Mesopotamian archaeological sites.)

There's an intimate relationship between this politicized representation of "Kurdishness" and Öcalan's political challenge to state capitalism. Though the Kurdish movement may have formally abandoned its statist ambitions, many Kurds in Rojava certainly have not, including many working directly for the movement itself. The Kurdish movement both struggles with and benefits from this reality. It mobilizes nationalism against external threats, while simultaneously engaging in ideological work to deconstruct chauvinistic nationalism and implement a more broad-church concept of "nation" as democratic, multiethnic confederation. Öcalan's hybrid metanarrative proves able to fulfill both contradictory functions, synthesizing a centralizing nationalistic cause with a decentralizing anti-nationalistic vision. This type of adaptable, hybrid theorization can help the Left to escape its present horizontalist malaise and speak a language ordinary people can understand.

It does Öcalan no disservice to say his treatises lack the rigor of Bookchin's trained academic prose. Rather, as Graeber writes when introducing Öcalan's *Manifesto for a Democratic Civilization*, the Kurdish leader is actively engaged in mythmaking but not in myth's "(positivist) colloquial sense of 'story that isn't true.'" Instead he is necessarily organizing the facts "to tell a larger, meaningful story."[7]

If some subtleties are perhaps lost in translation, more are certainly ironed out in the process of propagating Öcalan's ideas to Kurdish militants, youth, and women through Rojava's network of educational academies and ideological training programs, and again as they are disseminated through Syrian society. Bookchin's name is familiar to few people in Rojava save the more ideologically committed Kurdish militants, and that indirectly.

But one need not grasp critical theory to die for democracy—as any glance at the historic successes of revolutionary movements demonstrates. An ability to reach a revolutionary commitment without logical proofs or empirical data is fundamental to the psychological and political process of constituting hope in hopeless times. To this end, it's necessary to simplify, reduce, and close one's eyes to certain facts. Bookchin similarly feels "obliged to recover the authentic utopian tradition" from the past, as a counter to the nihilistic predictions of modern environmentalist literature.[8] Like Öcalan, he consciously crafts a myth of history intended to serve a particular end.

The Kurdish movement adapts Bookchin's image of a "double helix" to describe "two rivers" of history, tracing a "democratic" current of resistance and struggle in opposition to a mainstream history of worsening repression.⁹ (Recall that the Kurds live in what was once Mesopotamia, the "land of two rivers" between the Euphrates and the Tigris, the cradle of civilization.) These similar descriptive frameworks each require us to search the past for proofs of horizontal, democratic-social organization, operating in opposition to an ever-mounting tide of hierarchical exploitation.

Both Bookchin and Öcalan therefore valorize ancient modes of localized communal social organization that predate the rise of the city-state. This trope—of antediluvian societies enjoying forms of proto-socialist solidarity and anarchist community now irrevocably lost to modernity—has a long intellectual history in post-Enlightenment thought. It's known to Marx as "primitive communism," Rousseau as the "state of nature," Bookchin as "organic society," and Öcalan as "natural society."

Whether life ten thousand years ago really was any kind of an Eden is ultimately irrelevant. This idealized state of nature can best be understood not as any literal or utopian epoch, but on the converse as an ideological concept constructed to serve contemporary political agendas, particularly legitimizing the repressive counterpower of the modern state.¹⁰ As Rousseau puts it, the true state of nature "no longer exists, perhaps never did exist, and probably never will exist."¹¹ In the hands of Marx, Bookchin, and Öcalan, the concept of a lost, blissful state of nature is therefore reclaimed and wielded as a blunt instrument, used to castigate modernity and muster support for societal transformation.

The resultant version of history may prove somewhat simplistic, essentialist, or caricatured. But this simplification serves a revolutionary purpose. For example, when describing this prelapsarian society prior to the emergence of gender-, age-, and class-based hierarchies, Bookchin makes clear he "do[es] not wish to imply that women exercised any form of institutional sovereignty over men."¹² But militants in the Kurdish women's movement are likely to conceptualize this "natural society" in a more idealized light. Overlooking Bookchin's caveats, they instead envisage a literal matriarchal utopia based on an essentialist understanding of woman's unique harmony. So be it: this myth of history equips them for the daunting task of revolutionizing sexist, conservative society from the ground up.

Öcalan's diversions from mainstream archaeological and academic consensus, and in particular his obsessive political focus on Sumerian culture and its perceived links to contemporary social organization in the Middle East, are contextualized by his critique of Western historiography. To understand history through the prism of democratic or anti-hierarchical values is no more or less an error than understanding history as we are taught it in the West, that is, through the prism of anti-democratic and hierarchical values.

Graeber describes the Kurdish leader as a politically committed, Gramscian organic intellectual who refuses to play the liberal-academic game and is thus marginalized and denigrated by the academy. His writings are "meant to have an impact on the world, not just to state a truth but to state it in a certain manner to a certain audience in such a way as to lead them to act differently than they had before."[13]

In other words, many post-Marxist philosophers have hitherto only interpreted Marx in various ways. The point, however, is to change him. Recognizing the contingency of mainstream liberal or Marxist historical narratives has a freeing effect on Öcalan, Bookchin, and their followers, enabling them to explore democratic forces and modes of social organization obscured from more hegemonic narratives.

To Öcalan, and therefore to the Kurdish movement at large, there are few dirtier words than "positivism"—the post-Enlightenment ideology that values as true only scientifically verifiable facts and holds that all of human society can therefore be understood through scientific analysis. Conversely, Öcalan joins those critical theorists who believe positivist thought dangerously elevates science above its proper role as a tool for emancipating society. Instead, positivism places society itself at the mercy of a blind, self-perpetuating, dehumanizing, capitalist logic.[14] To put it another way, capitalism has its own myths—including the fundamental meta-myth that its myth alone is worth learning from.

As Öcalan puts it: "The capitalist economic and societal form is not a social and historical necessity; it is a construct, forged through a complex process. Religion and philosophy have been transformed into nationalism, the divinity of the nation-state. The ultimate goal of its ideological warfare is to ensure its monopoly on thought. Its main weapons to accomplish this are religionism, gender discrimination and scientism as a positivist religion."[15]

Many international friends of the Kurdish movement initially balk at this anti-empiricist tendency in Öcalan's thought, and it's certainly possible to poke holes in Öcalan's broad-brush analyses and grand historical claims. But to do so misses the point. No one denies that positivist science has saved and improved countless lives, but this science has also brought with it dehumanization, instrumental exploitation, mechanization, industrialized slaughter. It, too, must be unmasked and transcended.

The Kurdish women's movement, which further attempts to deconstruct authoritative male accounts of history, both helped inspire Öcalan's critique of instrumental rationality and continues along that same critical path today. As leading scholar of the Kurdish women's movement Dilar Dirik writes, despite a "common tendency . . . to judge the [Kurdish] movement's theories . . . on their scientific accuracy," it is "more interesting to consider the subtext and spiritual meaning, affect, and purpose, pedagogical and political, of such theses."[16] Those grounded in the Western academic tradition often struggle to decolonize their reading of history and recognize the contingency of our own grand historical narratives.

To this end, the women's movement practices what it calls "Jineology," or "women's science." If it were understood as a literal attempt to disprove the foundations of modern rationality, Jineology would appear self-evidently vague, insufficient, and spiritual. But Jineology is a science in the same sense that Marxism-Leninism presents itself as a science—a provocative epistemic claim that the liberal teleology of history is not the only show in town.[17]

Jineology therefore operates in a broader tradition of postcolonial critiques of positivist Western science: "Methodologically, [Jineology] values a diversity of approaches that can transcend the object/subject dichotomy rooted in much of Western intellectual thought, and holistically account for emotions, experiences, intuitions, notions of truth relating to . . . the non-material . . . This 'broad approach to meaning-giving' allows for the possibility of multiple interpretations of phenomena."[18]

Jineology challenges the positivist assumption that Öcalan's myth-making delegitimizes his analyses: first by pointing to the contingent, myth-like nature of all historical and political narratives, and second by actively reclaiming myth as politically, analytically valid.

Both Öcalan's critics and his advocates recognize this mythmaking quality in the Kurdish thinker's approach, and his advocates therefore do themselves no favor when they try to deny the fact. Based on interviews with internal dissidents who have quit the Kurdish freedom movement due to political, strategic, or moral disagreements, the PKK's critical biographer Aliza Marcus finds that "for Öcalan, the conclusion was always more important than the factual details that preceded it."[19] But sympathetic writers like Graeber and Dirik effectively reclaim this critique, situating it within Öcalan's critique of orthodox historiography.

Öcalan's ideology was crafted to put fire in (Kurdish) bellies, not pass peer review. Caviling over historical details is understandably taken by Kurdish organizers as demonstrating a counterrevolutionary inability to set aside personal reservations and skepticism, to take what the absurdist philosopher Kierkegaard would call a "leap of faith" from the bounds of rationality into a productive political future. The time for academic rigor is not when ISIS is at the gates, still less when a new world cries out to be born.

Kurdish political educators working with Western internationalists in Rojava were therefore prone to castigating the egotism, liberalism, and individualism of their students—for example, asserting that whereas fifteen liberals might give fifteen different answers to a given question, fifteen revolutionaries should respond as one. These deliberately provocative, Nietzschean onslaughts sought to shake the assumptions of Western anarchists comfortable with provoking the liberal order, comfortable with left-melancholic posturing, but rather less willing to scrutinize the extent to which anarchist thought or the values of the identitarian contemporary Left are determined by the liberal order's orthodoxies.

When critiquing positivist, post-Enlightenment liberal rationality, Rojava's political educators sometimes spoke in terms that recalled Nietzsche's reflexive condemnation of the smug, Richard Dawkins–style new atheist. Nietzsche famously mocked Christians, but he also mocked the "unsuspecting, simple certainty with which [the atheist's] instinct treats the religious man as a lower and less valuable type."[20]

Nietzsche was no more a friend to orthodox Christendom than the Kurdish movement is to state socialism. But this does not prevent either from a simultaneous critique of those atheists and anarchists who smugly think themselves superior to these preexisting orders, without undertaking the intellectual work needed to truly liberate themselves from their own imbrication in the repressive traditions. Just like Öcalan, Nietzsche saw that faith in science and historicism was often just that—another faith.

The Kurdish movement encourages us to recognize that we all have our own foundational myths—one for each nation, movement, comrade, if not more. By recognizing, deconstructing, and reconstructing our personal myths, we can divest ourselves us from the dead weight of capitalist hegemony and left melancholy. In conversation with comrades from the libertine, anarchistic Left, therefore, Kurdish political educators proudly recall the PKK's Leninist roots. But in conversation with Marxist comrades, conversely, they emphasize the Kurds' historic abandonment by the USSR and maltreatment by the nominally socialist Ba'ath regime. Each foundation myth serves a particular purpose.

The new or reformulated myths we light upon through this process can liberate us for bold, hopeful political action. When delivering education programs in working-class Kurdish communities, the party engages in a Paolo Freire–style process of consciousness raising, emphasizing the social and intellectual contributions of Middle Eastern women and Kurdish society. Freire's *Pedagogy of the Oppressed* encourages us to seek out, learn from, and animate localized metanarratives capable of synthesizing socialist ideals with regional reality.[21] The movement has literally appropriated and reframed myths and legends from Kurdish and Middle Eastern cultures to muster young Kurds and women to its cause. For example, it lays claim to anti-establishment folk hero Kawa the Blacksmith; venerates Mesopotamian goddess Ishtar as a symbol of women's repressed creativity, knowledge, and power; and draws creative links between its own female freedom fighters and the heroine of a *Romeo and Juliet*–style seventeenth-century Kurdish epic, *Mem û Zin*.[22]

A "Natural" Society: The Reactionary Undercurrent of Utopia

Öcalan challenges the liberal metanarrative of history by valorizing his lost natural society, representing the Kurdish people as particularly historically destined to rejuvenate a universally ailing society. Such selective historic accounts are not without their dangers. A vanished past is all too easily imagined as an ethnically homogeneous Eden, prior to the degeneration occasioned by the corruption of a national ideal—as at the ecofascist, survivalist extreme of contemporary ecological movements. Through the fetishization of a vanished, primitive-communist, communal way of life, the Kurdish movement risks indulging in its own left melancholy, retreating from the realities of capitalist modernity and the contemporary Middle East. Öcalan is therefore right to warn against the "reactionary form of localism against globalism" as opposed to what he calls "local, democratic, cultural, feminist movements."[23]

Likewise, Bookchin knows his alternative metanarrative of history might lead his followers to a blood-and-soil primitivism. He therefore warns against "the glorification of prehistory" and any misguided desire to recreate prelapsarian modes of social organization, which could easily serve to reinforce of racial, familial, and gender-based hierarchies tending toward white nationalism.[24] On the same point, Bookchin repeatedly turns Marx's maxim "the social revolution . . . cannot take its poetry from the past but only from the future" against both Marxists themselves and eco-capitalists.[25] He argues that the primitive past must be selectively deployed to open up a politically productive future, in a "forward-looking" rather than "backward" utopianism.[26]

For an understanding of the dangers of backward utopianism and the potentials of forward utopianism, we can turn again to Nietzsche—a man as committed to radical, forward-facing transformation as any Marxist or Kurdish revolutionary. In *Beyond Good and Evil,* Nietzsche remains alert to the danger that his polemic against the Christian moral order preventing humankind from achieving its full potential will be misconstrued as a mere call for conservative reaction. Nietzsche is clear there can be no half measures, knowing his thought can turn reactionary if it is not taken all the way to its limit. He therefore warns his fellow skeptics of modernity against any retreat into a desire for their "old God," seeking in the vanished past the vigor and joy which they quite rightly identify as lacking in modernity. To Nietzsche, when these half-baked philosophers betray a wish to retreat back into reactionary politics, what they really mean is they want to go away, retreating from the radical implications of their own critique of positivist logic.[27]

"A little MORE strength, swing, courage and artistic power, and they [the critics of modernity] would be OFF—and not back," he writes. His terms echo both Marx's desire for an unwritten poetry of the future and Bookchin's call for a forward utopianism. Here, as always, Nietzsche is seeking the negation of the negation, a radical critique that leads us to construct a new society, rather than merely pursuing personal power within present-day social structures and moral confines.

The danger lies not in too extreme a critique of modernity but in the direction this critique leads. For it can all too easily falter and be placed into the service of either chauvinistic reaction or tried-and-failed, left-melancholic politics. Certainly, such is the power of his disgust with modernity that Nietzsche himself was not immune from the trap of looking back rather than beyond. The philosopher was infamously fated to suffer just the kind of fatal misunderstanding he warns against, as the Nazis appropriated his critique of liberal modernity to serve their own retrograde, totalizing politics.

If we want to land beyond rather than behind the ailing liberal order, articulating a true, forward alternative, we must instead find a productive, dialectically produced third way. This distinction is vital to constituting hope in the face of historic decline and contemporary political malaise. Critiques of modernity are productive when they lead us through despair to the bold conclusion that only (socialist) utopia is an adequate alternative. Mishandled, such critiques can easily founder in the shadow of capitalist hegemony, social catastrophe, or climate collapse, leading us to retreat to our sundry leftist cliques, petit bourgeois domiciles, or ethnically homogeneous communes.

With typical far-sightedness, Bookchin recognized that "any self-managed community . . . that tries to live in isolation and develop self-sufficiency risks the danger of becoming parochial, even racist."[28] And certainly, ethnic chauvinism does creep into some Kurdish revolutionaries' speech as they exhort the Kurdish youth to battle ISIS and Sunni-Arab-supremacist militias hellbent on ethnic cleansing. ISIS's own Sunni Arab chauvinism means the region's Arabs are sometimes dismissed in turn by indignant Kurdish locals as *gişt çete*, "nothing but [Islamist] bandits." These sentiments can easily feed into a spirit of Kurdish supremacy, becoming actively harmful in the extent to which the long-suffering Kurds are now the autonomous region's determinant political and military force and hampering efforts to build multiethnic regional federation.

More broadly, a strong element of Kurdish nationalism is indispensable to the AANES's enduring survival. As a quantitative survey has shown, the Rojava Revolution is necessarily understood by most ordinary local Kurds as entrenching basic Kurdish rights.[29] In particular, the fight against ISIS was understood as a struggle to defend values coded as Kurdish (democracy, freedom of expression, women's rights) against theocratic violence.

This shouldn't imply a condemnation of the Kurdish masses for failing to grasp their political vanguard's emancipatory message, incorrectly interpreting Öcalan's paradigm change in chauvinistic terms. Rather, Öcalan's teleology of history inherently suggests a world-historical role for his long-repressed people. For many Kurdish locals, Öcalan's attempts to restage history as the struggle of democratic forces against hierarchical elites are significant only insofar as they speak to present-day struggles for Kurdish autonomy.

But this worrying current of Kurdish chauvinism is countermanded by an ongoing commitment to pluralism, remarkable in any context, let alone in response to ISIS's naked cruelty. The AANES's handling of Rojava's internal Arab-Kurdish tensions has overall been marked by a willingness to look forward and not back, as they define their new political project. Throughout the years, the AANES has therefore opened its borders to hundreds of thousands of Arab refugees; allowed low-ranking ISIS members to return home through regular amnesties; and compromised with conservative local Arab communities and powerbrokers, among other measures. Here, again, the Kurdish movement has been both motivated by objective circumstance and driven by its subjective ideological commitment to pursue a forward, third-way utopianism. It's precisely these continued pressures that have steered the Kurdish movement to eschew a politics of retreat or mere Kurdish self-determination in the years following ISIS's defeat, instead dwelling in the more productive ground of their unexpected, third-way venture into majority-Arab confederation.

Nonetheless, this tentative consensus remains under extreme internal and external pressure—all the more so following HTS's capture of

Damascus. It remains to be seen how many Arabs will prefer the uncertainties of life in the Kurdish-led autonomous zone to the relative security offered by the Turkish-influenced Islamists who are now Syria's internationally recognized rulers, leaving the AANES facing its gravest challenge yet. Any such crisis can easily produce authoritarian reaction as well as its unexpected utopian reverse, and any utopian vision emerging from social catastrophe must again be tested in the crucible of practical implementation. The Rojava Revolution has been undergoing the slow, painful process of evolving from a parochial Kurdish project into a broader federation. Whether this difficult and ongoing learning process can be carried into the new Syria remains to be seen.

A Myth Among Many

For better or worse, grand historical metanarratives have power. We may be wary of the nativist implications of Öcalan's historical account, or of classical Marxism's exclusionary claims. But we should also ask whether our own apologetic accounts of British, American, and other national histories could ever prove capable of motivating millions or challenging statist hegemony. In our telling, these national histories are likely defined by legitimate guilt over imperialism. But we also have a revolutionary duty to find ways of telling this history that demonstrate the relevance and possibility of revolutionary transformation. This might variously mean searching in popular history and culture for our country's own second, democratic "river" of proto-socialist, peasant, or working-class resistance to state and capital; turning to regional or local histories of resistance to the center; or celebrating contemporary, metropolitan multiculturalism as a wonderful, inadvertent byproduct of colonial violence.

For it is not only the Kurdish movement that adopts a particular historical teleology to undergird its political proposal. Rather, to recall Aliza Marcus's critical assessment of Öcalan's thought, both mainstream and radical political philosophies systematically place the facts at the service of their chosen conclusion. As Nietzsche knew, and as the great twentieth-century liberal philosopher Richard Rorty has also argued, there can be little justification for the essentialist belief that our political values are anything other than wholly contingent.[30]

Most of all, in making a philosophy of the supposed facts alone, positive science masks the liberal order's own grand, ideological conclusions. Recognizing this universal contingency frees us to adopt those interpretations that fit our own political agenda—as Rorty attempts, in his case arguing for an ironic liberalism that freely admits there is no inherent good or evil to human nature.

For example, Bookchin makes the rather extraordinary claim that the guiding principle of evolution is "mutualism, not predation," following Peter Kropotkin in representing mutual aid as an inherent fact of nature. Both thinkers might therefore be accused of politicizing evolutionary science to suit their own agenda. But if so, these anarchist thinkers are being no more or less dishonest than other thinkers who interpret evolutionary tenets to justify a reactionary belief in social Darwinism or liberal progress.[31] Liberal thinkers look at the free-loving, egalitarian bonobo and see proof that social justice and liberal humanitarianism are in our very DNA; conservatives look across the Congo River to its cousin, the patriarchal, violent chimpanzee, and derive precisely the opposite conclusion.[32] Who knows which is more accurate? What matters is which of the two comparisons we *choose* to draw. Perhaps particularly when it comes to the study of socialization in the natural world and in prehistory, subjects about which we still know so little, any interpretation necessarily adds political color.

Again, the question of whether we seek a forward or a backward utopia is fundamentally political, not scientific. When pursuing a given future, we cannot help but reinterpret the past. What nature (or history) "is" matters far less than what we make of it. Liberals, communists, anarchists, free market ideologues, fascists, religious believers—all can and do mold the raw materials of nature and history to reflect their own ideals. Knowing this, we need not shrink from radical reassessments of history, biology, or archaeology, as Graeber and his coauthor David Wengrow attempt to show in their monumental *The Dawn of Everything: A New History of Civilization*, arguing that the ancient history of human political and social organization is far more diverse and undetermined than conventionally thought.[33]

Indeed, the Rojava Revolution itself is open to interpretation as part of a broader political-historic myth, as witness its overdetermination by competing anarchist, feminist, socialist, liberal, and nationalist ideologies. In another recent contribution to the literature on Rojava, two international volunteers argue that the lessons imparted by the Kurdish movement are therefore best understood and communicated not as positivist lectures or academic articles but rather as stories and parables.[34]

The Marxist Myth

No discussion of the attempted (re-)definition of human nature through grand historical metanarrative would be complete without reference to the Marxist project, harshly castigated by Öcalan as a "noble struggle that has raged for the past one hundred and fifty years . . . on the basis of a vulgar, materialist positivism doomed to failure."[35]

Marx famously sought to "stand the dialectic on its head" and analyze history on the basis of class conflict in order to prove the world-historic significance of his political vision, rather than seeing history itself as animated by some grand, preexisting idea, ethics or values.[36] This is the "negation of the negation" once again. A social system is liquidated under the pressure of its own internal contradictions to create a more dynamic future alternative. In a sense, Marx's historical materialism therefore seeks to open up all of history in the service of a forward utopianism, placing historical fact in the service of a future dream.

It might seem contradictory, but the very concept of presenting a materialist analysis as preceding his political idea is part of Marx's profoundly political project. Marx's ideology had such extraordinary, unparalleled power precisely because it made myth out of the materialist analysis of a rationalizing age—mystifying the process of demystification itself. Marx and Engels transfigured a "scientific" account of historic class struggle into pure prophecy, successfully convincing millions of workers and scores of nations that revolution was their inevitable historic destiny.

When reading historians of the twentieth-century, it's easy to find instances of faith in the inevitable, ineluctable nature of Marx's proposed teleology of history, quite staggering to modern ears. Where can we now find the bizarre resolution of the Bolsheviks in the months prior to the Russian revolution, doggedly refusing to seize power on the basis of their slavish commitment to Marxist dogma, even at the risk of violent assault by armed masses of their *own* supporters, demanding, "Take power, you son-of-a-bitch, when it's handed to you!"[37] Which modern public intellectual would think like German economist and Nazi fellow traveler Werner Sombart, who claimed he was subjectively opposed to the communist assault on his own material interests but objectively forced to accept the inevitability of communist revolution?[38]

These anecdotes suggest the astonishing force of Marx's own willful refashioning of history as the terrain of class conflict. Reaching deep into prehistory, Marx molded the worker, golem-like, from the muddy swamps of Mesopotamia, placing its hand on the lever of historical change.

But the extent to which a metanarrative is capable of transforming reality is the same extent to which its failure precludes future transformation. This is the great tragedy of any totalizing historical narrative, Marxism included. If the worker did indeed stand at the fulcrum of history, the slow death of the workers' revolution necessarily means the death of any hope in future change. State communism's ultimate failure has marginalized the proletariat as a meaningful political force. To read confident, latter-day predictions of incipient proletarian revolution in Western states is to read the predictions of a tiny doomsday cult proclaiming that the end is nigh.

Little wonder many post-Marxist thinkers legitimately feel the "saddest legacy that the twentieth century leaves us is disillusionment, loss of hope"; that we must freely admit there is no new, emergent, revolutionary subject capable of remaking the world; and that our post-Marxist politics has all too often regressed into localism, horizontalism, and melancholic resignation.[39]

Ernst Bloch: Excavating Hope from Defeat

And yet even after the failure of Marxist state socialism, we continue picking through the dustbin of socialist history for scraps of hope, seeking reasons to keep on organizing toward our "horizontalist horizon." In this grim but necessary task, there's no better guide than political philosopher Ernst Bloch. Born in Germany in 1885 and working throughout the establishment, global spread, and authoritarian betrayal of actually existing communism, this unorthodox visionary developed a unique mystic-Marxist hermeneutics expressed via an idiosyncratic range of philosophical and theological references.

Ecstatically preaching communism as the "faith without lies," Bloch both captures the mystical potency Marx granted his proletarian followers and expresses the self-deluding willpower needed to maintain a belief in the Marxist proposal.[40] Bloch's eccentricity and mysticism have been the subject of reasonable criticism by other, more reasonable thinkers, but they're precisely what we need if we are continue working for socialist revolution in a post-socialist, post-revolutionary age. Bloch's unique understanding of Marx models a productive relationship with the tragic, inevitable current of history. It therefore suggests ways we can reckon with the tragedies of the twentieth century as we tentatively imagine our own latter-day metanarratives.

In Bloch's terminology, Marxism is possessed of both "warm" and "cold" streams. Marx instigated the cold science of historical materialism and thus demonstrated communism's logical inevitability. But he also urged Marxists to uncover a hidden current of utopian hope surging through history, a "warm stream" that closely resembles the Kurdish movement's "second river."

Marx's task is the "unmasking of ideologies and disenchantment of metaphysical illusion" on the one hand, and yet the unleashing of a "liberating intention and . . . strong appeal to the debased, enslaved, abandoned, belittled, human being" on the other.[41] Through his critique of metaphysical illusion, Marx instigates what might, paradoxically, be defined as the new metaphysical ideology par excellence. The warm river flows into the cold and vice versa, cool dialectics instigating the white heat of revolution.

This paradoxical relationship equips Bloch for his curious magnum opus, *The Principle of Hope*. Writing after his exile from Nazi Germany, the Jewish intellectual surveyed history, culture, geography, and cosmology for proofs of the inherent dynamism and mutability of the universe. He quotes an extraordinary range of evidence, from the flight of a swallow to the Babel myth to pulp pirate novels, as supposedly containing or encoding this inherently revolutionary quality. Ultimately, he finds a meta-level utopianism in humankind's inherent desire for meaning in a meaningless universe. Humans see faces in rock formations, angels in marble blocks, freedom in everything.

To Bloch, this inherent dynamism is proof of what he calls a "not-yet-conscious," located in the future and set against the regressive *past* unconscious of Freudian psychoanalysis.[42] Just as our brains work to suppress drives with their origins in the personal, sexual, and evolutionary past, so too (Bloch argues) do they suppress a drive toward an as-yet unachieved utopian socialist future. Why should analysis focus on the repressed past and present dreams, when our daydreams and fantasies in fact equally reflect the clash between our reality and repressed hopes for the *future*?

"More than one daydream before now has . . . remodeled reality," Bloch observes, recalling Marx's famous comparison between the unthinking labor of a beehive and the qualitatively distinct achievements of human craftspeople, who must necessarily imagine what they then go on to create. In this sense, humankind is precisely distinguished from other beings by our ability to labor toward an as-yet unrealized Babel.[43]

One of Bloch's favorite phrases is "thinking means venturing beyond," always and in everything.[44] For example, he reads a sense of transformative potential even into Columbus's voyage to the Americas. The philosopher isn't blind to that foolhardy, predatory venture's genocidal ramifications. But he believes we have a revolutionary duty to identify the revolutionary values it simultaneously entails: an unjustified, absurd, and therefore emancipatory willingness to venture into the unknown.[45] Bloch's work is marked by just such a revolutionary willingness, a meta-level pursuit of the revolutionary in any and all circumstances.

Bloch's brand of Marxism recalls Öcalan's own mystic belief that freedom is the fundamental goal of the universe, inherent in the very relations of quantum physics. Like both Öcalan and Bookchin, Bloch projects a confident ability to read his political project into biology, chemistry, nature itself. There is certainly important academic work to be done in reassessing archaeology, history, and even the natural sciences in light of a radical political agenda. More generally, Bloch shows us how much of seemingly everyday culture and apolitical science is ideologically captured by capitalism, and he challenges us to imagine ways of reclaiming these fields as sites of valid ideological contest.

Walter Benjamin was another early twentieth-century Jewish intellectual possessed by the metaphysical allure of Marxism. (Both Bloch and Benjamin were clear-eyed as to the USSR's failings, however.) In a famous essay, Benjamin similarly points out the revolutionary potential of playful, pleasurable, and libertarian moments in everyday life.[46] But he also urges his readers to undertake the radical task of imagining how these moments could become organized and "win the energies of intoxication for the revolution," rather than be dissipated into apolitical art and culture, drug use, or liberal-humanistic idealism. And indeed, in the post-socialist era all three outlets have drained much of the Left's potentially productive energy.

As well as lending itself to overly individualistic, apolitical, or mystic interpretations, this type of socialist thought can easily be appropriated by the Right. Bloch saw the Nazi regime as justifying itself through reference to a Jungian "collective unconsciousness" and racial archetypes.[47] He wanted to excavate the deep past, to uncover a universal sense of political destiny, but he also recognized the risk of unearthing a sense of racial destiny instead. This risk was precisely why he viewed repoliticizing the universe and human psyche as urgent, lest this quasi-mystic task be left to the Nazis and essentialist nationalists.

Bloch therefore prefigures Bookchin's demand for a forward rather than backward utopianism, stubbornly insisting that Marxism offers us "the horizon of the future to be attained." There is a fundamentally Jewish, messianic aspect to Bloch's version of Marxism in its pursuit of the transcendent through the immanent matter of time and space. In Bloch's poignant phrase, philosophy itself constitutes the pursuit of a "still-unachieved homeland."[48]

This type of grand analysis can also appear so zoomed out as to lose all political relevance. Bloch's philosophy brushes aside slaughters under Nero, the Holy Roman Empire, and Hitler as "merely misfortunes, not dialectical change."[49] There's an interesting comparison to be drawn here with twenty-first-century positivist ideologue Steven Pinker, whose *The Better Angels of Our Nature* conversely seeks to justify end-of-history liberal humanism. Pinker deploys statistical analysis in a highly ideological attempt to prove society has overall grown less violent and therefore somehow "better"—in the process describing the Holocaust as a mere "statistical fluke," with the Second World War nothing but "an isolated peak in a declining sawtooth." Similarly, he finds room for just over a page on the "gloomy scenario" of climate change.[50] With these two "flukes" dismissed, one might reasonably ask, what violence remains to explain away?

Bloch engages in similarly grim rationalizations. To him, even suicide bespeaks a sense of hopeful anticipation, in its terminal revelation of a hope that things must be better on the other side.[51] (Schopenhauer and Camus have made similar claims.) From opposite political standpoints, Bloch and Pinker are equally guilty of placing all evidence in the service of their chosen political project, to the point where this becomes quite tasteless, the fact their political goals are so distinct only serving to underline the dangers of such oversimplification.

Bloch is able to read cause for hope into even the epochal catastrophes of the twentieth century. Similarly, to Öcalan, while history is indeed a "true apocalypse," this apocalypse itself produces its eventual vanquisher. What he terms a democratic history of society necessarily emerges in resistance to the antidemocratic repression of actually existing civilization: "Democratic civilization's initiative to build historical-society arises from the need to end the capitalist network's deceit . . . not only because we can imagine new worlds, but because they are absolutely indispensable."[52]

As with Bloch's determined reinterpretation of historical defeats in the light of a future utopia, Öcalan's approach to history is ambiguous. Are we merely cherry-picking brief moments of hope from a history of continuous defeat, or recognizing the subtler Marxist dialectic through which "history advances by its bad side"? Sometimes, it feels as though Bloch reads history rather as we might watch a trashy movie, knowing that whatever hardship comes up will be justified by an inevitable happy ending. This type of thought functions as a secular theodicy—that is, a theology justifying all suffering as creating the necessary conditions for God's omnibenevolent love, or in this case communist utopia.

Bloch's bloody-minded hope has been condemned as overly romantic, "indefeasible because it is without reason."[53] It's no coincidence that the "Orient" recurs time and again in Bloch's opus, representing his idealized concept of the human consciousness and the revolutionary future.[54] Like any Orientalist, he simplifies his subject matter, projecting his fantasies onto it and thus escaping into an idealized and unobtainable future. At times, he therefore effaces his vision of genuine political content—just as Orientalist, idealistic conceptions of Rojava actually deny the region political agency.

To Bloch and Benjamin's contemporary Theodor Adorno, the dialectic of history is better understood as a series of tragic, catastrophic, failed efforts at political transformation.[55] We might well find this a more appropriate response to the long shadow of the Holocaust.

Or maybe not. There is a desperation to Bloch's thought, an effort of will that explains his enduring appeal and potential relevance to the contemporary Left. Again, perhaps the ultimate lessons his thought has to offer are less theoretical or organizational than they are psychological. His work suggests the effort of will and scale necessary to construct new theories of revolution, particularly in a counterrevolutionary age. In particular, he can help us rethink our received narrative of the twentieth century as an era of irrevocable left defeat. Perhaps this logic is, as Eagleton complained, "indefeasible because it is without reason." But is an unreasonable inability to be defeated really such a negative trait?

Toward a New Metanarrative of History

Marx represented human history as standing or falling on the basis of the proletarian class and its subjective ability to form the conduit for global socialist revolution. Post-Marxist theorists like Öcalan must necessarily take on a daunting task; their theories of history must place even the historic defeat of the workers' revolution in service of the continued pursuit of revolutionary hope.

Indeed, it's not only Marx. All totalizing, civilizational metanarratives that grant humanity a world-historical role must necessarily put history on an all-or-nothing footing—and *all* seems an increasingly vanished possibility. In the eighteenth century, Rousseau described civilization as a gross catastrophe in which the stage was set for slaughter and immiseration once the "first man" pointed to a piece of ground and said, "This is mine."[56] In the twentieth, Adorno and Horkheimer theorized self-aware man's mastery of nature as leading us ineluctably to the instrumental reason and rationalized butchery of the twentieth century. In the twenty-first, James Scott has argued that the invention of agriculture imposed a crash in living standards on doomed prehistorical communities, which were nonetheless forced to accept the agricultural mode of production or face eradication.[57]

These diverse, pessimistic accounts have several key themes in common. Each identifies human development as gripped by an irreversible, ineluctable logic. They all represent humankind's Promethean gift of consciousness as a blessing concealing a curse, with coming down from the trees an irreversible mistake. But at the same time, there is no sense in going backward—we cannot. All three accounts speak to the terrible curse of human self-consciousness, which precipitates a historic race toward catastrophe while also leaving us as helpless observers in the grip of these currents.

Rousseau's *On the Origins of Inequality* is paradigmatic in its pessimism. It is from the Stoics, much mangled by modernity, that Rousseau inherited his vision of a vanished state of nature marked by universal equality. Thus nature itself cannot be blamed for our present plight. Rather, "as there is scarce any inequality among men in a state of nature, all that which we now behold owes its force and its growth to the development of our faculties . . . and at last becomes permanent and lawful by the establishment of property and of laws."[58] While this "unlimited faculty is the source of all human misfortunes," there is no possibility to "go back."[59] This is why Rousseau famously argued we need a social contract to temporarily shore up civilization in the face of our ongoing, irrevocable demise.

Metanarratives without a total, all-or-nothing claim cannot hope to remake history, and yet any narrative that *does* grant humanity such world-historical significance must logically leave humans responsible for the subsequent catastrophe of global development. It's an impossible bind.

Correspondingly, therefore, the post-Marxist Left has struggled in vain to recreate a similarly potent historical teleology, or to marshal any political constituency with the coherence of the industrial working class. Whether it's Graeber's "99 percent," Jacques Rancière's "part of no-part," Michael Hardt and Antonio Negri's "multitude," or John Holloway's "rabble," numerous post-Marxist thinkers have sought to identify the social or political group(s) that could constitute the crux of contemporary political struggle in a postmodern era. Each of these descriptive theories attempts to recapitulate the theoretical and organizational force that Marx granted to the urban proletariat, and Mao to the peasants, by informing them they were destined to overthrow capitalism.

But as Nunes observes in *Neither Horizontal nor Vertical*, no such collective agent can now exist. In an era of affective labor there is no clear, paradigmatic center of value production that can be targeted by would-be revolutionary organizers, as they once targeted the industrial factory. Rather, these postmodern theorizations are efforts to articulate the reality that capitalism's uneven but hegemonic reach now encompasses us all.

Indeed, those postmodern horizontal concepts of political subjectivity offer an uncanny mirror image of strict Marxist dogma. Whether placing absolute faith in history's inevitable evolution toward socialism or rejecting (state) power outright in favor of a retreat into an individualized and localized politics, both approaches deny the need for strategic organization toward our socialist goal.[60]

Deleuze and Guattari's concept of one global and total class, in which "none escapes participation," offers another classic expression of total capitalist hegemony operating on the level of our individual relationships and psyches.[61] Worker, capitalist, militant, lover, artist: like it or not, we are all complicit in capitalist value production through the very fact of existing in society. And yet when compared to the industrial working class, once rigid as iron, this global "class" is as diffuse as sand. One cannot easily imagine a mass revolutionary movement organized on the basis of these critics' postmodern political philosophy.

Öcalan is profoundly aware of these challenges. As he knows, neither the classical Marxist-Leninist proletarian class, the colonized nation, nor these postmodern formulations have proven an effective starting point for global emancipation. On one level, his response is straightforward enough: "Liberating life is impossible without a radical women's revolution which would change man's mentality and life."[62]

This is more than a feminist slogan. Öcalan suggests that a subjective, ontological revolution is needed, deconstructing hierarchies founded on male domination of women, before society can be liberated in turn.[63] He therefore aims to establish a new civilizational, revolutionary fulcrum on the basis of a feminist critique of modernity. This analysis forms part of a broader wave of postcolonial social movements and feminist analyses, which understand decentralized, networked, women-led resistance struggles as the only mode of organization capable of overcoming rather than replicating the failings of hierarchical, centralized states.[64] This conscious attempt to create a new world-historical class from the subaltern margins is open to critique along similar lines as the post-Marxist class analyses sketched above. While such theories are perhaps analytically valid, they generally remain too diffuse and postmodern to constitute a class capable of instigating true revolution.

Yet simultaneously, Öcalan happily presents Kurdish struggle in more familiar terms, as a national struggle for self-determination. And crucially, this struggle takes place in a region of extreme geopolitical over-determination, amid paradigmatic Great Power conflict. Here concepts of nation-as-class, woman-as-class, and state-subjects-as-class overlap in a powerful formulation. Again, this union between a local struggle and a broader global subjectivity has a precursor in the fraught Marxist national question, linking nationalist or anti-imperialist sentiment with a broader internationalist, proletarian vision.

Öcalan's vision has been fairly charged with downplaying the continued economic exploitation of Rojava's agrarian and laboring classes. But this latter-day concept of a revolutionary subject class is nonetheless extremely potent. Öcalan advances a dual political subjectivity, at once Kurdish and internationalist, transcendent and immanent, horizontal and vertical, idealistically anarchist and pragmatically Leninist, blending localized nationalism with global calls to all subjects of capitalist nation-states.

This dual subjectivity has both granted Öcalan's vision the power to launch revolution in Rojava and earned it a hearing far beyond Mesopotamia. Through inscribing a local struggle with global and world-historical meaning, Öcalan suggests one way other movements can respond to the global crisis of metanarrative. At the least, climate catastrophe and incipient state collapse will furnish other global movements with fresh opportunities to frame their particular struggles in terms of the universal—to think globally and act locally.

The Revolutionary Religion

Nietzsche cautions us: "Every philosophy that lets the religious comet gleam through the darkness of its last outposts renders everything within it that purports to be science, suspicious. It is all probably religion."[65] It's a fair description of the Marxist and Öcalanite metanarratives of history, proletarian subjectivity and Kurdish national destiny. It also, surely, describes Nietzsche's own mythmaking.

Any philosophy capable of inspiring social or global transformation needs such a comet of faith somewhere in its skies. The Kurdish movement's struggles and sacrifices are justified with reference to the utopian, transformative Not Yet that Öcalan promises his followers. This type of revolutionary commitment is shot through with a streak of pure religion, unobtainable through reason alone. Partisans of a revolutionary "faith without lies," they follow Öcalan not as a critical theorist, but rather a secular prophet.

Öcalan therefore places himself in a potent, dangerous revolutionary tradition—that of the millenarian visionary, warning his followers that the signs foretell the end times, when all must necessarily be remade.

Chapter 5
Apocalypse as Revelation
The Millenarian Organization of Despair

Whenever the horizon has been consumed in the flames of social collapse, messiahs have come. This is particularly the case when isolated religious, national, or ethnic communities feel their very existence threatened by imperial powers, threatening the effective destruction of a local environment that is their entire world. It often requires such an existential threat for a population to ask existential questions about its own condition. When conquistadors, F-16 warplanes, or chemical deforestation threaten a people with imminent hell, they naturally turn to gods, cults, prophets, movements and ideas promising heaven on earth as the only possible response.

The ancient Christian idea that a "city of God" is imminently to be established on earth, as the necessary precursor to an eternal paradise, is known as "millennialism." The related term "millenarianism" refers to a broader spiritual tradition, which takes earthly turmoil as a sign that human society is about to be totally overturned through divine intervention.[1] This concept is lamented by its critics as "the most powerful, volatile, imaginary force in human history."[2] And indeed, it has perhaps animated more social unrest and postcolonial resistance than any other single idea.

The names refer to the coming thousand-year reign of Christ on earth predicted by Christian tradition, but such predictions are far from a solely Christian practice. Judaism, Islam, and Buddhism all emerged as disruptive, more or less revolutionary millennialist movements.[3] Indeed, the thousand-year millennium makes an early appearance in the Zoroastrian faith, which Öcalan represents as a precursor to Kurdish culture and a key influence on his Manichean vision of historic struggle between democratic society and repressive forces.[4]

More than that, the millenarian concept of successive historic ages tending inevitably to cosmic renewal has provocatively been described as a precursor to both Marxism and Nazism.[5] And with our own world lurching toward ruin, reformation, and renewal, similar religious and political ideas animate struggles in the Middle East and beyond.

The Kurdish movement, too, forms a part of this revolutionary millenarian tradition. Facing genuinely existential threats, Kurdish leaders reassure their people that the shocking catastrophes they endure are proof the global order is about to be reversed. Through its own unique formulation of the revolutionary millenarian idea, the Kurdish movement boldly places itself in the long tradition of a political concept uniquely capable of transforming despair into hope.

Öcalan's Kurdish Apocalypse

For leading scholar of (medieval) millenarianism Norman Cohn, revolutionary millenarianism is defined by a totalizing, all-or-nothing narrative of social transformation. The present crisis of a nation, group, or people is treated as an "event of unique importance, different in kind from all other struggles known to history, a cataclysm from which the world is to emerge totally transformed."[6] Öcalan's hybrid concept of the Kurds' world-historical role clearly stands in this tradition.

As in Bloch's perversely hopeful account of suicide, there is a strange optimism in the millennialist response to the end times. By definition, a prophetic warning means there is yet time to mend our ways, however late the hour may seem. Such ideas can scarcely be but transformative.

On a literal level, of course, each individual millenarian prophet has failed to herald any such cosmic transformation. Though promised by Jesus Christ, cult leader Jim Jones, and ISIS caliph Abu Bakr al-Baghdadi, among others, doomsday has yet to arrive. Histories critical of millenarian thought often form part of an intellectual effort to discredit the

Marxist idea or anti-colonial resistance. Nonetheless, skeptical historians are correct to identify the severe negative effects the intoxicating millenarian idea can have on a suffering people, inspiring needless sacrifice, violent excess, or the exploitation of deluded followers.

But even short of cosmic reversal, the millenarian idea also has a genuinely transformative side. First, it can give momentum to real-world social revolution. Second, and more profoundly, it can grant a suffering people their longed-for access to a world-historical metanarrative, justified precisely with reference to their suffering.

For Cohn, the millenarian idea is marked by the certain expectation of collective, terrestrial, imminent, total, and miraculous salvation.[7] These qualifiers can readily be transferred and applied to secular, world-historical ideologies like Marxism or democratic confederalism. The Rojava Revolution, and particularly its successful resistance against ISIS, is commonly presented as a "miracle."[8] How else, save through the language of divinely mandated social reversal, should the Kurds make sense of the way in which ISIS's attempted extermination of their people led directly to their long-sought-after autonomy?

Öcalan's famous 2014 May Day address makes clear the pivotal, epochal role he expects both the Turkish-Kurdish conflict and his own ideas to play:

> In the era of the hegemony of finance capital the assault is not only on labor, but on the entire society, its history, ecology and future. It has reached the stage of either socialism or barbarism, either society or a void. . . . The Middle Eastern region is the weakest link in the present hegemonic system. Kurdistan is at the centre of this region, where a kind of Third World War is being experienced. The [Kurdish] freedom movement is in the vanguard of the struggle of all peoples, nations and communities against this hegemony.[9]

Öcalan here offers an eschatology or account of the end times. Through a time of trials and tribulations, society will arrive at a day of judgment when it will either perish or be wholly remade ("either society or a void"). History, especially, is read in a light that places the Kurdish people's suffering at its crux, with the Syrian Civil War serving as a crucial latter-day sign that Öcalan's prophecy of a coming end times battle ("World War Three") is accurate. The millenarian idea binds the localized, Kurdish narrative to a generalized, world-historical metanarrative. It's a deeply effective motivational strategy.

Existential War and Genocide

As with the broader Turkish-Kurdish conflict, regional political leaders commonly figure Turkey's occupation of Kurdish regions in northern Syria as a "*şerê hebûn û nebûnê*" (a war of existence [or] nonexistence)—or sometimes, more simply, as "genocide."[10]

Turkey's occupation of northern Syria has not witnessed the campaigns of systematic executions that would typically mark a genocide, as when Baathist Iraqi forces exterminated up to 100,000 Iraqi Kurds in the systematic Anfal genocide. Yet "genocide" and "ethnic cleansing" are always politically loaded terms, applied to some unspeakable massacres and not to others. "Genocide" perhaps serves its proper function as a qualitative descriptor of an event as experienced by its victims, rather than as a quantitative way of objectively sorting massacres. And the Turkish operation is nonetheless experienced by its victims in existential fashion, as a struggle not just for a parcel of land, but over a political idea and way of life inextricably bound up in a particular ethnic identity.

After all, most international institutions refuse to even use the phrase "ethnic cleansing" when describing Turkey's military operations in Syria. But how else should one describe the brutal violence that has seen the Kurdish population driven down from 97 percent to under a third, to be replaced by Turkish-controlled Arab and Turkmen militias?[11] This excessive caution itself inspires heightened rhetoric in turn, and indignation over what ordinary Kurds perceive as unfair, politicized treatment allowing NATO member Turkey to get away with murder.

Certainly, living under Turkish occupation is not necessarily a death sentence for a Kurd. Some Kurdish collaborators, plus the elderly and indigent, endure. On the contrary, anyone suspected of working with the AANES—whether Arab, Kurd, or Yazidi—can expect to be disappeared into one of the region's black sites.[12] The Kurdish movement correctly argues Turkey is opposed not only to Kurdish self-determination but also to the broader federal political project being trialed on its borders. But at the same time, this multiethnic project is understood by both parties to the conflict as fundamentally Kurdish in nature. The movement must appeal to the Kurds' sense of existential threat to justify its prophetic self-conceptualization as the answer to totalizing state violence, and the correspondingly total sacrifices it demands of its loyalists.

Without an existential threat, that is, there can be no existential answer. Again, Cohn's analysis of medieval millenarian movements offers a useful illustration. He argues that newfound population movement and social exchange paved the way for an epochal resurgence of the millenarian idea, creating a shocking break with ancient customs.[13] These terms are readily applicable to the colonial invasions that have provoked more recent millenarian movements—Turkey's colonial occupation of Kurdistan included.

Millenarian fervor is inspired by the spectacle of extraordinary wealth, accompanied by simultaneous "hazards . . . not only menacing but altogether outside the normal run of experience."[14] Like the starving peasant class driven into a booming medieval city-state, a colonized people often find their colonizers offer a model of both hellish violence and heavenly possibility, capable of standing the existing social order on its head.

Driving through Rojava means driving alongside the Syrian–Turkish border, where it's impossible to escape this fundamentally colonial sense of struggle at the mercy of an omnipotent, transcendent power. The border is demarcated by the world's third-longest wall, stretching over 750 kilometers. Newly constructed after the declaration of Kurdish-led autonomy, it divides cousin from cousin, wheat field from wheat field, (Syrian-occupied) Kurdistan from (Turkish-occupied) Kurdistan. The wall is militarized with EU money; patrolled by armored cars; monitored by unblinking watchtowers; and equipped with remote-controlled weapons; light, movement, and acoustic sensors; jammers, radar, and laser-based detection technologies.[15]

By contrast, the Syrian Kurdish force's tanks are cobbled together from rusty scrap iron. The market streets are covered with tarpaulin in a vain attempt to shelter from the all-seeing eye of Turkey's ever-hovering

Bayraktar drones. The seasons before the last Turkish invasion were spent digging little rat-run tunnels that turned into death traps as the bombs started to fall.

The Turkish Armed Forces themselves are invisible, secreted far away behind drone control screens, only occasionally sallying forth to take pot-shots at shepherds or airstrike another meager border town into quick submission. Rojava's defenders are made to feel medieval, outmoded, outmaneuvered, surrounded from the start. Many vanishing peoples must have felt just the same when first faced with cannon and horse. Knowing it has found itself at the end of an age, the Kurdish movement has no choice but to fight for the new.

Baptists and Maoists: A Radical Tradition

Throughout my time working in Rojava, it was hard to escape observations that inspired comparison with my own upbringing in a charismatic, somewhat radical Baptist Christian tradition. Long evenings spent re-arranging plastic chairs to facilitate low-budget movie projections, awkward singalongs, and tired party games; fire-and-brimstone sermons interspersed with cheesy anecdotes; off-brand Pepsi offered to restive youths as a gentle bribe for their participation in meetings; the adept deployment of parables; mission work in febrile zones where any hope is a lifeline; commendable efforts to live, speak, and operate on the level of the people, the Baptist "in but not of the world," just like the Maoist revolutionary moving through the people like a "fish through water," while engaged in equally conscious efforts to mold selfish, liberal personalities into militant, recruitment-focused "fishers of men"; and an absolutist claim to represent the sole path from certain death to certain redemption.

These commonalities are not merely superficial, still less metaphorical. Rather, they emerge from Öcalan's "second river" of democratic, emancipatory politics, running submerged but never totally vanished from the radical early church through two millennia of religious and social upheaval to modern-day Rojava.

On arrival in Rojava, I was apt to criticize my religious upbringing as stifling and repressive, contributing to the various personal issues I faced later in life. But to my surprise, during frequent conversations about region and politics, Kurdish comrades didn't accept these sentiments—almost truisms to the modern, atheist Left. Instead, in line with the Kurdish movement's concept of revolutionary self-criticism (tekmil) as a reckoning with one's class, background, and upbringing, I was told: you have to ask yourself how this religion made you who you are; you cannot remain angry with your people forever, but take your anger and grow with it.

This bold challenge brought me to the collectively-written Italian novel _Q_, which follows an Anabaptist radical through the conflicts and uprisings of the sixteenth-century Protestant Reformation.[16] A PDF copy circulated among internationalist volunteers in Rojava—particularly among Germans, who felt they had to do more work than most to identify the democratic river in their own country's twentieth-century history. Like the German volunteers, I had my own reasons for learning more about these historic religious conflicts that had led to the dissenting tradition in which I was raised.

The novel vividly depicts religious dissenters' vain struggle to overthrow the hegemonic Catholic and latterly Protestant forces that divided Europe between themselves and outrun the bloody violence of the Counter-Reformation. At their extreme, radical religious movements took on a social character, envisioning and seeking to establish a Europe remade along dissenting, anti-authoritarian lines. Naturally, they were rapidly and violently destroyed by state power.[17]

_Q_ is partially intended as a political analogy with the authors' contemporary Europe, where, as of 1999, radical movements were similarly being smothered by globalist hegemony. But _Q_ also left me with a clear sense of continuity between the communally minded Anabaptist insurgents, my own religious background, and the political commitment of Rojava's revolutionaries.

The novel reaches its peak in an account of radical Anabaptists' 1534–35 efforts to establish a communal government in the city of Münster. By its end, the Münster uprising is said to have recalled the dying days of ISIS's own eschatological caliphate, marked by summary executions, torture, and the personality-cult rule of a crazed few conducted in the name of the kingdom of God.[18] These lurid descriptions may be colored by subsequent Catholic propaganda. Nonetheless, *Q* depicts the dark, dangerous side of millenarian tradition, just as much as its revolutionary power.

But as *Q* makes clear, the end times also engender a "collective madness," a heady and freeing sense that the old order is dying, that a new one must be born, that there is no time to act but now and nothing to lose in the pursuit of heaven on earth.[19] And so perhaps it was precisely my Baptist upbringing that drew me to my work in Rojava. I could well understand the appeal of the Kurdish movement's grand promise of revolutionary transformation rather than mere reform, and its demand for a secular, millenarian leap of faith.

The Revolutionary Millenarian Current

The millennium does not solely inspire isolated, insular cults. This revolutionary current survived the Anabaptists' sixteenth-century defeat to arrive in both Rojava and the quietly anti-authoritarian tendency of the modern, dissenting church, albeit in radically different forms. In the fourth century after Christ, Christianity completed its transition from suppressed revolutionary movement to formal religion of the Roman Empire. Under the watchful tutelage of Saint Augustine, millenarianism was excised from official church doctrine. From now on, good Christians would be taught that the imminent City of God would not entail any material upheaval in social norms, but rather God's spiritual presence in the hearts of his believers. This concept persisted for well over a thousand years, as the dominant position in Christendom.[20]

This was perhaps a rather poor substitute for the early church's promise of an incipient thousand years of justice, brotherhood, and abundance realized on earth. And so the millennial idea lingered on, in apocryphal prophecy, popular culture, and the biblical Book of Revelation.

For example, at the cusp of a calendar millennium in 989 CE, a medieval social movement known as the Peace and Truce of God broke out in response to the catastrophic collapse of Charlemagne's empire. The Peace has been described as one of the most potent, widespread peace movements in history, uniting commoners, peasants, and clergy via proclamations of temporary truces and immunity from intercommunal violence.[21] The Peace was followed by a dazzling sequence of iconoclastic preachers, mystical and antinomian religious orders, peasant's revolts, and flagellant movements. Many of these revolts and movements were marked by anti-Semitic violence. All were ultimately more theological than proto-socialist in character. Yet to varying degrees, these radical religious movements also used the millenarian idea to push beyond sectarianism and dissolve traditional social hierarchies, with the most radical holding property in common and challenging contemporary moral and gender norms.

These premodern millenarian communities sometimes served as more organized, communitarian alternatives to what historian Eric Hobsbawm calls "social bandits," the Robin Hood–type rebel robber bands preying on feudal society, who therefore became heroes of that society's oppressed classes.[22] Just like Hobsbawm's peasant heroes, millenarian movements emerge at times of economic and social crisis as an expression of premodern resistance to exploitative, centralized power. To Hobsbawm, social banditry and millenarianism are intimately linked as primitive responses to the cataclysm of capitalist social organization entering the premodern world.

As in Rojava, social and political crises understood as apocalypse engendered not bloodshed but kinship, enabling the partial transgression of long-standing hierarchies. Though limited and imperfect, the millenarians' early utopian experiments provided crucial blueprints for later socialist endeavors. And just as in latter-day Syria, wars driven by counter-hegemonic millenarian ideologies became the very proof of these ideas' urgent relevance, with the subsequent violence and catastrophe proving the prophet right.

The idea reappears and evolves throughout the centuries, right up to the Levellers, Ranters, Seekers, Fifth Monarchy Men, and other dissenting movements of the seventeenth-century English Civil War. This war is often overlooked in contemporary leftist accounts of history. But it marked a crucial turning point, where the democratic current already present in the radical, anti-authoritarian Protestant fringe of the European Wars of Religion began a turn toward its secular, liberal expression. Both the French and American Revolutions were defined by a profoundly millennialist expectation of secular social transformation. Thereafter, the idea would travel via Marx's theory of history to the twentieth-century Leninist party, the PKK, and modern-day Rojava.

Öcalan's Revolutionary Millenarianism

Millennialist movements typically viewed history as divided into several successive ages, culminating in apocalypse and transformation. Cohn argues this pervasive idea finds its modern expression in the classical Marxist dialectic of history, which likewise identified successive historic phases following inevitably one after the other along the path to full communism. He also views the Nazi conception of their own totalitarian rule as the Third Reich, or Third Age, in this light.[23]

These arguments, which were intended to discredit Marxist claims to herald a new and better era for mankind as totalitarian and deluded, can be challenged in their particulars. On the other side of the fence, communist thinkers like Bloch have drawn productive parallels between latter-day socialist movements and the medieval Christian millenarians, without always claiming a literal inheritance.[24]

At the least, it's impossible to deny the similarities between the teleological accounts of history offered by Öcalan, Marx, and their radical religious forebears. Like Cohn, Öcalan warns that the Marxist communist movement's own world-historical claims of imminent social transfiguration are a dangerous reflection of religious ideology.[25]

But though he sometimes seeks to place his own political project outside the millenarian tradition, Öcalan elsewhere sets this revolutionary, eschatological tradition against the "new . . . religion" of science and positivism.[26] When he attempts to articulate the Kurdish cause as the fulcrum of world-historical change, rather than one more nationalism among many, he himself is steeped in the revolutionary millenarian tradition that takes present tribulations as proof of coming eschatological transformation.

When he speaks of capitalist modernity as the "age of unmasked gods and naked kings," Öcalan preaches the potential end of that age, and he foresees a crucial war beginning in the Middle East that will expand across the globe.[27] Öcalan's vision is made real through the flames of a Third World War many Kurdish militants would claim their leader has accurately foreseen, and which appears ever more real following Israel's 2023 invasion of Gaza and subsequent spiraling regional confrontation.

As we've seen, there is a mystical element to Öcalan's analyses. But the extent to which his word is received as genuine prophecy by his followers is less relevant than the political commitment or activity it subsequently inspires. For example, the 1923 Treaty of Lausanne, which laid out new state borders in the Middle East and established the contemporary Turkish Republic, was the subject of a quasi-millenarian folk belief among the Kurdish movement, as it was in Turkish society at large. It was falsely claimed that the treaty would be revised or renewed in 2023, a century on from its establishment, potentially paving the way for a new order in the Middle East. Among the Kurdish movement, this idea was sometimes stated (incorrectly) as geopolitical fact, sometimes as conspiracy theory, sometimes as metaphor.[28] And like all millenarian predictions, it failed to come to pass as 2023 came and went. But the claim of imminent geopolitical renewal in the Middle East nonetheless proved capable of motivating the Kurdish people to action, regardless of how literally they took the idea.

Rather than denying or over-stressing the historical links between religious and socialist millenarian movements, it's perhaps more instructive to ask what the millenarian idea can offer us today. How can this potent idea be harnessed to revolutionary ends in a secular movement? What can we learn from the role this idea has played in improving ordinary people's lot? But also—how can totalitarian catastrophe, like the terror in Münster, ISIS's caliphate, or the Nazi Reich, be avoided? If both ISIS and its secular, leftist Kurdish opponents see themselves as engaged in a millenarian, all-or-nothing struggle, what makes the difference between the two sides' radically different praxis? After all, any religious belief could be categorized as a hope without hope. To put it another way, "false prophet" is an oxymoron. What should any prophet promise but that unobtainable better world?

The false prophets, demagogues, and anti-Semitic charlatans should never lead us to discount the possibility that a new world order is approaching us today, as it has in past crises and will do again. To say otherwise is to deny history. But care must also be taken to distinguish between different forms of social organization established on the basis of this most dangerous idea.

Organizing Anti-Colonial Resistance

Europe's Wars of Religion are far from the only time the millenarian idea has had continental repercussions. China's mid-nineteenth-century Taiping Rebellion, one of the bloodiest conflicts of all time, exemplifies the millenarian idea's intoxicating power to organize resistance to imperialism and exploitative overlords, with an obscure villager's visionary dream giving form to a struggle costing up to thirty million lives.[29] Economic grievances took form through a millenarian vision into a brutal conflict deadlier than the First World War. A fanatic army carried through widespread social-revolutionary reforms—socializing the land, suppressing private trade, and banning foot-binding. They left a permanent impact on power structures in the late Qing Dynasty, influencing subsequent Chinese revolutionaries up to Mao.

The point here is not to enter any historical debate over the revolutionizing of Chinese society. The revolutionary significance of the millenarian idea lies less in its material ability to encourage a group of medieval renegades to hold their property in common, or inspire foot-binding reforms, than in its superlative ability to give hope to indigent, hopeless masses. And nowhere has this proven a more effective organizing strategy than in the context of anti-colonial struggles.

Colonial contact is often marked by extraordinary violence so dehumanizing it naturally leads the victims to assume their conquerors must be either subhuman, superhuman, or both. Moreover, it's almost inevitable that colonial conquest will lead to a collapse of the known world. These wars are marked by the arrival of unknown technology from beyond the horizon, in a manifestation of superior power (and unobtainable wealth) as brutal and unavoidable as the great colonial wall that divides Kurdistan. In such a context, national resistance frequently coalesces around the millenarian idea.

This is indeed a catastrophe, the new messiahs say: it can only mean that a new world is imminent for our people. These movements are as diverse in form, potency, and millenarian flavor as the cultures that gave birth to them. They include Jewish revolts against the Roman Empire; the White Lotus Rebellion against the Qing Dynasty: the Boxer Rebellion directly targeting Western colonialism in China; the Sudanese "Mahdi," just one of many Islamic leaders to have taken up that eschatological title in an anti-colonial cause; Korea's Donghak Peasant Revolution; Prince Dipanegara's resistance to Dutch colonial rule in Java; Apolinario de la Cruz in the Philippines; Rastafarianism; the Jehovah's Witness–inspired Watch Tower movement in sub-Saharan Africa; German East Africa's Maji Maji; the Xhosa cattle-killing movement; and the movements around the Delaware (Lenni Lenape) Prophet and the Ghost Dance among Native Americans. Alongside hundreds of other such movements, each provides a distinct study of how despair in the face of colonial power can be organized into resistance through the millenarian idea.

The most notable wave of anti-colonial millenarian resistance came in response to Spain's colonization of the New World. (Some conquistadors also understood their own mission in millennial terms, notably the arrogant and deluded Columbus.[30]) This conflict was one of only three in history more deadly than the Taiping Rebellion, by some counts.

These were among the most spectacular, brutal, and effective military campaigns in history, effectively eradicating continental civilizations—true apocalypse. For the best part of half a millennium, resistance to the Europeans both within the empire (the seventeenth-century Tepehuán and Pueblo Revolts) and beyond it (Apiaguaki Tumpa, the Eunuch of God) repeatedly expressed itself through the expectation of millennialist, post-apocalyptic revival.[31] Some won military victories. Some implemented communitarian ideals in spite of the imperial authorities. Some inspired the subsequent liberation of their nations. Many suffered swift and bloody liquidation, as forecast apocalypses failed to materialize.

Reclaiming Liberation from the Colonizer

One particular feature of postcolonial millenarianism is worth emphasizing here. In the Brazilian backlands, to cite a new example, the excommunicated priest Antônio Conselheiro relied on a millennialist vision to inspire practical social measures of the sort often associated with millenarian movements—redistribution, moral reforms, common land, government by committee, a healthy living wage.[32] In Conselheiro's ideal community, as so often in Latin America, resistance to colonialism took the form of a mystic version of its official ideology—Catholicism. His movement proved capable of what the state-backed religious authorities were not, pursuing earthly salvation from their hellish suffering rather than waiting quietly for redemption in the hereafter.

Many postcolonial millenarian movements demonstrate this remarkable ability to recoup the emancipatory elements from the religion of their conquerors. The corrupt medieval church was the subject of millenarian social revolutionaries' rage, yet they naturally expressed this rage with reference to the Bible and Christian tradition. Likewise, postcolonial prophets find a democratizing, egalitarian spirit on the basis of often idiosyncratic readings of scripture. In this light, the often misunderstood Melanesian "cargo cults" thought to worship Western figures and material artifacts have been reassessed. Critics see in the cults an attempt to both recoup the material benefits of Western (imperial) civilization and express the pursuit of autonomy in opposition to that civilization.[33]

The Kurdish movement likewise attempts to identify the emancipatory factors in hegemonic religious and social traditions, even where these traditions simultaneously justify repression and hierarchy, and deploy these emancipatory ideas in the critique of that very tradition.

On the Western Left, we're more accustomed to think of Islam as the persecuted religion of racialized minorities in our own countries. But from its Middle Eastern perspective, the secular Kurdish movement naturally views things differently. They view Islam as a colonizing force that arrived from outside Kurdistan, particularly via the Ottoman conquests, to supplant Indigenous, animist beliefs. (Often, this argument is expressed through the claim Kurds were originally Zoroastrian, or with reference to the Kurdish-speaking Yazidi people's unique pre-Zoroastrian faith.)

But at the same time, it's clear the Kurdish freedom movement has been marked by its incubation in conservative, Islamic, rural regions. From its secular martyr culture through to the value it places on hospitality, it recoups what is positive from the local culture it's seeking to revolutionize. For example, Rojava's Women's Houses and reconciliation committees attempt to solve social crises through dialogue, without recourse to bloodshed or the courts. They do not attempt to forge these new principles of social justice from nothing, but rather in conversation with a preexisting respect for community elders driven by Syria's Islamic culture. The Kurdish movement therefore recalls the praxis of Marxist educators in the Global South, animating anti-capitalist organizing through the terms of the pueblo and Indigenous Catholic practice. Rather than engaging in an infantile, knee-jerk rejection of Islam, the movement seeks to preserve the social and liberatory elements of a religion and culture that have often proven oppressive in practice.

Elsewhere, this transmission of values occurs in a dialectic, oppositional fashion. For example, the Kurdish movement insists on strict norms of moral conduct for its militants, including teetotalism and celibacy. These standards are in part an attempt to distance the Kurdish movement from Turkish propaganda claiming the movement liberalizes and corrupts Muslim youths. The movement therefore ends up appropriating Islamic values in an attempt to appeal to the local population.

More concretely, the AANES valiantly strives to establish a "democratic Islam," advancing a self-consciously political argument for a poly-ethnic "brotherhood of peoples" as expressing inherently Islamic values. They have therefore established an Academy for Democratic Islam, intended to train young imams to preach democracy and tolerance in northern Syria's mosques, under the tutelage of an affable Sufi Muslim sheikh who regularly makes public appearances with Sunni Muslim, Yazidi, and Christian counterparts.

These well-meaning efforts to represent Öcalan's political vision as the natural inheritor of the Islamic tradition have yet to make significant inroads among the Sunni Arab majority, to put it mildly. Young Kurds who faced down ISIS might sometimes express a more humanist conception of faith inflected by their bruising contact with radical Islam ("I believe in God but not religion," and so on). But overall, Syrians' generally traditional interpretation of Islam remains unaffected by the upheavals of the past decade.[34]

It's perhaps too early to predict the results of the interface between radical, secular post-Marxist philosophy and Islamic tribal traditions under the AANES. But there are certainly instructive lessons to be learned from the movement's respectful, open approach to the very culture it aims to revolutionize. Could we imagine deriving similar lessons from institutional religions and traditional cultures in our own countries? For example, might we seek to emulate the social role of a rural Anglican Church or learn from our aunts' Midwestern hospitality, rather than rejecting these traditions outright? This, the Kurdish movement's practice suggests, is a part of revolution too.

Storm in the Lifeboat

The millenarian sense of social catastrophe also presents clear dangers. For one, the threat of imminent catastrophe can paradoxically produce political passivity and submission—as in the primal myth of a flood forcing a supposedly wicked people to mend their ways. This is particularly the case with straightforward religious millennialism, as Engels warned and history amply demonstrates.[35]

A total rejection of the sociopolitical order can result in political terrain being relinquished to the state, as the faithful "give to Caesar what is Caesar's" and place their hopes in a new world where their agonies will finally end. Leaders from Alexander through Caesar Augustus to Emperor Constantine were able to use millenarian imagery to discipline their subjects into quietude. For Friedrich Nietzsche, this Christian idea of an ultimate justification through faith has anesthetized the human spirit, preventing transformative struggle.[36]

On the secular level, overly dogmatic interpretations of Marxism can have much the same effect. A reductionist Marxism disciplines us to wait effectively forever in the patient expectation of a proletarian revolution, distributing our pamphlets, staging our left-melancholic marches. Bookchin is just one thinker to point out this risk of "indefinite postponement" in Marxism, identifying it as an ideological inheritance from Augustinian Christianity.[37]

Nonetheless, in the secular revolutionary millenarian tradition inherited by the Kurdish movement, there is no life everlasting or spiritual City of God to be inherited, only victory or defeat. The revolutionary movement rather stands in the more dynamic, immanent millenarian-ist tradition, which looks to the establishment of paradise on earth—as witness Kurdish militants' commonplace description of the PKK's mountain retreats as "paradise."[38] Veteran militants in Rojava spoke wistfully of their life in the mountains, reminiscing about holding property in common, baking bread in the snow, drinking from mountain streams. To Öcalan's faithful followers, Turkey's ceaseless bombing campaigns against these mountain lairs were only further proof that the Kurdish guerrilla lived a rarefied, utopian existence.

This embattled mentality comes with its own dangers. Like the related concept of a lost natural society, the millenarian idea can easily engender exclusivism, ethnic purism, and murderous dogmatism. In particular, it can find moral justification through what ecologist, ethno-nationalist, and eugenicist Garrett Hardin lovingly referred to as his "lifeboat ethics." Hardin was thinking of the rich Western nations, which he believed should refuse to offer a hand to those "drowning" in the Global South in order to save themselves. The same logic, marked by a utilitarian refusal to help outsiders or the less fortunate, can infect millenarian movements. If catastrophe is upon us and only the elect will be saved, those lucky few should not run the risk of ethical, spiritual, or material contamination through association with desperate, impoverished, "unsaved," or racially excluded outsiders.[39]

In the contemporary US, a millenarian brand of Protestantism is poisoned by a belief that the US is the last chopper out of global Armageddon. This inflects and reinforces anti-immigrant policies, finding extreme form in rhetoric about the supposed "great replacement" and an impending "white genocide."[40] These white-nationalist ideas are rooted in that broader American tradition where Manifest Destiny expansionism scrapes up against small-government isolationism. America's white, rural Christian Right is therefore left with a confused sense that the state, whose government it despises, must somehow be God's chosen vehicle for redemption from global catastrophe.

These are not fringe ideas. About 40 percent of US adults believe humanity is living in the end times, while many also believe in the Antichrist, the Rapture, and the Battle of Armageddon. These phenomena are often correlated to 9/11, Middle Eastern wars, the Israel–Palestine conflict, and other televisual spectacles.[41] Like the early Christians, the late Americans cannot help but interpret the signs and wonders of a decadent empire and a world in flux as proof of imminent social transformation. Unlike those early Christians, this interpretation appears to have provoked little desire to hold their goods in common or repudiate their decaying empire.

In fact, America's most extreme fundamentalist Christians have come to resemble ISIS, as they demand the "reconstruction" of literally interpreted biblical law through the tools of theocracy and capital punishment.[42] An intoxicating sense of divine mandate naturally leads these extremists to exclude others from their theocratic state-building project. Survivalism can easily breed hate of the outsider. Recall Bookchin's sensible warning that retreat into anarchist communes could mark the "first steps toward ecofascism."[43]

In particular, for centuries the Jewish people have often suffered the worst of millenarian violence, scapegoated as profiting from new and exploitative modes of social and economic organization. This tendency reached its utmost expression in the Third Reich. Nazi ideologues were able to organize a disaffected population by representing the Jews as the embodiment of a demonized global society, thus producing the very apocalypse the Nazis craved through their "*Endkampf*," or final struggle.[44] From cult compound to concentration camp, responses to crises perceived as apocalypse have themselves taken on apocalyptic form.

The Kurdish Movement as Cult

The Kurdish freedom movement (and particularly the PKK) is sometimes condemned as a cult.[45] And indeed, a quasi-religious sense of calling is readily apparent throughout the Kurdish movement. As Marcus's interviews with ex-PKK members suggest, "the thinking inside the PKK was that we were doing something that was holy, sacred."[46]

This quasi-religiosity is present in the veneration of Öcalan; in the way his writings, and the Kurdish movement's broader corpus of parables and myths, are deployed as holy texts; in the monastic lifestyle demanded of Kurdish militants, who indeed resemble mendicant monks in their clandestine passage from village to village, reputedly carrying nothing save a notebook and a little dry bread, dispensing knowledge and promises of inevitable, total revolution; and most of all in the movement's secular martyr culture.

The Kurdish movement is generally opposed to the active pursuit of martyrdom. Secular Kurdish militants do not believe in any literal afterlife. The movement therefore attempts to distance itself from the familiar spectacle of suicide bombing committed by radical Islamists. As the Kurdish movement understands this distinction, whereas Islamist militants sacrifice their lives in the hope of attaining paradise and personal reward, their own militants' sacrifices are made through necessity, in order to defend comrades from harm.

Nonetheless, once a fighter falls in battle or willingly sacrifices their life to save their comrades, they are immediately elevated into the pantheon of heroes. In theory at least, these martyrs are venerated and memorialized not for their death but for their life and struggle. Rojava, and the mountains of Kurdistan, is dotted with graveyards, monuments, and gardens, and decorated by red-, green-, and yellow-liveried martyr posters. They symbolize a paradoxical revolutionary ability to find life in the very moment of death.

For example, early PKK militant Kemal Pir died during a 1982 hunger strike, protesting the abuse and torture of Kurdish militants incarcerated in the notorious Amed prison. He is thus celebrated by the Kurdish movement as one of its preeminent martyrs. During his death-fast, Pir is reputed to have been asked by the prison governor whether he no longer loved life, and to have responded: "There are those who love life so much they are willing to die for it."[47]

This slogan is paradigmatic in suggesting how, and why, the Kurdish movement venerates its dead; and more broadly, how it derives hope through the very fact of the awful violence it suffers. The prison memoir of iconic female Kurdish militant Sakine Cansız documents her incarceration alongside Pir. It's a harrowing account of sexual abuse and physical torture specifically intended to break the spirit, in which bold assertions of hope nonetheless recur time and again.[48]

More than any other single factor, the sense that the deaths of comrades, children, and family must be justified through eventual victory has equipped the movement to endure decades of Turkish brutality. Latterly, this spirit has also played a crucial role in uniting the AANES's diverse communities. The Rojava Revolution is soundtracked by the polyglot, ululating wails of the Kurdish, Arab, Christian, and Yazidi mothers of the martyrs, omnipresent at every protest.[49]

This ability to read hope into loss is clearly inflected by the Islamic context, but also by the sense of an impending, revelatory, secular apocalypse that will justify present sacrifice. Many Kurdish militants therefore felt an understandable sense of almost spiritual justification following the outbreak of the Rojava Revolution, which suddenly made sense of the loss of so many comrades throughout three decades' thankless struggle. This martyr culture often serves a disciplinary function—"Our comrades died for this struggle, and you can't even get out of bed for guard duty?" and so on. But it also serves to liberate militants from their grief. This martyr culture is quintessentially millenarian: perhaps partially in the way it enables the Kurdish movement's leaders to maintain close ideological control of the living but more fundamentally in the way it uses existential crisis in order to motivate a suffering people to struggle toward resolving that crisis.

This existential context can also help us to understand the extreme commitment that the movement demands. Historically, the PKK followed the pattern of other Marxist-Leninist guerrillas by centralizing power and imposing severe disciplinary measures, particularly during the bloody war years of the 1980s and 1990s. On occasion, the party leadership even made use of execution or assassinations to ensure loyalty, unity, and commitment. These practices have long since been recanted in the course of Öcalan's self-critique and the PKK's subsequent "paradigm change."[50] "To apologize shows greatness," the PKK declared during this highly unusual transition, after Öcalan had issued his own courtroom apology for historic violence meted out against the PKK's dissenters.[51]

No one is being executed anymore. But on a less radical plane, the Kurdish movement's millenarian sense of its world-historical role and subsequently radical concept of revolutionary commitment continues to mark the lives of young recruits. Those who make a commitment to the movement are expected to submit to any and all directives until all four parts of Kurdistan are liberated—that is, effectively for life. These high-pressure recruitment tactics and lack of a straightforward off-ramp later in life have been the subject of legitimate external and internal criticism, and other movements and organizations may well choose to recruit and organize differently.

But at the same time, this disciplined commitment has proven pivotal in enabling Rojava's unlikely victory, offering hope and a better existence to millions. Rather, Western social movements and activist networks could explore ways to restore these concepts to their own political practice, while also learning organizational lessons from their attempted implementation and adaptation in Rojava. The Kurdish movement has moved from pure verticalism toward its present novel synthesis; perhaps more disorganized, despairing, horizontalist movements can approach the same delicate balance from the opposite side.

Recent critical work like *Revolutionary Hope in a Time of Crisis* has sought to muster "Afromodern, queer, Latinx, and feminist . . . Indigenous, Islamic, Arab, and Buddhist perspectives" often excluded from contemporary political discourse.[52] These heterogeneous traditions can all equip us to better reckon with loss, failure, and defeat as a fundamental aspect of leftist organizing. Likewise, the Kurdish movement's own insights into how to politicize death and defeat can help challenge our perhaps unexamined individualist fear of discipline, sacrifice, and truly collective politics. Indeed, any knee-jerk reaction to this tough, organized concept of revolutionary commitment is likely to be tinged with Orientalism or colored by Turkish propaganda. In a liberal, postmodern world none of us are really supposed to believe in anything. Any true faith or commitment appears cult-like to liberal eyes. But from the Kurdish movement's perspective, those serious about organizing toward revolution must be willing to risk the charge.

In fact, the loaded word "cult" is derived from the Latin *cultus*, which has a distinct and seemingly relevant meaning. In ancient Rome, the *cultus* was a set of devotional practices embedded within political activity and everyday life, whereby nominally religious practices were used to enshrine a particular mode of social organization through a diverse range of modes of political engagement, with all but the most basic gestures of fealty generally optional. The English word "culture" has the same root. Perhaps this historic concept better expresses the realities of the modern-day, broad-church Kurdish movement, which is marked by a set of shared formal commitments to a unitary concept incarnated in a venerated leader on the one hand, and a wide range of commitments, beliefs, and attitudes on the other. The Kurdish movement is less a cult than a culture, a diverse society in microcosm.

Outward Unity

Along with the need for a forward rather than backward utopianism, a politically productive millenarianism must be marked by an outward rather than an inward unity. It must seek universal social transformation rather than the elevation of an elect in-group. And indeed, the militant guerrillas are just one wing of the broader Kurdish movement. Without the Kurdish movement, the Rojava Revolution could never have come to be; but the realities of political organization in Rojava have also profoundly impacted the movement's militant vanguard. The Kurdish movement's continued engagement in Rojava therefore pushes it to avoid the dangers of a cultish, inward-looking ethics, reducing the risk of their remote mountain strongholds becoming exclusionary, ethnically pure lifeboats amid the storm of capitalist modernity.

In the mountains, the PKK can go its own way. In Rojava, the Kurdish movement must necessarily work with Kurdish housewives, Arab sheikhs, young people who want to both risk their lives in defense of the revolution and some day start families of their own. The militant movement is once again being forced to reassess its more Leninist, verticalist tendencies as they rub up against pragmatic social realities. They are pushed to pursue pragmatic compromises and new hybrid modes of communal life, adapting their utopian ideology to accommodate both Arab and Kurdish locals who are certainly grateful for the movement's protection and support but typically rather less willing to relinquish worldly possessions and family relations, as the party requires of its militants.

Nunes warns us against the fallacy of sharply distinguishing between the (vertical) vanguard and the (horizontal) masses.[53] As the experience of mass political organization within a common culture in Rojava suggests, all political actors and social groups lie somewhere along the spectrum.

Between the party chiefs and the armed opposition lies a whole range of experiences and degrees of commitment to the revolutionary cause. Indeed, Rojava is home to thousands of spaces (academies, military bases, civil society institutions) where lifelong militants live and work side by side with ordinary civilians. These little-studied spaces further facilitate the continued dialectic process of intellectual and political exchange.

An analysis that discounts individuals as a legitimate part of "the people" the moment they start working with the AANES (or another political organization) is always going to end up by detecting a sharp divide between a cult-like core of loyalists and the alienated masses. By treating any participation in the revolution as proof that individual has abandoned the popular masses and joined the revolutionary core, this type of circular, reductive logic prevents any useful analysis of the Kurdish movement's ongoing democratization. On the contrary, when ordinary people join in the revolutionary process, they may indeed be drawn away from their roots in a given village or neighborhood, but can simultaneously also test and challenge the verticalist, centralist core. This organic engagement, and the revolutionary movement's necessary reliance on ordinary civilian families to survive, further prevents any retreat into paranoiac insularity.

In a sense, the Kurdish movement is even fortunate that its own millenarian prophet remains confined to a prison island. Öcalan's confinement and maltreatment remains the rightful focus of political activity seeking his liberation. But despite the personality cult around the leader, he remains practically unable to be tempted into even the most minor accretion of material wealth or power.

This accident of fate has certainly contributed to the Kurdish movement's unique version of networked Leninism. If this movement is a cult, it's one where the leader genuinely reaps no personal gain whatsoever. Nor can the PKK's central committee, hiding in remote cave networks, be said to enjoy the luxuries of power. The AANES certainly offers more opportunities for nepotism and corruption than the PKK's mountain retreats, and locals complain about Kurdish militants wearing costly Jack Wolfskin–brand pants, stockpiling energy drinks, or driving 4X4s. But compared to many previous (millenarian) revolutions, the AANES has witnessed a remarkably low concentration of wealth in the hands of its nomenklatura. If anything, the AANES has adopted a policy of excessive caution toward preexisting social institutions, landowners, and tribal powerbrokers. This focus on building popular consensus has enabled ideologically non-aligned, tactical allies to enrich themselves at the expense of the AANES's broader interests.[54]

The potentially destructive quality of millenarianism is centripetal, driving unity around a leader and the panicked stockpiling of wealth and accretion of power. In Rojava, this trend is tempered by the centrifugal force of outward, real-world political engagement.

A Productive Millenarian Imaginary

More broadly, the Kurdish movement is kept from defaulting to a toxic lifeboat ethics since it fundamentally views the Kurdish people's emancipation as inextricable from a coming revolution in the regional (or even global) order. The millenarian mentality can lead doomer survivalists to withdraw to ethnically homogeneous compounds. But for billions of people worldwide, everyday life already *is* survivalism, and nowhere more so than in Syria.

In Western contexts, those who have the luxury to stockpile goods, retreat to a commune, and build walls are often precisely those for whom catastrophe is least imminent. This is true of the US's property-owning survivalist hobbyists and ultra-rich doomsday preppers. More broadly, it's an apt description of the US, UK, and EU as a whole, militarizing their borders against a perceived external threat. In contexts like Syria, conversely, the apocalypse is necessarily universal, filling the known horizon with flames. In a self-evidently universal catastrophe, it's therefore imperative to seek universal solutions, as the Kurdish movement attempts through its own revolutionary ideology.

Again, a brief comparison of the Kurdish movement to ISIS can help illuminate this crucial difference. In different ways, both are revolutionary millenarian movements. But ISIS's concept of the millennium (or end times) turns inward and backward, not outward and forward. Indeed, ISIS has actively sought to manifest the signs of the end times as prophesied in Islamic eschatological literature, not least by slaughtering Kurds, Yazidis, and Shia Muslims.

ISIS policies, strategies, and propaganda have often been implemented with an eye to the Islamic eschatological literature, intended to fulfill (or appear to fulfill) Islamic prophetic precepts heralding the end of days. ISIS's emergence under black standards, quest to conquer the otherwise-insignificant Syrian town of Dabiq due to its prominent place in millenarian Islamic theology, and rhetorical gestures toward the prophesied capture of Istanbul (Constantinople) can all be understood in this light.[55] Rather than feeling themselves to be the *victims* of social collapse, ISIS sought to become its harbingers and executors.

Some of these gestures and symbols may have been mere propaganda. Nonetheless, ISIS demonstrated a shocking will to endure beyond its own Jonestown-style last stand in 2019 in the AANES's eastern desert. Some acolytes detonated suicide belts. Meanwhile, surrendering fighters streamed out in their tens of thousands, in full knowledge they had just witnessed the birth of a new and potent legend of resistance in the face of empire that would serve them well as they began the slow process of rebuilding and rearming. Like the Kurdish movement, ISIS's ideologues are well aware that a millenarian account of history can make victory out of defeat.

In contrast, the Kurdish movement is not seeking to spark the apocalypse through dramatic acts of violence. Rather, its members recognize the inevitability of state, social, and political collapse and are therefore seeking to recoup a better future in the face of this violence. Accordingly, this catastrophe is articulated as facing not just the Kurdish people, but the *peoples* of the region as a whole. The AANES's bold and generous commitment to the "brotherhood of peoples" places them in the generous, outward-looking millenarian tradition, long downplayed by the historians of millenarianism. This is not their apocalypse, but they will make of it what they can.

Compromise Millenarianism

Utopian depictions of the Rojava Revolution must also be understood in this light. Beyond their clear rhetorical function, stereotyped descriptions of Rojava as "a dream of secular utopia" or "a utopia in the heart of Syria's chaos" also play a role in justifying the total commitment required by the Kurdish movement's millenarian project.[56]

All apocalyptic prophets must promise a new world, and the AANES has witnessed both the catastrophe necessary to justify millenarian political prophecy and the corresponding flourishing of new modes of social organization. As Cohn wrote of the AANES's millenarian medieval forebears, "in the very afflictions descending upon them the millenarians recognized the long-expected messianic woes; and the conviction gave them new militancy."[57] When Rojava's defenders represent their home as utopia, they aren't ignorant of the bitter hardships they face. Rather, this rhetoric forms part of their revolutionary project. They seek to turn war, climate catastrophe, and social collapse into the proof of an imminent better world.

More nuanced accounts of the Rojava Revolution, which depict it in more qualified terms as "a relative oasis," "a growing utopian crack," and so on, speak to this tension.[58] The millenarian end times are not themselves a utopia, but a period of trials through which the new is born.

And the Kurdish movement's analysis is not the only millenarianism on offer. With the Middle East in flames, we will see more millenarianisms emerge into our uncertain century as ways to make sense of disaster and chaos: ISIS-style radical Islamic eschatology, Christian Zionist millenarianism, and Israeli state millennialism, to name but three.

But we will also witness secular millenarianisms, and the crisis factor need not be war or occupation. For example, in US's nineteenth-century Adventist movement, an urgent belief in the impending millennium in the context of nationwide economic depression motivated people to wipe out debts and give away their property. It's therefore possible to imagine a revolutionary, millenarian debt jubilee breaking forth in response to a global economic crisis. In particular, the climate change eschaton will surely one day inspire national, continental, and global millenarian movements anticipating a revolutionary transformation in the global order.

This is how prophets of millennium speak. But why do their followers listen, even knowing that all previous millennia have failed, that each date forecast for apocalypse has come and gone without incident?

The following chapters will look in closer detail at the bold psychological contortions undergone by Kurdish militants, socialist organizers, and other willful utopians as they pursue their own impossible, eagerly anticipated earthly paradises. Their diverse responses to epochal catastrophe and the attempted extermination of their political projects are self-deluding, cynical, defiant.

In this spirit, they recall the tale of Middle Eastern trickster-figure Mullah Nasruddin, who is told he'll be hanged if he cannot prove his dubious credentials as a mystic visionary.

"I can see strange sights . . . stars in the daylit sky . . . demons under the earth," the Mullah hastily splutters.

"But how is it you suddenly came to perceive such extraordinary sights?" demands the suspicious king.

"Oh, that's easy. Fear is all you need."

Chapter 6
Copium Strategies
Cynicism and Naivety

In chapters 1 and 2 we looked at the Kurdish movement's political praxis in the AANES, arguing this program is defined by adverse circumstance and crisis, paradoxically driving a continued, determined utopianism. In chapters 4 and 5 we explored the movement's deployment of meta-narrative, ideology, and rhetoric to organize pessimism and combat despair. But the most fundamental challenges our contemporary Left faces are perhaps less organizational or ideological than existential. How do we, personally, continue to hope in hope's absence?

As Mullah Nasruddin suggests, when placed under extraordinary pressure the most unlikely figures can prove capable of vision, valor, and revolutionary boldness. From mischievous trickster figures to delusional aristocrats to contemporary hipster leftists, the history of anti-authoritarian thought and political organization is full of ambiguous antiheroes.

So, too, in Rojava. Besides the unlikely alliances forged between socialist-feminist insurrectionaries and conservative tribal power brokers explored above, a rogue's gallery of internationalist volunteers also felt compelled to answer the call to travel to a previously obscure corner of Mesopotamia and build a better world. Hard-bitten Foreign Legion rejects with shady criminal records fought and died alongside starry-eyed queer, vegan activists, and born-again Christians broke bread with anarchists, Maoists, Trotskyists, unreformed Stalinists, trade unionists, idealists, cynics, addicts, suspected agents, confirmed cowards, heroes, villains, and a positive superfluity of Germans. All found their own ways to keep struggling onward.

Revolution is not a dinner party, but the Kurdish movement places hospitality and grassroots social interaction at the very core of its praxis. As a point of political pride, whatever the present crisis there was always time for tea and a chat. Unexpected interactions between internationalists, Kurdish militants, and ordinary civilians threw into relief the remarkable psychological processes everyone underwent so as not to buckle under the weight of despair.

While addressing the psychological survival mechanisms Kurdish militants rely on, therefore, I'll also suggest four representative psychological types encountered among Rojava's internationalist volunteers.

The *disillusioned veteran* has spent years on the frontlines face to face with the revolution's shortcomings, and they choose to insulate themself through sneering detachment and gallows humor—which equip them to continue their struggle. At the opposite extreme, the newly arrived *naive utopian* is wholly incapable of seeing the revolution's shortcomings, full of infectious revolutionary fervor as they are.

The *total loyalist* takes a similar approach, but their initial naivety becomes a permanent condition. They decide to swallow the Kurdish movement's grandest ideological claims at face value, a one-shot tonic for any nagging doubts. And finally, the *cynical idealist* takes a similar path a step further. Undertaking a true absurdist commitment, their eyes are open to the contingent and limited nature of the revolution, yet they nonetheless choose to struggle anew each day.

Each type overlaps with the others in various respects, even though internationalists of different types might frustrate, disagree with, or undermine one another in their daily interactions. And each has their clear avatar in Western leftist movements; all model attitudes you might recognize in your own comrades or movements, though they also stand in particular relation to Rojava's revolutionary conditions. All come with dangers. We can learn from and critique each model of revolutionary commitment, exploring a novel range of practical survival strategies all leading us toward the absurdist, revolutionary leap of faith.

Tricksters: The Organization of Cynicism

Many of these survival strategies are far more ancient than our latter-day left movements. For example, many cultures have venerated or traced their origin to trickster figures: Loki, the spider Anansi, Brer Rabbit. Much like the social bandit, the trickster incarnates a popular rebellious spirit, the anti-authoritarian conscience of the masses. But more fundamentally, these figures also represent humankind's ability to make a virtue of our fallen, hand-to-mouth yet defiantly upright existence. They variously celebrate our self-awareness, our pluck, our status as the weakest and most cunning of the beasts.

The trickster model can thus help us shake off despair and engage in meaningful political organization, by deploying survival strategies particularly prevalent among the first type of internationalist volunteer, the *disillusioned veteran*. The early years of the war against ISIS attracted hundreds of volunteers without any particular ideological affinity to the AANES's progressive program—ex-military men looking for an adventure or frontline experience, and others angered by perceived Western indifference in the face of ISIS's attacks on European metropoles or genocide of the Yazidis. Some heroically lost their lives, joining the pantheon of the martyrs. Others served their tour of duty and returned home. But some stayed on, accustomed by now to the hardships of military life in AANES, growing ever more grizzled and world-weary and looking with a jaded eye on subsequent waves of more ideologically motivated leftist volunteers.

On the one hand, these men (and they are usually, though not always, men) sometimes denigrate the revolution's ideological dimensions, perhaps mocking socialist aspirations as deluded or even denying the significance of women's autonomy in Rojava. But at the same time, many have proven willing to endure all the boredom and frustrations of militant life and to risk their lives for their comrades. Many managed to stick it out in Syria for longer than their ideologically purer leftist counterparts, who were sometimes more easily dissuaded as they came to recognize the revolution's various shortcomings and compromises.

The cynical, knowing attitude of the trickster enables these disillusioned veterans to face catastrophe. As arch-trickster Bugs Bunny explains, in an unexpectedly profound meta-analysis: "When momentarily I appear to be cornered or in dire danger and I scream, don't be [concerned]. It's actually a big put-on. Let's face it, Doc. I've read the script, and I already know how it turns out."[1]

The trickster knows the terms. He can fool you, but more importantly he won't be fooled. Rojava's seasoned cynics won't let themselves be tempted into the murky waters of ideology. Just like Bugs, they know the score, know the system, know all the tricks of the game. They know how to make sure they get enough packs of cigarettes with their rations, know where to find diesel in Raqqa—but that's where their investment seems to end.

Sometimes, these men might perhaps feel more ideological sympathy than they let on, particularly after fighting alongside and losing leftist comrades. But sincerity is anathema to their survival technique. Perpetually self-aware, simultaneously self-aggrandizing and self-deprecating, the seasoned cynics tell jokes so they can get up each day and continue the struggle. Perhaps only once or twice, late at night, will they reveal the sorrow or hope in their heart. In the face of real violence more brutal yet than the cartoon bloodbaths endured by Bugs, they demonstrate how a fundamentally human trickster cynicism can be deployed to militant ends.

Rather than disqualifying us from the task of revolutionary organization, personal bitterness can help us weather hard times. Knowing how the story ends, expecting failure and catastrophe, we want nothing more than what we have. In this way, like battlefield soldiers who've already accepted their fate, we can endure hell until an unexpected victory dawns.

Quixote: Self-Narrativization

As Bugs suggests, the tricksters have read the script. They are aware of the conventions of narrative, myth, and war story and are thus able to short-circuit and circumnavigate all threats. (Spider-trickster Anansi is also God of Stories.) This meta-level ability to retell the story of one's own life can help us all endure hardship.

The paradigmatic example here is Don Quixote, the delusional, penniless nobleman who believes he's a knight errant sent to defend a profoundly disinterested world from evildoers. Quixote is both popularly understood as a foolish, perennial optimist and beloved by philosophers of the tragic, pessimistic absurd.[2] This dialectic relation, between utopian dream and humiliated reality, makes Quixote an ultimate embodiment of hope without hope. Time and again, Quixote makes the decision to act without a choice as though there were a choice, justifying the tragic mishaps and calamities that befall him by retroactively fitting them into his knightly self-image.

In this sense, the pessimistic quixotic soul finds a natural home in the twenty-first-century revolutionary movement. As partisans of an internationalist socialist movement now a shadow of its former self, we may well recognize something of our own self-delusion in Quixote's quest on behalf of a noble order vanishing from the world, if it ever truly existed at all. It's been claimed that pessimists "could never plant a bomb, plan a revolution, or shed blood for a cause," but the history of socialist struggle proves quite the reverse.[3] What is more pessimistic than a belief the world must be utterly remade, even and especially when that revolution seems more distant than ever?

True Quixotism motivates bold action by making successive defeats and humiliations into further proof that our struggle is heroic—whether against Quixote's windmills and various imagined nemeses, Turkey's NATO army, or capitalism itself. Quixotism is characterized by a lack of self-awareness bound up with a profound narrative awareness.

This self-narrativization functions similarly to Öcalan's construction of a new, Kurdish-focused myth of history, but on a more personal level. It's a way to overcome postmodern despair and the death of meta-narratives, as internationalists and Kurdish militants alike lay claim to personal myths they may rationally know to be false.

It's easy for internationalist volunteers in Rojava to slip into rhetorical grandstanding or performative heroics. Left-melancholic storytelling about an idealized past can take the place of concrete organization. But this all-too-human tendency can also be reclaimed for higher ends. For example, some arrogant volunteers of the disillusioned veteran type could be heard claiming to have played a personal, pivotal role in defeating ISIS.

These grand claims might be delusional, but they also override an individual soldier's effective irrelevance with a grand narrative of personal heroism, enabling them to continue playing their small and vital part in this broader movement.

More generally, the most effective organizers across the Left are often those best able to convince themselves and others that a given eviction resistance, land struggle, or shop floor unionization drive offers a pivotal turning point capable of landing a significant blow against the state or the capitalist system. We've all been in meetings with a comrade making overblown promises and grand appeals to lofty sentiments—but these are often also exactly the comrades with the charisma to encourage others to action, and the bloody-mindedness to stick with a struggle to its end.

Today's hardships are tomorrow's boasts, anecdotes, and rewritten personal histories. When arguing that the false recollections he calls "screen memories" evolve as a way of shielding us from childhood trauma, Freud quotes the Latin poet Virgil: "Perhaps even this, some day, will be pleasurable to recall."[4] The very act of narrating, of transforming suffering into a story, alters the immediate quality of that suffering.

This narrative urge might sometimes be self-indulgent, but it enables the quixotic disillusioned veteran to endure deprivation, shelling, jail time, and personal losses without complaint. The worse things are now, the better they will one day appear. On a more personal level, this approach therefore also reflects the millenarian, Marxist-Leninist, or Öcalanite sense of history as advancing through revolutionary crises.

When Friedrich Nietzsche celebrated *amor fati* or love of fate, he wasn't urging us to turn the other cheek like mild-mannered Christians. On the contrary, true *amor fati* willfully accepts and actively makes the most of the arbitrary hand we've been dealt by fate, serving "to redeem what is past, and to transform every 'It was' into 'Thus would I have it!'"[5] The fact that there is no essential truth or cause for hope lying beyond the veil of existence could inspire a despairing fatalism, or it could enable the knowing, willing construction of a personal narrative capable of leading us out of that fatalism.[6]

Too Far: Gallows Humor

The disillusioned veteran frequently resorts to gallows humor as a way of coping with loss. To Freud, humor often functions rather like a screen memory, creating an outlet for or enabling us to avoid working through past trauma; humor thus "assumes a place in the great series of those methods created by the human psyche to escape the compulsion of suffering."[7]

As in familiar memes circulated by US brocialists that valorize Stalinist communism rather than engage with its failures, the comic regurgitation of cruel, painful experience can characterize left melancholia. Once again, melancholy is typified by repetition that works to psychically evade the task of processing and overcoming trauma.

For example, in the quieter months following one Turkish invasion, combatants who had fought in the unsuccessful defense of a now-abandoned front line staged a mock raid on their own base as a birthday surprise for one of their number. Similar pranks are relatively commonplace throughout Rojava, as doubtless on the front lines of other armed struggles.

Crucially, defense mechanism humor should bind us to our comrades and help us endure harms we cannot overcome, not shield us from reckoning with our own failings. There is, accordingly, a place for gallows humor on the Syrian battlefield or among refugees facing deportation; less so when it's used to denigrate any effort at left organization in our own national contexts.

For the disillusioned veterans among Rojava's internationalists, nothing was off the table. But as another internationalist adroitly observed, Kurdish comrades themselves are far more apt to joke about suffering and defeat than about their victories or goals. A combat amputee might use his disability to clown around; ISIS, naturally, was the frequent butt of wry jokes. But from the Kurdish movement's perspective, mockery of the women's movement, the "martyrs," or Öcalan was always beyond the pale. Kurdish militants could, and did, laugh under enemy fire—but never during the serious process of self-criticism, intended to mold them into better revolutionaries.

Sometimes, international volunteers laughed about an aspect of the struggle in one moment, only to be criticized for taking the joke too far in the next. "Too far" in the sense of allowing the joke to run on from a bitter history and a harsh present reality, into the far future when the Kurdish movement's grand promises will eventually be realized. But until that day of transformation, sometimes all you can do is laugh.

Borrowed Mustaches: Idealization

Knowing cynicism about our present circumstances can usefully combine with a utopian idealism about our revolutionary goals, preventing that cynicism from hobbling us into inactivity. To this end, a renewed internationalist sensibility can help Western comrades to draw inspiration from both historic socialist struggles and contemporary mass movements in the Global South, using them as a goad to effective action.

The Right fails to understand the Left's intersectional, internationalist solidarity. For example, right-wing critics famously mock declarations like "Queers for Palestine" as analogous to chickens protesting for KFC, given Hamas's well-known theocratic tendencies.[8] These bad-faith critiques ignore the validity, coherence, and legitimacy of a principled solidarity that achieves its true significance precisely at the point when it departs from a like-for-like identification. More than that, a dash of romantic utopianism over distant armed struggles can charge domestic organizing in the West with renewed potency. Internationalism is not a one-way process but provides benefits to those standing in solidarity as well. One need not agree with or even wholly understand the positions of a given militant group fighting oppression to feel invigorated and inspired by its example.

Many newly arrived international volunteers in Rojava idealize or even fetishize the Kurdish movement, using their notional example as a stick with which to castigate their fellow international volunteers ("Well, actually, the Kurdish comrades do it like this."). Non-Kurdish internationalists were commonly spotted sporting Kurdish national dress and tragicomic attempts at the bushy mustaches associated with the Kurdish national identity, or else striding around affectedly in combat trousers despite never having visited the front line.

Though clearly open to charges of Orientalism or straight-up ridicule, an idealized, militant Kurdishness simultaneously plays a serious role in motivating internationalist commitment. A naive over-identification is often present in other international solidarity movements too.

Similarly, the mountains where the PKK are engaged in their desperate armed struggle against Turkey come to represent that impossible hope to comrades in Rojava. In Kurdish, these remote guerrilla hideouts are simply referred to as "the mountains," in a rarefying metonym. "The mountains" are both deployed as disciplinary concept and held out as representing the utmost limit of hope. Constant references to the truly militant commitment of lifelong revolutionaries far off in the mountains are intended to caution, discipline, and remind Kurdish militants on the ground in Rojava how far they have to travel before their ideal world is achieved.

Rojava encodes a utopian, unrealistic hope of a better world to portions of the Western Left. Within Rojava, some internationalists similarly idealize their Kurdish comrades. In turn, the mountains play an idealized role for Rojava's Kurdish revolutionaries themselves—effectively becoming the "Rojava" of Rojava.

"I Do Not Know If I Have Entirely Recovered": Revolutionary Madness

As Don Quixote makes clear in word and action, it's better to "live a madman, and die sane" than the other way round.[9] Better to delude ourselves now as we pursue a perhaps unobtainable goal than make a sincere investment that will ultimately drive us insane on our deathbeds as we recognize our failure to remake the world. Revolutionary history and calls to arms are marked by the language of insanity, sickness, stupidity. As Bloch argues, "the paranoiac is often a project-maker."[10]

Indeed, when we read Bloch's dogged efforts to interweave all manner of historical, cultural, and Gnostic evidence into proof of a coming Marxist utopia, it sometimes feels like we're reading the delusional schemes of a paranoiac who sees connections invisible to the rest of us. Yet in conversation with a paranoid schizophrenic, we sometimes see the mists clear, as they reveal they're partially or occasionally aware of their own delusions. Likewise, Bloch's less than utopian critical awareness sometimes seeps in, as he admits how far we have to go before the Not Yet becomes reality. He praises lunacy, and yet he finally admits "no one has yet been satisfied by mere wishing. It does not help at all."[11] Bloch's lunacy is politically productive because it is elective, programmatic, and shot through with bitter sanity. Like Quixote, he is mad of his own free choice.

This interplay, between willful, insane, public expectation of utopia and quiet, private admission of our political insanity, is crucial. For example, individuals who make a lifelong commitment to the Kurdish movement undertake not to criticize one another's actions and decisions in public. In public, both the Kurdish vanguard class and their international recruits can indeed appear deluded, unwilling to brook any talk of socialist or Kurdish defeat even when the odds appear insuperable. But in private, Kurdish militants of course criticize one another, while also expressing misgivings and regrets. Their apparent insanity is organized into a revolutionary bipolarity.

To understand the psychological role a willed sickness or insanity can play in revolutionary struggle, we can take a brief detour to explore an extraordinary text: Russian aristocrat-turned-anarchist-revolutionary Mikhail Bakunin's confession to Tsar Nicholas.[12] This letter, written to plead for clemency while Bakunin was jailed in solitary confinement following his participation in the pan-European revolutionary movements of 1848–49, is endlessly fascinating. Excerpts from the text were circulated in an attempt to discredit Bakunin, while it's also possible to read the Russian emperor's personal annotations scrawled in the margins. Is Bakunin capitulating to try to save his neck? Or is he trying to trick the emperor into securing his release, while also protecting his comrades from harm? Does he actually believe what he's writing? Opinion has been divided ever since.

To Camus, Bakunin's admission that he was never able to engage in political activity "except with a supernatural and painful effort to stifle forcibly the interior voice which whispered to me that my hopes were absurd" demonstrates that utopian political thought can be toxic and dangerous, dissolving all present ethics in pursuit of a still-distant goal.[13] As with the politicized insanity invoked by some millenarian prophets, the social order is liquidated in the name of a never-to-be achieved Not Yet, paving the way for chaotic and disorganized violence.

But Bakunin's true stance is indecipherable, incoherent, perhaps unknowable even to himself. He believes and simultaneously does not believe, often seeming unable to resist confessing his continued revolutionary commitment, bursting the fetters in which he has attempted to confine his defiant spirit.

Thus Bakunin describes his political commitment as an "intoxication," a "political fever," what Tsar Nicholas himself annotates as "political madness."[14] "EVEN NOW I DO NOT KNOW IF I HAVE ENTIRELY RECOVERED," he laments (in all uppercase letters) in a direct message to the emperor he is nominally trying to convince to let him go.[15]

His revolutionary fervor is described in terms familiar to the addict: He hates and yet craves it, cannot resist it, knows it is killing him and yet wants more: "My will, or better, my stubbornness, grew as the difficulties grew, and the numerous obstacles did not frighten me, but on the contrary inflamed my revolutionary thirst, inciting me to feverish, untiring activity. I was doomed to destruction: I had a presentiment of this, and I moved gladly toward it. I was then already weary of life."[16]

Bakunin's despairing death drive is deployed to political ends. The question whether he was acting out of a suicidal inclination or simply throwing himself into insane revolutionary fervor out of desperation is beside the point. The two sensibilities—despair and resistance—are inextricable. Rather than simply believing, he "wanted to believe."[17] Faith is here the subject of the will, not its object. His text is at once terribly self-aware and marked by a relinquishing of logic—the sane, intentional deployment of insanity.

Of course, Bakunin was writing under duress and direct observation, knowing his words would be read by the emperor, which partially explains this strange ambivalence. But under empire, under hegemony, in an age of mass surveillance, we all operate under similar conditions. We are all pleading for clemency and striking contradictory postures in response to an all-seeing, almighty power. Our resistance is inextricably shaped by hegemony which by its very definition defies any alternative.

Resistance under hegemony is insanity. And indeed, as modeled from Quixote onward, insanity under hegemony can be resistance.

As is frequently reported, those on the political Left are more likely to be depressed—hence the phenomenon of so-called activist burnout in the racial justice and climate change movements, among others.[18] There isn't room here to explore the full causes and implications of these bleak statistics, though endemic, melancholic attachment to ineffectual modes of organization is certainly part of the problem. But the statistics also suggest that individual self-care and bourgeois wellness can never cure our sick, mad, angry political commitment. Can the Left find ways to care for our comrades and keep up our morale, while also accepting a fundamental dissatisfaction with reality as inherent to transformative political action? Can we lay claim to a willful, world-refusing political sickness without dying from it—or being cured altogether? Can we accept that our personal goal is not to be stable, well, or safe, even as we strive to achieve these goals for our world? Can we stop burning out but keep on burning?

Certainly, many internationalist revolutionaries were primarily drawn to Rojava through an ideological affinity with the revolution's political aims. But the majority (regardless of "type") were also driven away from capitalist modernity through some deep dissatisfaction with this system, sometimes manifesting as mental health or addiction issues. "Volunteer fighters," the internationalists are commonly called, as though each militant did not feel absolutely driven to join the revolution—as though their sacrifices and revolutionary commitment were not absolutely *mêcbur*, compelled by circumstances beyond their control.

Bloch claims that suicide implies a forlorn hope in a better world, a vain protest against a capitalist system that we know cannot be all there is. His claim is tragically borne out by a rash of suicides among internationalist comrades returning to the West after years of struggle in Rojava. Having seen that a better, more collective, more hopeful alternative is possible, many returning internationalists struggle to readjust to their isolated existence in the West. (Untreated battlefield PTSD and repression by Western governments have also played a role in these suicides, with both factors again worsened in lonely and individualistic Western contexts.)

This doesn't necessarily mean all the internationalists in Rojava were mad or depressed. Rather, it suggests that madness is an expected and legitimate response to contemporary capitalist culture. The challenge is how to organize this fundamental pessimism and direct it toward bold sacrifice or mundane daily commitment, rather than letting it culminate in a bleakly "optimistic" suicide.

Deliberate Simplification

In an attempt to invigorate their followers and prevent this despair from setting in, many revolutionary movements have deployed a strategic simplification of politics—the simplified myths of history described above. As crisis worsens, millenarian messiahs invoke their followers to insane acts of sacrifice by promising them the violence suffered by their tribe, people, or nation is proof of imminent divine intervention or social transformation.

This type of simplification is a highly potent method of precipitating political action. But it's also been shadowed, throughout the centuries, by violent excess. An exclusionary, negative anti-intellectualism has often proven unable to achieve the negation of the negation by positively creating new modes of thought, creation, and intellect, instead licensing the brutality of Stalinism or the Khmer Rouge.

Yet simplification is also democratization. There is a subtler but nonetheless profound violence in technocracy and a mystification in reserving knowledge to an intellectual elite. The Marxist metanarrative of history therefore sought to provide a revolutionary simplification, demystifying economics on behalf of the industrial workers. Mao achieved the same for the peasant, anti-imperialist South. Christ suffered the little children to come to him, speaking in parables the illiterate masses could understand; the Zapatistas' Subcomandante Marcos writes children's stories; Öcalan makes myth of history to feed the Kurdish people's hunger for politically relevant truth.

It's in the dialectic relation of our political ideas to people's material reality that we're forced to truly understand, express, and clarify our arguments.[19] Democratization simplifies, and simplification democratizes. If we consider political education a fundamental transformative task facing the Left, we must therefore be prepared to adapt, alter, and simplify our messages to reach the broadest audience possible.

In the process of winning over a suspicious public, the Left is often hampered by what we could think of as the climate change paradox: it's far easier to point to a single unseasonably cold summer as proof that climate change is a hoax than it is to make the more complex, negative argument that this temporary cold spell is actually the result of generalized global warming.

The Left has long grappled with the challenge of communicating dialectical thinking to the public. Economic deprivation is falsely blamed on greedy immigrants, rather than neoliberal governance; an epidemic of male suicide is falsely blamed on feminism, rather than patriarchy itself; the global financial crash is falsely blamed on a shadowy Jewish-Masonic cabal, rather than legal and visible fiscal institutions. The truth is stranger than the simple, comforting fiction. We must find ways to express these nuanced, paradoxical complexities to a mass audience.

We therefore continue to seek a political vocabulary capable of the same reach as the simplifying, reductive Right. No wonder we're still waiting for a leftist mega-influencer capable of challenging Andrew Tate or Alex Jones. The necessary fury is there; our daunting task is to organize it. We must reckon with the paradox that many ordinary people hate capitalist elites more than almost anything save socialists, navigating through a hostile media environment and ideological consensus back to where we belong, at their side.

For Freire, "even when one must speak *to* the people, one must convert the 'to' to a 'with' the people."[20] This "with the people" approach is easiest to achieve when opposing an explicit, concrete enemy, but this type of simplified rhetoric should always be linked to a clear, careful, systemic socialist theorization. During the twentieth century, for example, the anti-imperialist concept of "proletarian nations" provided a radical, hyper-effective simplification of the communist analysis. In an era of decentralized, globalized finance capital, we should consider how to organize and direct a generalized resentment of elites, "the bankers," and the super-rich in a similarly revolutionary fashion.

Indeed, the West is experiencing an organizational crisis of populism, as evidenced by the generalized failure of social-democratic coalitions in Greece, Spain, France, the UK, and the US. There are valuable lessons to be learned from what recent critics of left populism tellingly call Jeremy

Corbyn's and Bernie Sanders's "quixotic" efforts to align themselves as anti-establishment voices operating within the political establishment.[21]

These left populist movements are commonly considered to have failed since they were too *un*popular, too far outside the Overton window of acceptable parliamentary politics. Yet for just the same reason, they were unable to go far enough in articulating a radical new subjectivity in opposition to the elite. Media hostility notwithstanding, part of the problem came from inside the house, with radical rhetoric and left melancholic aesthetics masking necessarily reformist political programs which left no one satisfied. All too often, as a result, these movements' ideologues appeared mealy-mouthed and confused. Trump, the simplistic right ideologue par excellence, has faced no such challenges.

Radical knowledge must be made available to all, in functional, emancipatory form. Successful and productive political organization is marked by the *deliberate, willed, temporary* suspension of complexity—thus the success of Leninism and Maoism in turning Marx's theoretical project into political reality. In *Capital,* Marx steadily extrapolates a global economic theory and political philosophy from the starting point of a few pounds of cloth. Lenin then distilled this philosophy back down into maxims every bit as deceptively simple as the fabric from which Marx began. The function of the political vanguard is to oversee this simplification process. Yet all too often "complexity becomes the great alibi," revolutionary metanarratives foundering against the reef of postmodern despair.[22]

To this end, the Kurdish vanguard have functioned effectively as what Gramsci calls organic intellectuals, remaining intimately connected with proletarian Kurdish society while offering it intellectual, political, and spiritual guidance. Insofar as the vanguard remains organic, it is able to navigate the tension between theoretical complexity and necessarily simplified explication, while simultaneously engaging in ongoing education and consciousness raising.

There is no Cultural Revolution–style assault on intellectualism in Rojava. On the contrary, the Kurdish movement is a mildly intellectualizing force. This is thanks both to its promotion of Kurdish-language education and culture, and to its programmatic introduction of feminist, socialist, and postcolonial thought to civil society, albeit primarily filtered through Öcalan's work.

As we've seen, Öcalan is adept at honing complex ideologies into highly transmissible, replicable maxims. But this reality goes further than Öcalan's knack for a catchy phrase. Öcalan's work *is* its distillation into a handful of slogans, heard throughout Kurdistan and worldwide—as powerfully demonstrated by the Kurdish movement's slogan "Women, Life, Freedom" (*Jin, Jiyan, Azadî*), taken up by Iranian anti-regime protesters and thus disseminated across the globe, although its original Kurdish and militant connotations are often censored by the reformist liberal establishment and Iranian opposition.

While Öcalan's followers have sought to extricate deep meaning from these slogans, their function is clearly centripetal rather than centrifugal. They are intended to be dispersed, spread like seeds through society, and any serious reading of Öcalan must take account of this productive dispersal.

More broadly, a simplified, utopian vision of Rojava has played an undeniably productive role in reopening possibilities long foreclosed to the Western Left. Mere utopianism alone is never enough, but neither should it be discounted as a weapon in the revolutionary educator's armory.

Our second set of internationalist volunteers, the *naive utopians*, therefore, represent the revolutionary possibility of simplification—as well as its limitations. Likely arriving from a standard anarchist milieu in Europe, the naive utopian spends six months in Kurdistan, fails to learn much Kurdish beyond the slogans, and seldom leaves their all-internationalist compound in the countryside. They therefore return home convinced that the revolution is an unambiguous, feminist, direct-democratic utopia, an unadulterated implementation of Öcalan's theory in practice.

On a limited, local level, these naive utopians often implemented Öcalan's vision rather more closely than seasoned, battle-weary Kurdish veterans, who were more given to pragmatism and cutting corners. The resultant interactions could be tragicomic, as exasperated eco-activists chided Kurdish veterans for burning camp waste using crude diesel, or in one extreme instance railed against the washing-up schedule as positivist, Stalinist, and repressive. Nonetheless, within the confines of their own commune, these naive utopians often managed to get the job done quite admirably. Naive enthusiasm helps!

But the naive utopian also represents the limits of a simplified politics: not, these days, anti-intellectual violence, but on the contrary quietist retreat. The naive utopian's understanding of the revolution is marked by ideological purity, theoretical simplicity, and disengagement from the material complexities of implementing democratic confederalism on a mass scale, as outlined in chapter 1. For example, they might ignore the fact that their revolutionary life in a "green" commune is underwritten by the oil profits that the AANES must pragmatically rely on to survive, creating a rarefied space to implement Öcalan's idealistic vision of communal life to an extent inaccessible to most ordinary locals.

The purely naive utopian will not be able to disseminate these ideals further into society and might appear ridiculous if they try. For example, internationalist volunteers sometimes attempted to describe the horrors of capitalist modernity in the West to young locals, encouraging them to remain in Rojava. But ordinary young Kurds have Instagram; they have cousins in Europe; and they can well perceive the admitted material difference between life in Syria and Europe. If naively utopian comrades praised life in Rojava while pouring scorn on life in London or Berlin, they risked distancing themselves from the struggles ordinary locals faced each day, or the legitimate anger ordinary Syrians might feel against the Kurdish movement.

Simultaneously, many locals recognize that their political project is unique and that there are things in Rojava worth fighting for that are absent in the West, for example a spirit of solidarity and community not easily found elsewhere. Internationalists could indeed make valuable contributions to the movement's critique of capitalist modernity. But negotiating these conversations requires a deeper, critical sensitivity to the grim challenges of both civilian life and revolutionary organization in northern Syria.

This danger has its parallel among Kurdish organizers, often manifesting as frustration when local realities depart from Öcalan's utopian vision. The less organic the vanguard class is, the more they become distant from and frustrated by ordinary civilians, whom they perceive as recalcitrant and backward. Kurdish comrades can likewise be tempted to retreat to (all-Kurdish) communes rather than continuing the harder, more vital work of building democratic confederalism from the ground up.

Preserving this vanguard mentality while maintaining a genuine love for the people is a challenge, of course, but one community organizers must not shirk. Can we find ways to convince ourselves of political claims we doubt, to assert victories we cannot foresee, to speak and even think in primary-colored anti-capitalism, while simultaneously perceiving the world in many shades of gray?

Again, a constructive engagement with their own religious, cultural and traditional contexts can help organizers to communicate with communities in language they understand, engaging in what revolutionary educator Paolo Freire called the "dialogic" process of open and two-way learning, which will in turn rejuvenate dry, academic socialist theory through its encounter with living struggles and traditions.

The Kurdish movement's concept of education as dialogic exchange offers instructive models of simplification as democratization, opening up new vistas of political activity. Simple lessons from village life illustrate socialist concepts, which are then implemented on the village level. Consciousness raising takes place on the streets during revolutionary upheavals, in prison cells, in mountain hideouts, and on the military frontlines, always with reference to the particular struggle at hand.[23] "*Tekmil*," the process of criticism and self-criticism, offers a way for petty, everyday squabbles, grievances, and acts of solidarity to form part of a broader communal political program. Education programs frequently rely on personal, written testimonies that are then analyzed in relation to the Kurdish movement's revolutionary ideology.

To Freire, this kind of education is hope in its very essence. It encodes a determined belief that change is possible, beyond deterministic belief in a certain Marxist utopia and beyond fatalist resignation to capitalism.[24] To venture into an embattled, impoverished community and seek converts to socialism or democratic confederalism, people must necessarily have a deep, organic sympathy with and understanding of realities in that community. Yet to remain motivated for this task and motivate others in turn, it can simultaneously prove useful to be, on some level at least, a naive utopian, analogous to what is known in the Christian tradition as a willing "fool for Christ." Like Bugs Bunny, like Bakunin, like Quixote, the most effective revolutionaries tell themselves the stories they need to get by.

Chapter 7

More Copium Strategies

Toward the Doomer Revolutionary

Existential philosophy has long recognized the paradoxically freeing effects of despair and cynicism. Absurdist philosophy likewise perceives the fundamental meaninglessness of the universe, the amoral, chaotic void into which humans have been thrust. But absurdist philosophers like Camus and Kierkegaard attempt to venture beyond this meaninglessness, exploring the paradox through which humans continue seeking truth and meaning, even when we fear, believe, or know that there is no meaning to be found.

A consciously politicized form of absurdist thought has much to offer the contemporary Left. It can help us make sense of our own ridiculous striving for a better, socialist world, in the face of the apparent reality that no such better world can be achieved. On the personal, organizational, and national levels, the Kurdish movement's theory and practice offer useful models of absurdist thought animating day-to-day political commitment.

To this end, both Rojava's internationalist volunteers and Kurdish comrades draw on a diverse range of potentially absurd tactics: self-delusion, self-effacement, deliberate forgetfulness, hipster posing, virtue signaling, even the aesthetic fetishization of revolution. Indeed, many of these tactics are already common practice throughout contemporary society and movements on the Western Left, suggesting productive ways to reckon with and travel beyond our despair.

As we've seen worldwide, young generations are demonstrating a willed commitment to political organization, even in the absence of

165

an organized and credible left movement capable of mounting a challenge to capitalism, statism, or imperialism. This quality is mocked by the Right as "cope," "copium," or "hopium": a self-delusion since we're unable to admit the scale of the challenges we face, high on the seemingly self-deluding hope endemic among the Left.

Opium is a narcotic, but, as Marx suggests with regard to religion, it's also an anesthetic. It can help us endure a surgical intervention and return to life—perhaps dizzy and weakened but healed and ready for renewed struggle.

So even if the Left does prefer getting high on "hopium" to reckoning with the scale of its defeat, this capacity for delusion should help equip us for the struggle ahead. Recall Bakunin's "supernatural and painful effort to stifle forcibly the interior voice" whispering to him that his hopes were absurd. When he speaks of sickness, madness, revolutionary delirium—don't we hear a hopium addict speak?

Everyday Absurdism

In Rojava as elsewhere, an absurd political commitment is not the preserve of an elite activist or vanguard class. And neither is it a philosophical nicety divorced from everyday life. Rather, absurdist thought patterns are a daily reality throughout society. Ordinary people frequently display an impressive radical political commitment—even to the extent that this might resemble self-delusion to skeptical, Western, or positivist eyes. A bloody-minded refusal to surrender is often most acute precisely where the Rojava Revolution has suffered the worst setbacks, forcing people to choose a radical commitment to its principles anew.

In 2018, the Syrian Kurdish region of Afrin was seized by Turkey, which forcibly displaced most Kurdish locals. Yet many of the 200,000 displaced Kurds chose to remain in an isolated exclave adjoining their occupied homeland, living in barren refugee camps rather than withdrawing to slightly safer cities elsewhere.[1] When I asked one elderly camp resident if she wasn't worried by living in range of the shells Turkish-backed militias regularly lobbed toward her refugee camp, she looked at me askance. *My tent isn't close to the front line*, she said. *It's close to Afrin.*

She wanted to at least smell the wind coming from her homeland's lost olive groves, she said, in a phrase often repeated by other refugees. And in turn, her defiant presence, pointless in the sense that there remains no realistic hope of her return to Afrin, was nonetheless able to create a real political impact, enabling the Kurdish movement to retain both a strategic military foothold and an ideological horizon to struggle toward.

Their occupied homeland, many displaced Afrini Kurds repeated to me wistfully, was "heaven," an Eden of olive groves sprouting from Syria's most fertile soil. As the metaphor suggests, Afrin remains ideal, unobtainable, and for this reason capable of motivating great personal sacrifice. This tension is inherent in the very materiality of Afrin's refugee camps, where canvas is slowly being surrounded by concrete supporting walls, potted plants, and ragged vegetable patches. Each home embodies the conflicted yet symbiotic relationship between hard years in the wilderness and the enduring hope of return. For as long as these camps remain, a potent and unfulfilled hope will continue to spring up, its unreachable source just over the front line.

This doesn't imply any superhuman proclivity for resistance on behalf of the Kurds alone, idealizing a diverse people too often treated as a monolithic bloc. Much the same mentality was present among civilian Arab families I met in the aftermath of the war against ISIS, who returned to bombed-out homes to hang up washing on lines strung between ruined walls still dirtied with ash and blood, willing community out of almost nothing.

As in the Palestinian refugee camps throughout the West Bank and similar sites of tenacious resistance worldwide, these displaced Syrians prefer to remain in limbo. The Palestinians clutch rusted keys handed down through generations as a mute symbol of their implausible belief that they will one day open their own front doors again, front doors they may never have seen. Neither vanquished nor with hope of victory, they remain, like the rebel in Camus's absurdist philosophy, suspended in the active and productive tension of continued struggle. "Resistance is life," the Kurdish slogan runs, but for many ordinary Kurds, it's more accurate to say that "life is resistance."

Life Lies

We might well admire the everyday resistance undertaken by displaced Kurds or Palestinians but struggle to imagine such a commitment in our own lives. For try as we might, we cannot all be utopian idealists. It can certainly be difficult to admit we suffer from political despair—we might be embarrassed, worried about letting our comrades down, scared the admission will leave us lacking direction and purpose. But this confession can also be the first step on the path to a renewed revolutionary commitment.

In this case, we must undertake the necessary psychological contortion to *lie to ourselves in full knowledge that we are lying to ourselves*. Again, even this type of meta-level self-deception, willingly denying facts we simultaneously know on some level to be true, is a part of our daily lives. Bloch identifies a sublimated yearning for a socialist Not Yet even within capitalist society: consider sports, gambling, or escapist media. At the same time, all these cultural phenomena inspire billions of people to willful self-delusion. When a fat old man pulls on his soccer shirt, he knows full well he will never be a superstar, and he enjoys the kick-around all the more. Perhaps he's fooling himself, but he is also freeing himself.

From Plato's "noble lie" through Ibsen's "life-lie" without which ordinary humans cannot endure existence, the idea that a degree of social or self-deception is a necessity for human survival has a long philosophical pedigree—albeit the philosophers typically lament the fact. We all find ways to weather indignity, endure discomfort, and elude despair by lying to ourselves.

As pessimistic philosophers have suggested, it's only by "artificially limiting the content of consciousness" that we evade awful cosmic despair each day—whether through religious commitment, capitalist distraction, or sublimation into human endeavor.[2] Bloch writes movingly of the need for a truly revolutionary analysis to reckon with the simple fables and white lies we tell ourselves each day, just as much as we need to reckon with the depths of our subconscious.[3] Indeed, while claims that raves or free parties constitute genuine spaces of resistance to capitalist hegemony clearly overstate the case, there is nonetheless something to be said for the way in which drink and drugs equip many Leftists to continue struggling in defiance of our self-evident organizational weakness, creating temporary but nonetheless meaningful access to community and a spirit of defiance we might not normally feel.

Leo Tolstoy memorably described various species of self-delusion in his *Confession*, where the great Russian writer meditates on how he endured a grave existential crisis. If the most honest response to the meaninglessness of existence is suicide, the absurdist response through which we manage to survive is a lie, an act of cowardice.[4] Yet this doesn't mean the lie is useless. Tolstoy knows he's lying to himself, just as much as the aging soccer fan knows it; or the hard-pressed single mother buying a lottery ticket with a weary grin; or the trans kid briefly feeling invincible on the dance floor. The lie told to the self frees the self to live.

To existentialist philosopher Emil Cioran, "to live signifies to believe and to hope—to lie and to lie to oneself."[5] At this extreme limit of existentialism, there is nothing to life beyond the lie. As all metanarratives of history necessarily add political spin one way or the other, so too any philosophical sense of self necessarily deludes. We need not experience such a total existential despair to ask how we might repurpose the fundamental unknowability of our existence to political ends, adopting and relying on a given political life lie while remaining alert to its potential falsehood or implausibility.

Indeed, this is one radical implication of the Kurdish movement's critique of materialist positivism, the school of thought that claims only scientifically proven facts are true or valid. As Westerners raised and schooled to worship positivism as a religion, we can easily find ourselves convinced that there's only one life lie worth believing—the lie of inevitable and rational progress toward capitalist liberal democracy. But if we can successfully reconsider our Western, academic skepticism toward grand metanarratives, we can open up a potential world of revolutionary possibilities.

The radical possibility brought about by a political life lie is well illustrated by the third internationalist type, the *total loyalist*. These comrades have made a single, life-altering decision to accept the Kurdish movement's particular political narrative. Accepting Öcalan's world-historical representation of the Kurdish struggle as today's paramount fulcrum of global revolution, they bid their prior political activity farewell and devote themselves permanently to the Kurdish cause.

This type has much in common with the newly arrived naive utopian. But the total loyalist's own utopianism is not naive. It's rather a conscious, willed, choice on some level at least. Having spent years in Kurdistan, they could recognize the revolution's shortcomings, but they consciously choose to overlook them.

Again, the ability to narrativize one's own existence emerges as a potentially revolutionary quality—the fundamentally transformative ability to imagine things as otherwise. There are reasons to be skeptical of the total loyalist, with their deliberate effacement of doubt and uncertainty. Whereas the naive utopian might simply be unaware of the contradictions of the revolutionary process and the everyday suffering faced by many ordinary Syrians, the total loyalist deliberately closes their eyes to the revolutionary movement's inability to relieve this suffering, try though it might.

Nonetheless, there are lessons to be learned from their single bold step into history. For example: Staunch Kurdish movement ideologues claim Western governments back Turkey's brutal assaults on Rojava because these powers fear the spread of democratic confederalism will result in the inevitable collapse of their own nation-states. When threatened with arrest or detention by their governments back in the West, internationalist volunteers in Rojava repeated this life lie among themselves. *See*, the internationalist volunteers reassured one another defiantly, *here's proof the "democratic confederalist" movement threatens imperial, capitalist power.*

In reality, of course, Western cooperation with Turkish policy is rather more concretely determined by joint security concerns with a key NATO ally and trading partner than any fear of incipient global democratic confederalist revolution. But this willfully chosen life lie, this jointly created narrative, served to motivate the volunteers' revolutionary commitment.

We ourselves might choose any one of a hundred life lies, variously seeking to convince ourselves that our sacrifices will be justified through revolutionary state capture; that our arms factory blockade can prevent an imperialist war; that queer solidarity smashes borders. These are just some of the political life lies told by our diverse left movements. Are they enough to overcome capitalist modernity's own life lie, its claim that capitalism is the only game left in town?

Auto-Placebo

Contemporary medical research offers a useful analogy, illuminating this psychological process. Earlier, we saw how the "hope industry" peddles the lie that hope is an equal-access resource, denying the reality of structural inequality. In fact, this liberal hope is a placebo—a sugar pill, offered in an attempt to delude us into believing there's a cure for our profoundly sick existence. But what happens when we recognize this fact, and choose to hope anyway? Can we treat hope as an "auto-placebo," a false cure that we knowingly administer to ourselves regardless?

The psychosomatic power of the placebo is only just becoming understood. Surveys have consistently shown that many modern doctors regularly prescribe placebos; the animist and shamanic traditions that predate modern medicine commonly operate by convincing true believers they've been cured by nonexistent magic; and we all know a quick pat or kiss can help a child get over a bump or scrape.[6] The point here is not to suggest that positive thinking can be any alternative to modern medicine. Rather, it's simply to recall that hope is *always* a placebo.

As recent surveys of the placebo effect have shown, placebo drugs work even if patients know the drug cannot help them.[7] "Open-label placebos" have been shown to alter brain chemistry even when the patients know (and yet simultaneously do not know) that the drug is just a placebo and can only help them if they willfully believe in its power.

As you might expect, the placebo phenomenon is particularly effective with regard to conditions with psychological and psychosomatic aspects—like depression, chronic pain, and fatigue—and less so for diseases like cancer. But psychological challenges are exactly what we are hoping to overcome. This research can comfort us with the knowledge that we need not discount false hope out of hand. Modern science proves the point: false hope works!

If we recognize the reasonable hope that the hope industry wants us to swallow is itself a mere placebo, we are freed to hope for what seems truly unobtainable. We can spit out the placebo of liberal hope for a life that is dignified, secure, and worth living under capitalism. And instead, we can swallow our socialist auto-placebo of total, irrational hope that we will see that system revolutionized and replaced.

Nietzsche: The Will to Stupidity

I've been repeatedly using the words "willing" and "willful" to describe a hope deployed in full knowledge of its hopelessness as strategic simplification or freely chosen life lie. These terms imply a courageous commitment to self-mastery; they deliberately recall Friedrich Nietzsche's complex relationship to the question of truth.

In seeming opposition to the life lies adopted by meek, unthinking Christians or the socialist total loyalist, the nihilist philosopher brags of his commitment to uncovering those truths that modernity enables us to avoid. The ideal Nietzschean thinker thinks things through, in totality and to their conclusion, recognizing and refusing all pre-received orthodoxies. They refuse to be comforted by false, lame, liberal hope in a better tomorrow.

With this self-conception in mind, what should we make of Nietzsche's provocative talk of a "will to stupidity"? How should we understand his claim that it's "a sign of strong character, when once the resolution has been taken, to shut the ear even to the best counterarguments?"[8]

Among other projects, in *Beyond Good and Evil* Nietzsche sets out on an anti-positivist mission that in some respects prefigures Öcalan's subsequent critique of positivism as the new religion animating exploitative capitalist modernity. Nietzsche, too, wishes to deconstruct the instrumentalist rationality that views only scientifically verifiable facts as true, exposing positivism as an idiotic, small-minded "will to truth" that makes a new religion out of supposed factual objectivity.[9] He seeks to demonstrate that all ideology is contingent, that there is no such thing as an "actual drive for knowledge that, without regard to questions of usefulness and harm, [strives] blindly for the truth." Rather, we all pursue a truth that serves our own particular ends.[10] The "will to power" relies on a "will to stupidity" precisely because it cannot be rationalized through false claims to objective truth, like those that might justify a naive positivist, socialist, or religious faith. The question is whether we will blindly submit to liberal rationality; retreat into cynicism; or become total loyalists for some greater cause.

Let's follow this logic to its conclusion. For even on a metaphilosophical level, Nietzsche contradicts himself. He both mocks all truths as illusions and styles himself the herald of truth—a contradiction that has baffled and provoked his critics ever since. If Nietzsche's paradoxical truth can expose the lies underpinning every school of thought, it must surely expose its own foundations. As the philosopher gleefully recognizes, even his own stance as the ultimate truth-knower and truth-teller is just one more contingent pose. On this point, he offers us another useful intellectual model for the politically productive self-delusion of agency. We recognize the contingency of our actions but interpret them as freely chosen acts, thus liberating ourselves precisely through the cheerful acknowledgment that we are not truly free.

One lesson Nietzsche has to offer revolutionaries is precisely this playfulness, this doubleness, which he at once advises and models throughout his work. On one page, he rages against selective readers who unthinkingly cherry-pick details of his work to suit their own agenda. Yet on another, he advises his followers to cherry-pick at will when interpreting their own experience.

Nietzsche is as replicable, quotable, and profoundly centripetal as Öcalan (and another subject of chaotic, scattergun appropriation on Facebook—a fact that would surely delight him). His aphoristic style implies an open, endless search for an unreachable goal, undoing itself with each self-sabotaging observation to open up new and unrealizable possibilities.[11] A knowing inconsistency lies at the very heart of his critique of liberal, positivist truth: "He who cannot lie, doth not know who truth is."[12]

This reading might seem to imply that Nietzsche can be used to any ideological ends whatsoever. But there are limits. He rightly encourages suspicion of any ideologies that lay claim to universal truth, and moralistic liberalism most of all. It's therefore the paternalistic, moralizing elements of our own politics that Nietzsche cautions us against, just as he loathed the liberal and moralistic tendencies that defined the utopian, pre-Marxist socialist (and anarchist) politics of his day.[13] Conversely, therefore, a truly revolutionary socialism must necessarily adopt a Nietzschean approach toward capitalist modernity. This Nietzschean socialism will be marked by a truly radical critique of modernity's positivist foundations; by a wholesale rejection of the notion of objective, universal truth; and by a corresponding messianic, transformative leap "OFF—and not back" toward a totally revolutionized future.[14]

Nietzsche's critique of the moralistic, paternalistic, and self-satisfied elements still present in contemporary democratic-socialist politics is worth listening to. But this doesn't mean we need to give any credence to those dull, dangerous readings that see Nietzsche as advocating for social Darwinism. Many figures on the contemporary Right fundamentally misunderstand Nietzsche, using his radical philosophy to justify a fundamentally petit bourgeois mentality and morality, clinging to liberal capitalism's social and moral norms as though they were the "objective" truth. There is nothing that the philosopher would have despised more.

Although Nietzsche would surely have mocked them too, Öcalan and Bookchin are two socialist thinkers who have recognized how Nietzsche's doomed search for a truly free and human life beyond the limitations of bourgeois society can and must illuminate the path trodden by latter-day revolutionaries. Nietzsche may have been anti-socialist, but he was wholly revolutionary.

Nietzsche offers us critique, not confirmation. We should not turn to him expecting consistency, or justification that our chosen ideology is correct. On the contrary, he cautioned his readers never to make the mistake of believing the ideals or goals we hope for must therefore necessarily be true, like meek Christians who believe their ardent desire for a good and moral universe must necessarily translate into the existence of an omnibenevolent God.

But once we recognize truth's universal contingency, we can begin to make new truths to suit ourselves. This is the daunting challenge Nietzsche sets us. Having recognized the implausibility of all universal truths, we must nonetheless learn how to venture out into the world cynically, knowing full well we cannot change it either, knowing full well our philosophy is *also* fatally flawed. This is what Nietzsche himself attempted, as he confusedly strove to envisage an elevated, transfigured humanity. Like Don Quixote, he willingly embarked on an impossible, self-maddening quest.

Thus Nietzsche cautions his followers to master, make use of, and discard their own beliefs as it suits them; to "make use of their stupidity as well as of their fire," acting freely on the basis of beliefs we know to be contingent. It's a challenge of profound relevance to the contemporary, anti-positivist, socialist revolutionary.[15] We must open our eyes to the unlimited possibilities implied through Nietzsche's liquidation of social and moral orthodoxies, just as we close them to the inevitable inclusion of our own beliefs in this process.

Nietzsche famously claimed to "philosophize with a hammer." His philosophy is destructive, not constructive. It therefore creates space for new thoughts and ideas through the destruction of the old. An extreme ideology like Nietzsche's, which takes apart all preexisting ideologies, will ultimately destroy its own foundations. In the final analysis the Nietzschean method itself can be subjected to Nietzschean critique and revealed as just one more orthodoxy. Nietzsche's famed nihilism too, was socially produced by the desperate conditions of his nihilistic, bourgeois age. And so even Nietzsche's own nihilism must be consumed, as he hoped and predicted it would be, not through any backward or reactionary retreat but on the contrary through a necessarily political leap into the future.

Nietzsche ventures beyond good and evil but falters at the point where he could actually create his own new system, the prophet of a world he could never manage to envisage. Presaging the fate of many twentieth- and twenty-first-century political movements, he stared into the void left by the death of metanarrative and the absence of objective or positive truth, wondering what could possibly fill it.

Reading Nietzsche, we sense his dissatisfaction with the vague alternative he advanced, and his longing for a new morality beyond Christian orthodoxy he would never live to see. Even if we accept a radical interpretation of Nietzsche that understands all real-world political and moral systems as devoid of meaning, this can help us recognize *even the ultra-cynical dismissal of meaning* as just one more way to avoid confronting the abyss. As a truly Nietzschean reading of Nietzsche implies, his own nihilism is just one more moral system. It offers people a way to survive, no more or less justifiable than absurdist socialist belief in a better tomorrow.

This radical destruction of meaning perhaps helped to drive Nietzsche mad. It led him to take up his own political life lie, placing a continued and ultimately Christian faith in a better world beyond the illusions he exposed—hence his "ridiculous" faith in the so-called Übermensch (superman), a supposedly superior form of humanity that Nietzsche hoped would emerge once we had shed our attachment to bourgeois Christian morals.[16] Unable to accept that nothing lay beyond the moral systems he destroyed, he eventually crumbled.

But at another point in history, Nietzsche's radical conclusions could just as easily have led him to follow his own advice to its limit. He might have leaped "OFF," joining socialist movements in a willfully self-deluding venture toward a messianically transformed utopia we know full well may never arrive. He could have found himself in the ecstatic, unexpected territory where other equally pessimistic but nonetheless socialist thinkers have landed.

Metamodernism: Gen Z as Übermensch

Nietzsche offers diagnoses, not prognoses. There is no concrete political sense of who this heralded Übermensch might actually be, how or when he will achieve his mission of superseding and transforming all preexisting ethical values, or what the resultant society will look like. The Übermensch offers us only a vague image of a revolutionized society freed from bourgeois moral constraints. Crucially, the Übermensch is not a bookish cynic like Nietzsche himself, and certainly not an Aryan Nazi Party member.

As the philosopher freely admits, "I am the reverse of a heroic nature. To 'will' something, to 'strive' after something, to have an 'aim' or a 'desire' in my mind—I know none of these things from experience."[17] Perhaps, he wrote despairingly in *The Antichrist*, not a single one of his true followers had yet been born.[18]

It could thus even be argued that the renewed revolutionary commitment of recent generations models one quality required of any Übermensch yet lacking in Nietzsche himself. Young people demonstrate an impressive ability to see the arbitrary, constructed falsehood of all systems yet retain the courage to keep operating through, with, and against these systems. They easily recognize the contingent nature of moral and political orthodoxies. But unlike Nietzsche, they don't allow this knowledge to cripple them into inactivity and prevent them from striving for a revolutionary goal.

Cultural critics argue that this ability to oscillate between two extremes of skepticism and sincerity is a defining characteristic of contemporary society. This so-called meta-modern sensibility is characterized by a "pragmatic idealism" and "informed naivety."[19] Just think of the typical left-wing social media feed, pivoting wildly between cynical, self-ironizing memes and sincere appeals to socialist, feminist, or liberal values. More broadly, this kind of meta-modern sensibility has enabled emergent generations of activists to make their renewed revolutionary commitment, engaging in political struggle even as they remain deeply skeptical over the grand political narratives on offer. They therefore avoid the twin pitfalls of both Obama-style liberal idealism and postmodern, despairing, Facebook-quote Nietzschean nihilism.

Just like their forebear Bugs Bunny, the meta-modern generations know the game is rigged; but they'll play it anyway. They know climate catastrophe is inevitable; they'll fight it anyway. They risk their lives fighting cops in their country's manifestation of the wave of horizontal revolutions, or campaign for an aging left populist politician, while simultaneously dismissing any actual prospect of systemic political change.

These emergent political generations prove quite capable of the self-aware and masterful will to stupidity. They despair one minute and organize the next. They contradictorily identify themselves as both suicidal and revolutionary, cynical and kind, making use of whatever narrative suits in a given moment.

Considering the Left's present impasse, this self-aware yet self-deluding sensibility is almost a prerequisite. As Nunes argues, contemporary generations are engaged in a growing critical search for a rejuvenated mode of political organization, "between fatalism and voluntarism, prudence and daring; between opportunism and dogmatism, firmness (of principle) and flexibility (in tactics); between sectarianism and reformism."[20] Perhaps this meta-modern ability to pivot between cynical despair and sincere hope can help us find some paths toward meeting these paradoxical challenges—not through a weak social-democratic synthesis but rather through self-aware and absurdist leaps between contradictory poles.

Thus emerges the shadowy figure of the doomer revolutionary, equipped to enter global internationalist struggle against capital, empire, and climate crisis precisely through their Gen Z, meta-modern, pragmatic idealism, equal parts cynicism and sincerity. Whereas past generations of comrades could rely on grand metanarratives of change and socialist revolution, consciously or otherwise, emergent generations of revolutionaries may find themselves adopting a meta-modern approach, struggling onward in knowing acceptance of their cause's ultimate contingency.

The doomer revolutionary is what we might call a "socialist ironist," offering a revolutionary advance on Richard Rorty's "liberal ironist." For Rorty, the radical acceptance that all narratives are contingent leads inevitably to a belief that only detached debate can be trusted to advance human society.[21] But through the meta-modern sensibility, we can return to the terrain of action, willfully reinvesting one of those debunked metanarratives with belief—socialism, anarchism, or democratic confederalism, for example.

Militants, Posers, Hipsters

The Kurdish revolutionary movement is skeptical of postmodern thought. But in their own way, they model a similar, meta-modern pragmatic idealism. The Rojava Revolution has endured thanks to its particular synthesis of sincere grand narrative and practical everyday compromise. A willed utopian belief equips its militants to deal with quotidian setbacks.

Kurdish organizers never shrink from the very meta-modern deployment of a diverse range of political metanarratives, picking them up and putting them down again like so many tools. When speaking to anarchist comrades, they justify democratic confederalism as more anarchist than anarchism; to trade unionists as more socialist than Marxism-Leninism; to Catalan comrades as the only vehicle capable of bringing true national liberation. Similarly flexible strategies are used to recruit ordinary locals. The Kurdish movement appeals to diverse communities on the basis not only of feminist, ecological, and socialist thought but also Islamic values, tribal culture, Kurdish-Palestinian solidarity, regional minority status, and normative human rights.

This meta-modern ability to advance a particular narrative while simultaneously remaining aware of its contingencies and limits is inherent to Paolo Freire's revolutionary pedagogy.[22] Rather than assuming a false liberal equality between all political and educational subjects, the Kurdish movement's political educators carefully adapt their discussions to particular local contexts, while simultaneously paying these communities the respect of believing they can grasp, understand, and implement a universal political program.

Like the storytelling trickster god, the adept Kurdish militant has a thousand guises, avoiding the one-size-fits-all ideological purism of the naive utopian. Following Nietzsche's injunction, they "do not shrink from the ordeal of being deemed inconsistent."[23] Yet these same Kurdish revolutionaries maintain a remarkably disciplined, strict internal culture. In their hearts they cling fast to those grand claims Öcalan holds to be essentially and inherently true, while simultaneously proving capable of adapting their language, style, and approach to a given circumstance. This approach suggests how grand metanarratives can adapt to survive in a skeptical and self-aware political culture.

Öcalan sharply critiques both (ideological) liberalism and dogmatism: to him, effective militants must learn when to be stiff, and when to bend. An inner, militant, revolutionary commitment should open the way to an external flexibility and openness. It's a difficult path to tread, with elements of the Kurdish movement still tending to inflexible organizational dogmatism, even as its pragmatically minded social and economic programs drift away from Öcalan's original ideological vision.

In our own Western Leftist scenes, meanwhile, we often get this complex political sensibility totally back to front. In public, we drive away potential newcomers to the struggle with performative verbal dogmatism, exclusionary identity politics, or overweening theory-bro grandstanding. At the same time, our left melancholy prohibits us from engaging substantively with those causes that require our sincere, unseen commitment.

As the example of our naive utopian strutting around in borrowed combat trousers makes clear, there's a clear costume, style, and even vocabulary associated with the Kurdish militant identity. As a riposte to regional stereotypes and Turkish state propaganda framing (Kurdish) communists as work-shy, dissolute, and morally corrupt, Kurdish militants are expected to wear crisp, clean clothes at all times, marking themselves out from the rest of civil society. (Historically, blue jeans were banned, and to this day one would never encounter a Kurdish militant with scruffy or gelled hair, revealing clothing, or off-putting piercings.)

To Öcalan, the ethical and the aesthetic are intimately linked.[24] A pose struck often enough becomes habit, then personality: hence the Kurdish movement's strong focus on personal ethics, manners, appearance, and even hygiene as the necessary precursor to the revolutionary transformation of society. As Nietzsche has cynically suggested, in the absence of innate, objective moral truths, hypocrisy and performance can lead to habits taking over and becoming the real: "When anyone, during a long period, and persistently, wishes to appear something, it will at last prove difficult for him to be anything else."[25] Whatever our inner sentiments, if we constantly act either welcoming or standoffish, we're likely to end up *becoming* truly welcoming or standoffish. To Nietzsche, the paradigmatic figures of hypocrite, priest, and actor represent the all-too-human reality that our behaviors can easily overtake us and become who we are.

Again, a Nietzschean self-awareness can help this admitted truth be reclaimed to revolutionary, militant ends. If the example of a privately self-doubting but publicly committed priest bears witness to the transformative power of performance, so too does the highly regimented, formulaic life of a Kurdish militant. For the Kurdish movement is well aware of the power of repeated, even hypocritical performance. It welcomes new recruits, however raw, and molds them through a particular set of learned behaviors.

In a similar spirit, we could perhaps reclaim those other slanders commonly leveled at the contemporary, Western Left: poser, virtue signaler, hipster, and so on. These negative labels imply a willingness to change one's style, appearance, and even morals to fit in with a given scene. But perhaps we should all be *more* willing to adapt our style, marking ourselves out as part of a particular, exceptional political culture. What is a desire to fit in but a desire for community?

An internal political culture, style, and code can all help foster a collective identity—so long as this formation of collective, militant identity once again functions outward, not inward. It should form the kernel of an organized group, not its hard outer shell.

For example, it's possible to imagine a Leftist Boy Scouts, responding positively to the contemporary crisis of masculinity by offering discipline, order, practical and even combat skills to a young generation otherwise at the mercy of the cynical, exploitative alt-Right, while simultaneously instilling respect for women and communal, anti-fascist values. The Left Scouts could thereby play a productive role in defending and strengthening broader social movements.

There are dangers here too, of course. An overly aesthetic conception of militancy can clearly lead us to a superficial, performative, exclusionary politics. For example, the highly performed, posed, militant Kurdish identity is associated with the movement's notably radical youth wing—especially Kurds who grew up in Europe before joining the struggle in Rojava, who therefore have a point to prove vis-à-vis their own corruption by the capitalist West. It's these younger, less experienced, more insecure militants who feel compelled to act as though their whole identity has been erased and replaced by what Öcalan calls the "militant personality."

Conversely, older and wiser militants often prove able to let their guard down and let others see their continued, inner complexities. They are more likely to operate outward, welcoming and understanding newcomers, part-timers, and hipsters on their own terms. These older comrades often display a meta-modern, storytelling trickster god's ability to wear the costume of militancy where useful to build discipline and community and yet set it aside where necessary. A certain veteran internationalist militant, her revolutionary credentials long since placed beyond doubt, once drew criticism from younger comrades for celebrating her birthday with '80s disco music rather than traditional Kurdish tunes. She didn't care; she knew how to strike a rigid, awe-inspiring, militant pose on the frontline where necessary, inspiring young local and international revolutionaries alike. But she also knew when it would be more productive to let her still-human personality shine through.

Militant Art of Forgetfulness

The revolutionary militant ability to adopt multiple personal and political narratives is intimately linked to the capacity for self-delusion outlined above—and in particular, to a militant, self-aware forgetfulness. As existential philosophers argue, memory is intimately bound up with the horror of self-aware human existence. Forgetfulness is therefore a necessary corollary of survival, or (in Freud's terms) self-preservation. Kierkegaard is just one philosopher to have emphasized the freeing quality of forgetfulness.[26] He discusses a self-aware, organized forgetfulness, rather than Freud's unacknowledged defense mechanism.

If we need a selective forgetfulness in order to endure daily reality, how much more might it be needed to endure the hardships and losses of revolutionary struggle? A certain dash of self-delusion and inconsistency, placed under the control of a consistent political program, can certainly help preserve limited reserves for the fight. A related concept of forgetfulness is developed by Jack Halberstam in his *Queer Art of Failure*, a delightful, provocative attempt to reclaim "low" culture, stupidity, and failure as encoding anti-capitalist thought and resistance.[27]

That Halberstam's arguments find a certain analog in Rojava is not necessarily a surprise. Despite growing and notable exceptions (especially driven through internationalist interaction between the Kurdish women's movement and other global feminisms), the broader Kurdish movement remains generally suspicious of an LGBTQI+ movement it often reductively frames as a product of individualistic late-capitalist culture.[28]

Though the movement's analysis of queer issues is generally one-dimensional, this perspective must always be contextualized by the movement's ongoing efforts to revolutionize gender roles and family relationships within a deeply conservative Muslim society. As Kurdish women's movement activists have written in an open letter to their Western comrades, Western feminists and activists should take care they're not "dictat[ing] the exact same conceptualization and practice of LGBTQI+ identities that exist in the progressive circles of the West everywhere in the world and devalu[ing] all radical movements that adhere to other conceptualizations."[29] Again, solidarity need not mean like-for-like equivalence.

At the same time, a number of parallels between the Kurdish and queer movements emerge, particularly in terms of those radical attempts to challenge the nuclear family and establish new modes of affection, intimacy, and solidarity. In an essay reflecting on their own experiences as one of many queer feminist internationalists in Rojava, a Western volunteer describes how difficult interactions and conversations helped them to find common ground and shared experience with Kurdish comrades despite their seemingly divergent perspectives:

> I was used to sexuality as a headline theme of liberation or a bat-tleground in itself. Here, that energy was channeled into a wider struggle for women's liberation: for a revolutionary rewriting of gender roles and a shaking up of traditional models of family and romantic love . . . I was living among people who had built a life outside of the nuclear family in order to fight capitalism, the state and patriarchy. . . . If I couldn't find myself here, what did these [queer] politics of mine even mean?[30]

The disproportionate number of internationalist volunteers claiming a queer identity is surely no coincidence but rather linked to the dislocation from patriarchal Western society mentioned above as a necessary precur-sor to joining the revolution.

Halberstam quotes a critic of positivist statism to argue that "illegibil-ity may in fact be one way of escaping . . . political manipulation," as queer people "fly under the radar" and become incomprehensible to straight society. There's a striking parallel here with the Kurdish movement's prac-tice of issuing all new recruits with new names, as a marker that the new revolutionary has chosen to shed their old identity, shake off statist con-trol, and enter into an alternative nexus of relationships.[31]

By joining the revolution, internationalists were all able to set aside something of their past selves. Shady pasts faded into the dark altogether. Queer or straight, the internationalists were illuminated by their new and revolutionary identities. In particular, the total loyalists often deliber-ately kept their background a mystery, obscuring what might well have been a run-of-the-mill past on Europe's anarchist scene. In this way, they embody the autonomizing and emancipating power of illegibility, the rad-ical power to walk away from one's old existence at the drop of a hat—or by pulling on a borrowed pair of combat trousers.

Though the relevant factors vary from case to case, the decision to leave an old identity behind brings with it a particular blend of pressure, expectation, and opportunity. Internationalist volunteers traveled to Rojava to experience a few moments of life outside the state; young Kurds are offered the chance to once again access their identity, now that they are outside states that formally banned Kurdish names, language, and culture; young women are enabled to leave the patriarchal home behind, enter an autonomous, all-female mountain camp, and take on the name of a slain female militant. In all cases, this attempt to leave behind a prior identity can also lead to ideological contradictions, personal misgivings, and inter- and intra-communal tensions. The radical demand that new recruits leave their homes and families behind has saved thousands of women from violent abuse and patriarchal repression, but it can also place a strain on the Kurdish movement's relationship with these communities. Internationalists' efforts to "borrow" a new and revolutionary identity might well prove an irritant to ordinary Syrians, who never asked to be born into revolutionary Rojava.

Both the Kurdish and radical queer movements are marked by a chosen, willing step away from a prior existence defined by rigid patriarchal social structures and into a less certain territory. Both movements call on their followers to abandon blood kinship, to keep walking along revolutionary pathways laid out by dead elders. These movements are thus simultaneously defined by a determined political commitment to archive and document their own history; reverence for older generations of militants; martyr cultures; and the imbrication of mourning and militancy. Little wonder that for some queer internationalist comrades, "what at first glance looked [to be] most different" between their prior political scene and their new life in Rojava often turned out to have "the most in common."[32]

The Kurdish and intersectional feminist movements each forcefully remind us of the need to keep our background and upbringing in political view. Borrowing or assuming a new identity shouldn't blind us to the realities of our privileged Western upbringing or the need to maintain productive relationships with our home communities.

But at the same time, the most freeing political and personal moments are surely those where we forget our past existence and struggles, and we're able to stand united for the moment, liberated by dint of this loss. This might take place through a queer chosen family, a moment of internationalist solidarity, or any revolutionary commitment to a communal cause or way of life. A willful ability to forget, erase, or elide our past can make a virtue of past tragedy, freeing us for the struggle at hand.

Either/Or: Revolutionary Aesthetics

If not carefully handled, this playful, meta-modern, self-aware approach to politics can prove toxic. In this spirit, politics can easily be reduced to an ineffectual, merely aesthetic or left-melancholic performance, denying the possibility of substantive change.

To help avoid this potential pitfall, we can briefly turn to one of philosophy's most ancient quests: the pursuit of a resolution between the pursuit of beauty, pleasure, and personal satisfaction on the one hand, and broader social, ethical, or political commitments on the other. Christian existentialist Søren Kierkegaard is just one of many great thinkers to have grappled with the contradiction between, and potential resolution of, what he called the "aesthetic" and "ethical" conceptions of life. The nineteenth-century philosopher was particularly concerned with the opposition between an upright, civic, Christian existence, and a life marked by the pursuit of aesthetic beauty and intellectual and physical pleasure, represented as leading to existential despair. But his arguments can help think through modern tendencies to individualism, liberalism, hedonism, intellectualism, or self-indulgent self-care and achieve a related commitment in the secular, political field.

"Everyone who lives aesthetically is in despair, whether he knows it or not," Kierkegaard suggests, in terms prefiguring a Freudian understanding of melancholy.[33] His assessment has direct relevance to a Western Left currently struggling to overcome the reduction of politics to repetitive and ritualized protest, alongside other forms of collective and individual performance. Kierkegaard lambasted the "disgusting sight of young men who are able . . . to play with the titanic forces of history, and unable to tell a plain man what he has to do in life."[34] We're probably all familiar with their contemporary incarnation—theory bros more interested in toying with Marx or Hegel than making a concrete personal commitment to political work.

Whether performed protest or stylized debate and discourse, an aesthetic politics risks becoming a mere pose. Kierkegaard's philosophical resolution of this contradiction is worth exploring. His opus *Either/Or* stages a debate between these two, seemingly opposed perspectives. Part I advances the aesthetic perspective as a diverse collection of essays and aphorisms, while Part II is conversely marked by a sustained defense of the ethical life, and in particular Christian marriage.[35]

It might seem obvious that Kierkegaard is going to endorse the ethical, Christian, married life. But in fact, nothing is so clear. Instead he wrestles with the conflict between these two perspectives. On the one hand, his aesthete sometimes displays a repressed, unfulfilled, melancholic yearning for the ethical. On the other, Kierkegaard longs for the purely aesthetic. As with Milton's representation of Satan in *Paradise Lost*, famously livelier and more sympathetic than his representation of God, the philosopher's impassioned engagement with the aesthetic reveals a clear sympathy for this standpoint.

As Kierkegaard once boasted, he doesn't "lack the courage to think a thought whole."[36] And, famously, Kierkegaard didn't follow his own advice in the "ethical" section of his book, breaking off marriage to the love of his life to pursue a lonely, philosophical career.

There are no easy resolutions here. But we can read *Either/Or* as advancing the ethical life as the *highest mode of aestheticism*. This suggests a way forward for those of us who (like Kierkegaard himself) find ourselves tempted by the admitted pleasures of an individualistic, intellectual, or aesthetic existence. The cynical, the too smart, and the too self-aware can nonetheless achieve an ethical mode of existence through—rather than in opposition to—their aesthetic egotism, reaching the ethical without denying the dark side's allure.

Ultimately, Kierkegaard suggests the ethical life has its own particular aesthetic appeal, more beautiful yet than the life of pure aesthetic sensation. On this point, the Kurdish movement would concur. As we've seen, Öcalan straightforwardly seeks to reclaim aesthetic beauty as emanating from an inner ethical commitment: if "ethics is the morality and the consciousness of freedom, aesthetics is to emanate in line with this consciousness."[37]

Kierkegaard sees the deep aesthetic appeal of a Christian, married life marked by duty and sacrifice: we could say the same about a life committed to political struggles we know stand slim chance of success. The mind that produced *Or* also conceived of *Either*, and perhaps there will always be a dash of egotism motivating even the most noble, self-sacrificing acts. Perhaps we must try revolution on for size and see if it scratches our aesthetic itch.

This reality was readily apparent in Rojava, where many internationalists were doubtless first attracted by the aesthetic quality of armed leftist struggle, only to find themselves swept up into something far larger than they had imagined. Thus many volunteers who originally arrived for the straightforward purpose of joining the Kurds to battle ISIS found themselves drawn into the broader ideological struggle for a Middle East free from state violence. These disillusioned veterans found themselves becoming total loyalists, working to implement democratic confederalism in diverse and unlooked-for ways. They found ways to critique and move beyond their initial adventurism or fetishization of the Kurdish cause, the initial aesthetic giving way to a genuine ethical, internationalist commitment.

As Kierkegaard elsewhere cautions his readers, we must be prepared for existential torment if we're to achieve true, transformative hope without hope. As the Kurdish movement also knows, the initial pose alone is not enough. People may end up choosing a life of political struggle as a pose because it looks good, because they're under peer pressure or from some other selfish motivations. But if their revolutionary commitment is not to wither on the vine, it must become deepened and strengthened through struggle, joint sacrifice, and comradely criticism.

From Pose to Sacrifice

In this sense, therefore, Kierkegaard's existential struggles are reflected in the Kurdish movement's own practice. The movement happily accepts new recruits driven by ambiguous motivations or the aesthetic lure of militancy, treating these desires as the starting point of a more ethical life. Posers are welcome, although those poses will later be put to stern test.

More broadly, the Kurdish movement represents disciplined, militant organization as beautiful, the peak of aestheticism, in contrast to an ugly, disordered, individualistic, liberal life. In this way, the Kurdish movement has appealed to Leftists dissatisfied with the organizational chaos, "lifestyle anarchism," and lack of seriousness endemic among horizontalist leftist movements of the West.

The total loyalists are just as likely as the newly arrived naive utopians to engage in a mimetic fetishization of Kurdish militancy: listening solely to Kurdish music, eschewing the company of other internationalists while earnestly seeking acceptance from Kurds, downplaying the importance of other (Western) political struggles, and so on. But their own mimicry of Kurdish identity differs qualitatively from the mimicry which the naive utopian indulges in, due to the quantitatively different extent of their revolutionary commitment. Their initially aesthetic engagement has brought them to the point of turning their back on their homeland forever, prepared to risk their life in an internationalist cause. Local comrades rightfully criticized the idealism, adventurism, or Orientalism that could characterize internationalist volunteers' approach to the revolution. But this didn't diminish their deep respect for those internationalist comrades who devoted their lives to the Kurdish cause.

As we've seen, Nietzsche uses the actor to illustrate his claim that repeated, even hypocritical behaviors can bring about genuine internal change. Similarly, Camus represents the actor as a paradigmatic example of the absurd man, self-aware as to the futility of his own existence even as he cheerfully plays this role anew every day.[38] The total loyalist deliberately assumes a role, turning their existence into a self-aware performance of revolution, their will to stupidity into a will to power, and their aesthetic pose into an ethical commitment.

The internationalist total loyalist could easily plunge too deeply into a full-scale identification with the Kurdish militant personality, choosing to forget ethical or political points where they previously maintained a comradely critical distance from the Kurdish movement's positions. Again, it's often these loyalists who would naively argue that the Kurdish movement has scarcely put a foot wrong in the course of the Syrian conflict or clumsily misrepresent the movement's highly contextualized perspectives on sensitive issues of gender identity, personal relationships, or political culture as universal truths. This type of naive idealization could certainly mean the total loyalists failed to live up to the Kurdish movement's own tough standards of criticism and self-criticism, excusing inexcusable behaviors and flawed policies rather than following Öcalan's admonition to constantly critique and renew our personalities and practices.

These risks should always be kept in mind. But comrades in horizontalist left movements are more likely to err on the side of excessively nervous caution. I suspect many on the Western Left are privately plagued with doubts over whether our revolutionary commitment is genuine and serious enough to count. We may feel like posers, performers, constantly fearing we'll be found out. On this point, we should draw comfort from Kierkegaard, who wrestled with analogous doubts throughout the course of his own philosophical journey, and who powerfully suggests how a doubtful, critical sensibility need not always result in sneering retreat.

Öcalan theorizes exterior aesthetics as emanating from an inner ethical conviction. But in practice, it's often the other way round. Even if you privately resent yourself for being a mere poser, even if you fear that genuine interior change is slow in coming, or even if you're too scared to admit to yourself that you may have undergone a truly transformative change of heart—no matter. Complicated, self-serving, self-narrativizing, half-ethical, half-aesthetic motivations can prove enough for today, at least. They have helped countless comrades to survive and continue making a limited, imperfect, yet nonetheless revolutionary contribution.

Chapter 8

The Revolutionary Leap of Faith

Self-delusion; selective simplification; the aestheticization of revolution. These interlinked copium strategies are all potential tactics. They offer ways to survive day by day, endure setbacks, and continue the struggle in extremis. Probably we recognize some of them in ourselves, or our comrades. But on a more fundamental level yet—why should we begin to struggle at all?

Can these ideas really provide us with the courage and sticking power of genuine ideological commitment—of pure hope? Can they be a substitute for that inner conviction we may secretly have found lacking? Or, as Kierkegaard warns in a memorable image, might they leave us skipping endlessly over the earth like a solo kayaker drifting on the ocean, without ever truly disembarking onto the firm shores of ethical commitment?[1] Like Kierkegaard's lonely aesthetic wanderer, many such comrades end up buffeted between scenes and struggles, from European squats to climate camps to stop-the-war marches to Kurdistan to the next big leftist cause célèbre. This is one way Kurdish comrades have criticized leftist internationalists. From a Kurdish perspective, the internationalist volunteers often seemed postmodern, cosmopolitan, divorced from their homeland, and unable to commit to long-term, grassroots organization in their own communities.

We can make an aesthetic case for revolutionary commitment even in the face of apparent hopelessness. But there's no readily apparent reason for a Nietzschean skepticism of all preexisting narratives of human existence to lead us to political organization, in particular. We may therefore be tempted to sink into despair like Nietzsche himself, waiting for a revolutionary change we know will never come in our lifetimes; to follow Kierkegaard in devoting ourselves to a more private or metaphysical concept of morality; to turn to drink or drugs; to give up our principles altogether, and find a way to get rich; or (perhaps most likely of all) to devote our limited energies to building a better life for our family and friends within the contemporary capitalist system, rather than striving for any greater material change.

The Leap of Faith

Again, Kierkegaard's profound struggles with the mysteries of Christianity offer us a startling, unexpected solution—the "leap of faith." This familiar idiom is derived from Kierkegaard's dramatic and paradoxical understanding of religious commitment. And the extraordinary and total commitment of Kurdish revolutionaries, among others, is underpinned by a similar, secular leap.

By definition, the philosopher argues in *Fear and Trembling*, we can have faith only once we acknowledge reason is insufficient. If we were able rationally to conclude that God existed, there would be no faith worth the name. Rather, we must relinquish ourselves in an "infinite resignation," in Kierkegaard's phrase, taking a step toward God that can only be taken when we acknowledge that step's fundamental impossibility.[2]

To Kierkegaard, this radical concept of faith is encapsulated in the Bible story in which Abraham agrees to sacrifice his own son to please God, even though he knows there is no logical or ethical justification for the act. As Kierkegaard recognizes, it's an abhorrent story. But if Abraham weren't revolted at the sacrifice being demanded him, he would not truly have been acting from faith. Faith must necessarily be a desperate transformative act, as we struggle through our fear, trembling, and doubt, overcoming them only through a wild leap into the dark.

Bloch is just one thinker to have imagined a similar leap of faith in revolutionary terms, as an irrational leap toward the utopian Not Yet of a socialist future.[3] More recently, theorists of leftist hope in the present crisis have argued for a renewed "political conception of faith."[4] Through our own infinite resignation, we acknowledge our doubts and skepticism, our left melancholy, the scale of the challenges we face. And we are thereby freed to undertake a secular leap of faith, toward our own unreachable socialist goal.

The Kurdish movement's own quasi-religious understanding of revolutionary commitment is derived from two key influences: the secularized faith that Lenin forged out of Marxist theory, and a secularized Islamic martyr culture. It thus forms part of a broader revolutionary current of socialism as the "faith without lies," a similarly radical all-or-nothing commitment translated from the divine into the political realm. While remaining alert to the perils of such totalizing and radical thought, we can learn valuable lessons from all these traditions.

Not Less Than Everything

The leap of faith is not cheaply or easily made. We must know what we risk. Kierkegaard is burdened by a profound sense that choices must be made seriously, with the full weight of consideration and conviction.[5]

But the important thing is therefore to choose, to reckon with the impossibilities of faith and human existence, to take a step forward despite the fundamental impossibility of knowing whether this step is justified. Like the Kurdish defenders of besieged Kobane, we must fight our own battles without a choice as though there were a choice, believing without rationally knowing that victory will come.

As we've seen, the Kurdish movement demands a total lifetime commitment from its most trusted recruits. This commitment is expressed through a simple sworn oath, as the necessary prelude to a lifetime's struggle. In the Kurdish struggle and socialist cause as in the domain of religious faith, true conviction necessarily lies beyond reason. When enlisting new recruits, the movement therefore doesn't demand total ideological conviction or rational acceptance of Öcalan's theories. Indeed, most haven't studied Öcalan's thought in any detail at all. There will be time for that later. Rather, all the movement demands is a single moment of revolutionary commitment.

On this point, the Kurdish movement's practice thus closely resembles Kierkegaard's description of how a doubting soul might come to Christ and the ethical life. To Kierkegaard, the "instant of choice" is in itself ethical. What matters is the internal reckoning with our ethical concerns, a struggle which is in itself inherently ethical, bringing us ineluctably to an inherently ethical choice.[6] The aesthete, by their very nature, will never be able to choose at all.

From a more revolutionary perspective, the Kurdish movement's single moment of commitment likewise constitutes an inherently ethical moment of decision, which cannot but be a decision to keep struggling till the end. By dint of its existential nature, then, the choice is never cheap; it necessarily costs "not less than everything," in T. S. Eliot's haunting phrase. At this radical turning point, even a partially selfish or aesthetic decision becomes ethical, public, and permanent.

We may well suffer a generalized sense of despair, quickened by our clear-eyed assessment of recent left failures and cynical postmodern skepticism over those political movements still promising revolutionary change. We may suspect that our activity cannot change anything, and that it therefore doesn't really matter whether we join a given struggle or movement, choose another path. Yet this need not render us incapable of political action. On the contrary, as Kierkegaard shows us, truly revolutionary commitment can *only* begin from a desperate point beyond reason.

This journey through disillusionment is therefore not an embarrassment, to be glossed over through melancholic protestations that we never once doubted the possibility of victory. If we don't doubt our cause, it isn't faith. To Kierkegaard, "it is an infinite advantage to be able to despair," since it's only then that we can hope to one day be cured of that despair.[7] As Öcalan once told his faithful followers: "You must believe, before everything else, that the revolution must come, that there is no other choice."[8]

It's only through our own infinite resignation we can leap into true, existential conviction, placing our hopes not in our day-to-day record of successes or defeats, but in a perhaps unreachable goal. This is what Kierkegaard calls the "double movement" of faith: first the infinite resignation, then the irrational leap.[9]

Our final type of internationalist militant, the *cynical idealist*, goes through just such a double movement. They may arrive in Rojava as naive utopians, bursting with hope; they may witness the compromises and flaws of the revolution and endure a difficult spell as disillusioned veterans, doubting whether revolutionary transformation is indeed possible. Through this process, they resign their naive, childish hope. But they thereby achieve a more profound commitment, dedicating themselves to the cause not despite but because of these flaws and compromises. The cynical idealist's hope is more serious, since it is informed by a clear-eyed assessment of the perhaps impossible challenges faced by the revolution and therefore more capable of equipping them for a lifetime's struggle.

As we saw, the total loyalist might too easily close their eyes to their comrades' failures to live up to the Kurdish movement's principles on either the personal or political level, thereby harming both their comrades and the revolution itself. Conversely, the cynical idealist recognizes and holds these contradictions, wrestling with them even as they continue their work in support of the movement's broad goals. For example, the total loyalist might downplay an incident of abuse, choosing to believe that Kurdish revolutionaries are immune from engaging in patriarchal behavior. But the cynical idealist would follow the Kurdish women's movement in recognizing that patriarchal power dynamics exist even within the radically autonomous women's movement itself, thereby proving the need for continual anti-patriarchal struggle once more. If the total loyalist were confronted with incontrovertible evidence of an abuse of patriarchal power or a lack of women's solidarity, the shock might drive them from the movement altogether. But the cynical idealist knows that individual failures only prove the need for continued revolutionary organization on the internal front. They are alert to contradictions and shortcomings and therefore protected from the shock of small defeats.

The same approach can help comrades to grasp and reckon with the severe political, economic, and geostrategic challenges facing the AANES, without losing faith in the revolution. The total loyalist might refuse to see these difficulties; blame them solely on hostile neighboring states or counterrevolutionary elements among the local population; or be pushed into despair should the weight of evidence against the AANES one day prove incontrovertible. The cynical idealist views the AANES's efforts to reckon with these challenges as potentially revolutionary in their own right yet simultaneously knows better than to expect perfection from any political movement. They are therefore less likely to treat the revolution as a mere springboard for their own revolutionary hopes, and more likely to acknowledge both the genuine suffering of ordinary locals and the movement's admitted organizational and strategic shortcomings.

Through its concepts of self-criticism and building a militant personality, the Kurdish movement makes a virtue of this active, ceaseless task of self-transformation. Kurdish organizers sometimes explain the importance of self-criticism to local recruits from Muslim families through comparison to the Islamic teaching that the greater jihad involves struggle against one's own fallen nature, as opposed to the lesser jihad of struggle against external enemies. The same holds for revolutionaries in the Kurdish movement, who are enjoined to prioritize the daily struggle to be humble, selfless, and anti-hierarchical over more dramatic acts of revolutionary valor.

Kurdish organizers are therefore fond of exemplars like the young revolutionary said to have peeled sacks of potatoes with as much gusto as though he were fighting on the frontline. In striving for a distant goal, we are freed to continue our daily, ordinary tasks and activities, even when they seem trivial or mundane. When internationalist militants are asked what they've learned in Rojava, the response is almost inevitably the same: patience.

More broadly, Rojava's militants are encouraged to "give meaning" (*wate dayîn*) to the minutiae of life, to remind themselves that thousands died to make free life in Rojava possible.[10] They should therefore grant revolutionary significance to their life in its smallest details, from an unexpected egg in the day's rations to the joyful revolutionary duty of cleaning the toilet.

Crucially, this approach should free people for a celebration of our common values and achievements, not bog them down in excessive nit-picking or performative purity politics. For example, if the word "martyr" is too quickly invoked, without fear and trembling, it ends up feeling cheap. This is an error many newly arrived internationalists make, striving hyperbolically to imbue toothpaste with the mystical value of the blood of eleven thousand martyrs as they criticize their comrades for unavoidable waste or another tiny error. As a cynical idealist internationalist once noted, whereas newly arrived naive utopians rattled off endless laundry lists of criticism and self-criticism based on the minutiae of communal life, seasoned comrades fighting on the frontlines could be done with tekmil in a matter of moments. They criticized one another only when it mattered, saving their words where unnecessary and trusting that their comrades were working steadily toward the same revolutionary goals.

As we've perhaps noticed in our own movements, it's often comrades who have passed through the cycle of defeat, despair, and renewed, cynical hope against hope who prove most willing to stick with difficult, ugly, boring organizing tasks. How many of us know a tough old leftist mother figure, jaded and cynical, who remains absolutely committed to a cause even as younger comrades come and go with the seasons? Through the leap of revolutionary faith, we're paradoxically equipped for the most ordinary and uninspiring tasks.

As Freud suggests, if we experience a generalized sense of fear or angst, we're then protected from sharper shocks.[11] Naive hope exposes us to the shock of defeat—a deeper, more profound fear shields us, enables us to continue.

This is where more liberal, optimistic philosophies of hope against hope fall down. For example, Rebecca Solnit's quest for "hope in the dark" is shot through with a need to seek out silver linings, local victories, the consolation of historical successes and putative future gains. These limitations suggest an inability to undergo a political version of Kierkegaard's infinite resignation to the existential challenges we face. Thus Solnit's political prognosis is also limited, culminating in an activist, Occupy-era fetishization of the horizontal and the hyperlocal, and therefore doomed to fail.[12]

These shortcomings notwithstanding, Solnit joins a small cluster of thinkers who have preceded this book by theorizing a turn back to revolutionary hope. John Holloway pursues "hope in hopeless times," Terry Eagleton explores "hope without optimism," while Kurdish critical theorist Saladdin Ahmed advocates for "revolutionary hope after nihilism," with repeated reference to Rojava's revolutionary alternative.[13]

These diverse thinkers all offer us ways to view contemporary generations' bold and unexpected commitment to apparently hopeless political activity. Across the Left, there's a growing sense that mere optimism must be relinquished in pursuit of a deeper, darker, and more profound commitment. The cynical idealist clearly remains open to charges of hypocrisy, or even of exploiting others' daily suffering to justify their personal sense of revolutionary justification—a particular risk faced by cynical idealist internationalists in Rojava. Yet there's an undeniable bravery in taking up a great political cause in full knowledge of its hopelessness.

The Promethean Scream

In his profound survey *Pessimism: Philosophy, Ethic, Spirit*, contemporary philosopher Joshua Foa Dienstag lays out a radical, though not revolutionary, philosophy of pessimism, in strong opposition to liberal teleologies of straightforward progress and progressive evolution.[14] Dienstag suggests we could imagine the very first thought through which humankind transcended our animal origins as a primal grunt of displeasure, a preverbal gasp of realization that things could be otherwise. This notional moment, marking the emergence of a truly human consciousness, is therefore simultaneously a death wish, expressing a refusal to continue living under present conditions: "Humanity only began to live when it wanted to die."[15]

This paradox again recalls Bloch's formulation of suicide as hope, and the despairing theories of historical progression advanced by Rousseau and Adorno. All subsequent human achievement and suffering can be dated from this epochal historic turning point. This primal narrative of becoming human is simultaneously the narrative of an irrevocable fall.

Dienstag's philosophy is concerned with equipping us to make sense of a fundamentally meaningless universe and to survive, perhaps even to live lives worth living; it is less concerned with motivating political action. In this way, it forms a more considered formulation of the problem of consciousness powerfully articulated by horror writer Thomas Ligotti in his manifesto *The Conspiracy Against the Human Race*. Pushing a century of despairing philosophy to its limit, Ligotti represents the universe as not merely amoral but "malignantly useless," the meaninglessness of existence itself an act of violent harm given the unwanted curse of consciousness.[16]

It might be hard to see the link between this extreme existential despair and our day-to-day political activity. On one level, the Kurdish movement's Leninist origins often lead its representatives to dismiss philosophical lamentations over our meaningless, useless existence as so much postmodern nonsense. Often, a nominal anti-positivism gives way to a crude essentialism, treating the Kurdish homeland, biological womanhood, and Öcalan's utopian vision as straightforwardly, inherently good.

Yet those of us interested in the active political formation of a better world can and must learn from pessimistic and absurdist philosophy, since we are placed under a triple existential burden. We must believe that the present world we're seeking to revolutionize is nonetheless worth living in; and yet we must also believe in a notional, unrealized better world yet to be; and we must further believe the struggle and sacrifice necessary to achieve that world are justified.

In this light, Dienstag's primal grunt theory recalls revolutionary theorist John Holloway's concept of hope as an essentially negative force. To Holloway, hope is "the moment of human refusal, the great NO" that defines humanity in opposition to the hell of existence and thus marks the very inception of truly human subjectivity.[17] A similar concept of inaugural human despair is here reclaimed as what Holloway calls the anti-capitalist "scream." If human existence began at the point when we revolted against our fallen condition, it follows that to exist is to resist.

This primal grunt theory effectively retells the most famous trickster myth, in which the Titan Prometheus steals fire from the Greek gods and gives it to humankind. In punishment for this cunning act, Zeus chains Prometheus to a crag and plucks his liver out anew each day, only for the organ to grow back overnight.

The myth represents human consciousness itself as a revolution, a rebellion against the natural order. (The name "Prometheus" means "forethought," while to the Greeks then the liver was the seat of the human emotions, a symbolic role it still plays in the Middle East.) It likewise describes that notional moment, buried deep in the prehistory of humankind, when we first dared to think that things might be otherwise. There is a profound link between the theft of life-giving, death-dealing knowledge; the first flaring of human consciousness; and our subsequent bitter self-awareness. To be become human is to become alive to the inevitability of suffering, and yet also to be kept alive each day by the ambiguous gift of hope, like Prometheus chained to his crag.

In turn, the Prometheus myth is intimately linked to the myth of Pandora's box. In one telling, Zeus allowed Pandora to open the famous box full of curses as a further punishment for Prometheus's hubris. The curses (sickness, death, suffering) spill out into the world, leaving behind only hope. It's therefore unclear whether hope, like consciousness, is a blessing or a curse. Subsequent interpretations have variously understood Pandora's hope as a great evil, deluding us into accepting earthly suffering, yet also as a virtue, our greatest redemption from these evils.[18]

As revolutionaries, we may well be haunted by the Pandora question—is hope actually worth it? Knowing all the evil in the world, might hope not cause us to suffer all the more? Hadn't we better be cynics, defeatists, reformists, and do without hope altogether?

But we are called upon to act like Prometheus. Prometheus crucially acted *without a choice as though there were a choice*, seizing the potential curse of human intelligence and self-awareness *as though it were a gift*. For Dienstag, Camus was wrong to suggest we must imagine Sisyphus happy in his labors: in the same spirit, we must recognize the subtler emotion behind Prometheus's endurance.[19] "Happy" is the wrong word. As in the Romantic poet Shelley's revolutionary retelling of the myth, it's this defiant spirit which enables Prometheus to endure his torment, in full knowledge of his apparent hopelessness.

Marx therefore celebrated Prometheus as the "noblest saint and martyr," incarnating not only humankind's fundamental rebellious spirit but also the demystification of religion and the subsequent celebration of creative human agency. And Bloch goes further yet. He describes the Marxist revolutionary project as the realization of a notional religion venerating Prometheus, the true faith implied by the spirit of Greek tragedy—the faithless faith of cynical idealists, of all those who know we are forever cursed for rising up against our fallen human condition and yet determined to make a virtue of that curse.[20]

When Öcalan dramatically describes himself as "chained to the rocks of [his offshore detention center] İmralı island. . . . Just as Prometheus was chained to a rock," he places himself in this revolutionary tradition.[21]

His illuminating philosophy, too, is inextricable from the tortures he suffers each day.

The Socialist Wager

You are probably familiar with the theological formulation known as Pascal's wager: given the terrible cost of God not existing, we might as well place our despairing faith in Him. Revolutionary theorists—Bloch, Daniel Bensaïd, Lucien Goldmann—have argued for an analogous political commitment. Asking whether it's actually possible to achieve a transformed socialist world through human struggle, they conclude that we have no choice but to make a socialist wager on a better tomorrow, given the potential cost of defeat.[22] The famous slogan "socialism or barbarism" carries much the same meaning, implying there is no choice but to choose resistance, rather as Kierkegaard argued there was ultimately no choice save choosing the ethical life.

Pascal's wager has also been used to theorize a revolutionary response to the incipient climate catastrophe. Urging massive social and political change rather than mere policy reform, a latter-day prophet of climate collapse, Jem Rendell, whom we will meet in the next chapter, chooses the following words: "I always come around to the same conclusion—we do not know. Ignoring the future because it is unlikely to matter might backfire. 'Running for the hills'—to create our own eco-community—might backfire. But we definitely know that continuing to work in the ways we have done until now is not just backfiring—it is holding the gun to our own heads."[23]

Once again, if we opt not to choose, we are already betting on defeat. The future's total unknowability means only a total response is justified.

Almost by definition, the climate crisis is returning a universal spirit to left politics, forcing us to act globally even when we believe we are thinking locally. Though the rate of change and the scale of the crisis vary from country to country, we are all increasingly placed in a frontline position where global defeat or global triumph once again become valid, expected political horizons—as they were from a Marxist perspective in the fervent days of mass communist organization.

The Authoritarianism of Hope

Earlier, we identified the dangerous and opiate-like quality of millennialist expectation in incipient global revolution, either inuring us to wait peacefully for a never-to-arrive better tomorrow or else numbing us to harm today as justified in the service of a coming utopia, that evanescent Not Yet.

The socialist leap of faith implies much the same dangers. Dostoyevsky's *Devils* offers one tragic satire on the dangers of political nihilism and mere posturing, in absurd pursuit of a never-to-arrive better tomorrow (though of course that new dawn would ultimately arrive in Russia, inspired in part by the violent nihilists whom Dostoyevsky scrutinizes).[24] Camus argues that "utopias have almost always been coercive and authoritarian." To the man who prophesies utopia in the one-hundred-first year, he asks, what does it matter if people suffer for a century?[25] And Nietzsche critiques both religious and political utopias as deadening present-day life, joy, and activity.

By placing irrational hope in a utopian future, we again risk a tasteless political theodicy, justifying today's hardship with reference to tomorrow's paradise. Revolutionary movements lay a socialist wager, betting that the harm they cause will be justified by a coming victory, retroactively making that suffering worthwhile. Hence the harm done by twentieth-century state-socialist movements and the errors of the Kurdish movement, particularly in its earlier, statist manifestation but also in pursuit of its current revolutionary goal. In our own horizontal and anarchist movements, meanwhile, this type of thought fosters both a tendency to personal burnout and a culture of covering up abuse.

What Kierkegaard has called fear and trembling is therefore particularly vital in the political context. A cheap optimism might lead us to deny or downplay present-day suffering. But a hard-won hopeless hope can help us acknowledge and make sense of these challenges. This spirit animates the Kurdish movement's martyr culture, which acknowledges the pain of present-day loss while simultaneously deploying it in pursuit of a better tomorrow. As we saw when comparing the Kurdish movement's generally productive and outward-looking vision of the end times to ISIS's toxic interpretation, it's possible to view today's suffering as justified by tomorrow's triumph without celebrating or hastening that suffering for its own sake.

Narratives of resistance and struggle can help us make sense of the pain. To Camus, "struggle implies a total absence of hope," which nonetheless "has nothing to do with despair."[26] Rather, "the absurd man can only drain everything to the bitter end and deplete himself . . . in that consciousness and in that day-to-day revolt he gives proof of his only truth which is defiance."[27] Like the Kurdish movement slogan "resistance is life," there's a sense in which this concept of political activity denies victory as a potential goal in favor of a melancholy fetishization of oppositional struggle. But this resignation to perhaps endless conflict lies very far from despair.

The Kurdish movement's narrative of resistance thus both recalls and challenges Camus's argument in *The Rebel*, in which the philosopher extends existential arguments raised in *Sisyphus* to the field of political organization. To Camus, as we've seen, any attempt at political perfection or the triumphal ending of history can result in terror. In a criticism of Marxist-Leninist orthodoxy that recalls Öcalan's doctrine, he argues that the truly rebellious figure is constantly in a state of struggle, neither wholly crushed by oppression nor wholly liberated to become a new oppressor in turn.[28]

This distinction was the cause of bad blood between Camus and his rival Jean-Paul Sartre. Sartre saw an attachment to mere rebellion as deferring the responsibility to achieve material (Marxist) revolution, instead requiring the perpetual continuation of repressive power structures in a mutually parasitic relationship—turning socialists into mere nonviolent delinquents, unable truly to shake the foundations of power.[29] (This preference for rebellion over revolution surely contributed to Camus's infamous, Eurocentric condemnation of armed resistance to French colonialism in Algeria.) Again, therefore, Camus's argument can properly be understood as a psychological rather than organizational strategy.

As we've seen, Kurdish and international militants have found various ways to remain productively suspended in struggle, caught in their leap from despair toward hopeless hope. By undergoing the trials of the double movement and having their eyes opened to the challenges the revolution faces, the cynical idealist is able to recognize the revolution as a process, a continued and complex struggle, ethical by virtue of its unfinished, open, continuing nature. Thus Kurdish comrades insist the Rojava Revolution is not a sudden armed victory but rather made up of countless repetitive clandestine conversations in Kurdish villages; the quiet sacrifices of revolutionary mothers; the lifelong approach toward the socialist Not Yet.

It never ceased to amaze me how regularly Kurdish civilians would casually lift their shirts after six months' friendship to reveal the shocking lacerations left by regime torture, or else suddenly share an anecdote of kidnap, sniper fire, or airstrikes while having previously affected a light-hearted distance from the revolutionary struggle. These tales and scars were markers of a utopian sensibility that necessarily suffuses the present, not to make light of suffering but to justify it with reference to a common tomorrow. Revolution, the mothers of the martyrs often declare, is as natural as the milk they offer their children. In this slogan, the redemptive and universal once again blend with the local and mundane. Relatedly, the "resistance is life" slogan is sometimes used with a knowing, half-cynical grin, encouraging comrades charged with peeling potatoes or another dull day-to-day task.

At the same time, the productive tensions that animate political life in Rojava remind us of the ethical and political imperative to remain dissatisfied, sick, ill at ease with the world. In what Freudian psychotherapy terms the nirvana principle, the death drive compels us to seek the total absence of stimulation, a blissful return to a state of total non-sensation, equilibrium, and non-being.[30] From opposing directions, naive optimism and cynical disillusionment bring us to much the same static end. Comfort is correlate to death, and contentment anathema to resistance. Rather than the Zen state of acceptance and seemingly egoless egoism that underwrites placid, capitalist pseudo-enlightenment, the resistance model enables us to welcome and live with our dissatisfaction.

On a broader political level, continual struggle between the poles of despair and triumph is likewise necessary to prevent the dangerous dismissal of suffering as justified by the utopian revolutionary dream. While the Kurdish movement has certainly made errors in the course of its partial, compromised victory in Syria, as we've seen the Rojava Revolution has thus far been kept from self-consuming reaction precisely due to the harsh challenges it faces.

In its ideal theoretical form, democratic confederalism runs the risk of indulging in a smothering nirvana principle through its proposed return to the static bliss of an imagined primitive communist utopia. But the AANES is necessarily kept from this retreat through its real-world crisis, practice, and compromises, engaged in the ongoing, complex, negotiated process of implementing its vision on earth in Rojava.

This concept of militancy as struggle particularly underpins the tekmil process, through which comrades engage in the greater struggle of challenging and revolutionizing potentially toxic behaviors or organizational practices, in a political culture intended to prevent left authoritarianism from taking root. It's for this reason that Kurdish revolutionaries are supposed to only critique one another's failures, not praise any successes. (Some Kurdish organizers are fond of the motivational slogan "the reward for work is more work," a cliché I've even heard attributed to Öcalan.)

For Kurdish theorist Azize Aslan, similarly, the Kurdish women's movement creates a crucial "negative antagonism" through continued internal struggle against patriarchy, hierarchy, and verticalism within the broader revolutionary movement.[31] Even Öcalan's continued imprisonment plays a similar productive role on the personal level: in his case, there can be no utopian-authoritarian assumption of power, forcing the Kurdish leader to choose continued struggle each day.

In all these ways, Öcalan, his followers, and his movement necessarily remain in a continued rebellious resistance. More broadly, this is perhaps the fate of stateless movements, able to extend the revolutionary moment and maintain their open, productive, rebellious spirit only at the cost of remaining forever at the mercy of greater powers.

Certainly, this reality can sometimes be used to downplay or excuse the revolution's failings, by both internationalists and Kurdish comrades, for example by denying democratic confederalism's struggles to take root in conservative Arab communities or the insufficiency of a cooperative economy as a dual-power alternative to market exploitation in Syria. As Öcalan's belief in an internal political women's revolution as the necessary precursor to broader social transformation makes clear, we cannot postpone the implementation of our ideals until the revolutionary Not Yet arrives. Rather, we must begin implementing them within our movements today, reckoning with our objective material circumstances as we meet them.

"*Yan serkeftin yan serkeftin*" runs another famous Kurdish slogan, "either victory or victory." It echoes the Latin translation for "either/or" that Kierkegaard quotes: "aut/aut." In both cases, the repetition implies a hidden correspondence between two apparently opposed perspectives.[32] In the same spirit, the Kurdish slogan in fact offers no alternative at all. There is no choice but to choose life.

The Inner Commitment

Many of these survival strategies are private, interior affairs—the socialist leap of faith perhaps most of all. These are philosophies of the soul, ways of managing our own doubts and insecurities, suggesting the complex and compromised ways we manage to survive from day to day. They don't necessarily make for comfortable reading, nor do they always show the Left, Rojava's internationalists, or the Kurdish movement in the most noble light. But they are legitimate, genuine, sincere responses to the severe organizational challenges we face.

They are offered to those comrades who find themselves each day, without quite knowing why or how, both struggling to continue and continuing to struggle. Many of us might empathize with Bakunin's attempted justification of his anarchist propaganda as an attempt to shelter his comrades from the realities of their weak position: "When I received bad news I held it back; but when the news was good I tried to exaggerate it for their eyes."[33] As Richard Rorty suggests with regard to his liberal ironist, a cynical inner skepticism can nonetheless free us for a productive and sincere external political commitment.

Nietzsche likewise cautions us to hide our self-aware cynicism and meta-modern emotional self-mastery from those around us, "for there are circumstances when nobody must look into our eyes."[34] But perhaps some of your comrades secretly feel the same way. Late at night, drunk or emotional, we might confess these copium strategies to one another and be comforted. Or perhaps we might conversely choose to hide them from even ourselves, swallow our auto-placebo, and convince even ourselves that our commitment is wholly sincere.

Vanguard Anarchism

At the same time, these existential considerations have organizational implications. As argued in chapters 3 and 4, the contemporary Left faces a two-part challenge. We must A) identify a political subject capable of articulating an effective response to the individualizing logic of neoliberal capitalism beyond the vague and inchoate forms of the multitude and the 99 percent, and B) find ways of effectively organizing this subject beyond the tried-and-failed models of nominally leaderless, prefigurative, direct-democratic horizontalism.

Keeping some aspects of our political analysis reserved to ourselves, a trusted inner circle, or even a vanguard party need not constitute a verticalist power grab—it can form part of a generous, self-sacrificing politics. Again, simplification can contribute to democratization, and education is a paramount revolutionary task. Knowing how to present our arguments in a straightforward, appealing way while privately acknowledging their inherent flaws and contradictions (and debating their potential resolution) is therefore a fundamental task facing any would-be mass, popular movement.

Certainly, our revolutionary duty might sometimes be to share our knowledge and acknowledge these contradictions. But our duty is surely sometimes also to struggle on with doubts in our hearts, even as we present a cheerful face to those around us, assuring them of those revolutionary truths we know to be false yet hope to be true.

As we take on this profoundly challenging task, we need never stand alone. Certainly, the Kurdish vanguard stands apart, seldom criticizing one another in front of civilians and maintaining a generally upbeat, assertive, united front. But internal criticism among the revolutionary class itself is correspondingly all the more severe, and in private these militants of course experience doubts and misgivings. They share a bonded kinship all the stronger for distinguishing the militant from the people they serve.

As they theorize a political subjectivity fit for our contemporary era of dispersed, decentralized value production, Hardt and Negri suggest that Saint Francis of Assisi could provide a model for the twenty-first-century militant, since the famous saint strove to become indistinguishable from the multitude of the common people he served.[35] But revolutionaries, like monks, have a dual persona. They are part of the multitude of humanity, and yet visibly and deliberately set apart. Like the wandering Christian monk, the true revolutionary is "in this world but not of it," moving through the people like a "fish in water" (as Mao demanded of his own revolutionary cadres), wholly in their element and yet distinct and self-contained.

The militant must speak to the people in one language while privately admitting their fears and criticizing or comforting their comrades in another. Rather than merely disappearing into the horizontal multitude, they must seek to organize their lives around values perhaps theoretically shared by the people but lacking or absent in day-to-day life. They are self-evidently held to a higher, alien, vertical moral standard, standing apart through their ethical and aesthetic unity.

The Kurdish movement deploys various tactics to ensure its own militants remain in the world but not of it, incarnating popular values while simultaneously seeking to implement and embody a distinct, alien revolutionary code. The requirement for an initial, explicit commitment to the cause; a unified aesthetic code; corporate, collective, internal discipline; learning from and borrowing social values practices in our local culture; the practice of criticism and self-criticism; strict standards on drug use, alcohol consumption, and sexual relationships—new interpretations of all these practices could be useful as we seek our own ways to become revolutionary fish in water. Could we have the courage to mark ourselves out as militants, as benevolent yet radical as latter-day monks, adopting a truly revolutionary ethic and aesthetic that shuns the trappings of lifestyle anarchism and social-democratic comfort?

Hevaltî: Hope for Our Comrades, If Not Ourselves

As the leap of faith can inspire organization and discipline, so too can revolutionary organization help us take that leap. Comradeship is absolutely fundamental in enabling us to live with our losses, without falling back into Nietzschean cynicism, melancholy or despair. This is what the Kurdish movement valorizes as "*hevaltî*" (comradeship).

Productive revolutionary commitment means we must avoid both static fatalism and blind naivety, rather remaining suspended and struggling in tension between these two extremes. Thus we typically manage far better when our comrades help us keep these opposing points in view. They temper our utopianism today and help us make light of despair tomorrow. And it's far easier to struggle for a cause we suspect to be hopeless on behalf of others than to do so for ourselves.

When Kierkegaard made his leap of faith and Pascal cast his bet on God's existence, the religious believers knew that they would be welcomed in paradise. The socialist organizer or climate activist has no such personal consolation. As Rojava's martyr posters remind the Kurdish movement's militants each day, we may well go to our graves without experiencing any concrete personal reward. The (eco-)socialist wager is made not for us but for the world. Yet it's just for this reason that the wager can help us keep struggling, even when we ourselves might suffer depression or despair.

Although many pessimistic philosophers are great advocates of friendship, their treatments of existential despair naturally describe these travails as isolated, individual experiences. They wrestle with the meaninglessness of existence in the stillness of their own hearts. Nietzsche is paradigmatic in this respect, craving a friendship so ideal he could find no suitable companion, thus dying quite alone.

Perhaps revolutionary commitment is also an inner, philosophical affair. But hope without hope loves company.

In the Kurdish movement's usage, the word for "comrade" is quite simply the word for "friend" (*heval*). When referring to full-time Kurdish revolutionaries, Kurds will often simply call them "the friends," as in "A friend needs a place to lie low in Istanbul," or "The friends have called for a protest." This allusive language, partially intended to preserve clandestinity, is suggestive of both the intimate links the revolutionary movement has forged in Kurdish civil society and the priority it places on interpersonal solidarity within its ranks.

The related term "*rêheval*" carries the further, special connotation of "companion traveling the same path." Joint struggle creates social bonds, and these social bonds in turn create the conditions for continued struggle. Earlier we heard the story of the two Kurdish revolutionaries in Diyarbakir prison, resisting their attempted sexual humiliation at the hands of their torturers by staring determinedly into one another's eyes rather than observing one another's degradation. Revolutionary friendship can preserve us through the worst outer trials and inner doubts. Like Don Quixote and his loyal follower Sancho Panza, we urge one other on, mutable as tricksters, each taking up the thread of the revolutionary narrative whenever the other threatens to lose the plot.

Kierkegaard says, a little dismissively: "Courage is the only thing that can save life and save man—unless a man expects to be helped by breaking off his skepticism capriciously and combining with several like-minded persons to determine what the truth is."[36] Yet that capricious act of breaking away to form a collective is a true act of hope without hope, denying our own inner doubts to place faith in an association of equally doubting individuals. As Frantz Fanon suggests, and as the Kurdish movement's example shows, all revolutionary and national liberation movements have begun with just such a moment of breaking away from skepticism, first on the individual or psychological, then on the collective, and finally on the national level.

Each commune, movement, or revolution is made up of a mass of ordinary individuals—egotistical, self-preserving, doubting humans. Yet even knowing this, we nonetheless choose to rely on our comrades. Comradeship takes away the doomed-to-disappointment expectation of individual pure inner goodness, saving us from reliance on the falsifiable liberal belief that people are fundamentally good.

In opposition to the depoliticization and individualization of hope in the hands of the liberal hope industry, and its weaponization to keep us small, scattered, and scared, the revolutionary movement reorganizes hope. Collective life and political organization require a defiant belief that other humans can be better than the individual selves we know all too well are limited and flawed.

Like soldiers on the front line, we cling together not because of our own individual courage but instead because we don't want to let our comrades down—or to be seen letting them down, which comes to much the same thing. In Rojava more than anywhere, comrades live in the auto-panopticon, striving to become a self-observing cell, ideally holding one another to an alien transformative standard. But the same is true throughout our own fragmented archipelago of leftist spaces, as it is in any social or political movement proposing a radically new ethics, monastic movements included.

This is the positive side of what's often called virtue signaling, or revolutionary posturing. In Syria, there were days when deeply depressed or disheartened comrades dragged themselves out of bed because they knew their comrades were expecting them to clean up before breakfast and didn't want to let them down; because they didn't want make others pick up the slack; because they didn't want to get criticized in tekmil; because they wanted to convince themselves or others they were true revolutionaries. This expectation to go through the motions and customs of a semi-militarized, semi-ritualized "collective life" (*jiyana kominal*), even when comrades were depressed or disheartened, could sometimes feel stifling.

Yet this disciplined, unstinting routine undoubtedly keeps many comrades alive, providing them with purpose, or at least the form of purpose. It provides daily encouragement and the conditions of long-term dedication. At best, it offers a model of truly collective self-care, with comrades motivated to keep themselves alive and well in order to keep their comrades alive and well in turn.

Again, monastic movements offer one potential model of the revolutionary and organizational benefits of a shared ethical and aesthetic culture. Kierkegaard's admiration for the aesthete shines through, his criticism of their egotism notwithstanding. Similarly, despite his general hatred of priests, Nietzsche admits his admiration for the highly disciplined Jesuit organization: "We may even ask whether, with precisely similar tactics and organization, we enlightened ones would make equally good tools, equally admirable through self-conquest, indefatigableness, and renunciation."[37]

Monastic movements insist on humankind's fallen, flawed nature but argue that it's precisely for this reason that we humans must be organized into a collective way life. Even if we're as cynical as Nietzsche, skeptical of humankind's ability to transcend its petty egotism, we can learn from the monastic example. Our left movements may often be constellations of egos. But perhaps it's through the organization of this individualism, rather than denying its existence, that we can supersede our social atomization.

Nietzsche suggests we will one day be able to overcome the moralistic, utilitarian organization of society, returning to the individual through the establishment of an enlightened, freely chosen "collective individuality."[38] This negative-utopian conception of the need to transcend bourgeois society reflects the ultimate goal of Marxism, pursuing an "association in which the free development of each is the condition for the free development of all."[39] In both revolutionary theories, unity is arrived at not despite but because of social antagonism, freeing us for a higher form of collectivity which enables rather than stifles individuality. Both Marx and Nietzsche hopefully predict anarchist freedom as the ultimate condition of humankind.

Socialism as Babel

With the goal of absolute freedom in mind, we can work toward a condition of enlightened socialist individualism through the paradoxical collectivity of socialist organization. It is through revolutionary organization that we can approach a socialism truly capable of answering Nietzsche's call to arms.

The Kurdish movement sometimes opts for a "prefigurative politics," with its day-to-day struggle organized along the horizontal and direct-democratic values that it aims to implement on a mass scale. This approach has certainly helped the Kurdish movement, among others, critique and reform certain harmful or ineffective elements of its own verticalist, Marxist-Leninist political culture. Yet it has also repeatedly contributed to the organizational failures of latter-day, would-be revolutionary movements to achieve lasting change. From Gezi Park to Black Lives Matter to a thousand smaller protests and occupations, nominal horizontalism leaves these movements at perpetual risk of being co-opted, subverted, or defeated. Melancholically fearing any lesson learned from the organizational successes of the twentieth century, they remain within safe and pre-defined bounds that leave the institutions they wish to revolutionize wholly untouched.

Like many effective revolutionary movements, therefore, the Kurdish movement is also willing to implement verticalist tactics while in strategic pursuit of its horizontalist horizon. Hence its militants submit to hierarchical party discipline, even as they work tirelessly and effectively to encourage ordinary Kurds to critique hierarchy wherever they find it. This process is full of challenges and contradictions, as we've seen, and can hamper efforts to foster a truly pluralist and democratic political culture. But at its best, the horizontalist horizon reflects back on relationships even within the verticalist party structure, charging them with love, mutual respect, and *hevaltî*. For example, while the movement encourages respect for the experience and learning of senior hevals, it's often precisely these comrades who are most open to structural critiques from young comrades or newly arrived internationalists during political debates or tekmil.

A politics that is truly prefigurative rather than merely figurative (that is, standing in for something else) is defined by its onward progress toward the Not Yet. It allows the communal pursuit of an evanescent political goal to illuminate and transform those constitutive practices, sensibility, and relationships that make up the movement. That *pre-* is crucial, basking us in the transformative light of a socialist tomorrow, justifying us as we hold one another to our alien, comradely moral code today.

In a more or less critical spirit, Dostoyevsky, Kierkegaard, and Bloch all use the Tower of Babel myth to represent their own takes on hope without hope.[40] In particular, the tower constructed in a vain attempt to reach heaven represents endless striving for an unobtainable socialist goal. (The Soviet Union's epochal, never-to-be-constructed Palace of the Soviets was modeled on Babel.)

As socialists, our attempt to attain heaven on earth is perhaps foolhardy, doomed to atomization, infighting, and collapse. But the very act of coming together, striving in full knowledge of our fallen nature, has revolutionary potential.

Perhaps socialism is indeed our atheist stand-in for true religious faith, "the Tower of Babel which is constructed without God's help, not to reach the heavens, but to bring the heavens down to earth."[41] But perhaps the real paradise lies neither in an imagined, authoritarian-utopian heaven, nor on a fallen, failed and fragmented Earth but rather in the continued socialist struggle permanently suspended between these two poles. A broken Babel stands as a tragic monument to squabbling and doomed-to-fail human endeavor. But it's also a monument to the unexpected diversity of opportunity and experience that very effort can create.

Chapter 9

Hope After the Holocaust

The socialist leap of faith may help us endure the darkest days we face. But any attempt to find cause for hope in our hopeless times must reckon with two catastrophes—the twentieth-century history of totalitarian, fascist, and anti-Semitic violence culminating in the Holocaust, and the twenty-first-century future potentially culminating in climate apocalypse.

These dual catastrophes cannot lightly be linked. The Holocaust shouldn't be reduced to a metaphor suggesting the planetary scale of the climate crisis, which itself remains unwritten and unknown, and the climate crisis in turn should not be written off in such terribly certain terms. Neither problem admits of ready answers, and even where they do suggest ways to survive and respond to catastrophe, these answers are not necessarily comparable.

And yet revolutionary theories of hope are inevitably tugged between these two dark horizons. Contemporary politics is haunted by the possibility that we are being drawn into a maelstrom from which all conventional or reformist political organization seems unlikely to deliver us. Even if the ultimate outcome of the climate catastrophe remains unknown, this very unknowability necessarily requires a revolutionary leap of faith, as suggested by Pascal's eco-socialist wager.

And at the same time, political thought about hope is necessarily marked by the twentieth-century reality of industrialized death. Adorno's negative utopianism emerged directly from the Holocaust. Like the ancient apophatic theologians, who sought to understand God only through what could not be said about God's perfection ("what no eye has seen, nor ear heard"), we must necessarily consider hope through its potential total absence.

Many writers have sought to muster the history of anti-fascist and Jewish resistance during WWII as proof of humankind's ability to endure its darkest hours, even as others have naturally concluded that humanity's hopes perished in the gas chambers. You don't even need to scroll far down the Wikipedia page for "hope" to find a picture of Auschwitz, where a rose has been laid to signify that dual and dangerous quality.[1] In our continual search for hope, we repeatedly feel compelled to return to this most hopeless era of human history.

In fact, that Wikipedia page about hope opens with a picture of a Syrian refugee girl editorialized as possessing "a hopeful expression." It's a further testament to both humankind's paradoxical, determined ability to seek hope in the most hopeless circumstances and to the intertwining of post-Holocaust narratives of hope with our own contemporary struggles. If we are truly to find hope in hopelessness, we must consider the extreme limits of hopelessness—and consider those survivors who have done the same.

Outside the Auschwitz Canon

Secular Auschwitz survivors have noted the extraordinary ability of both militant Marxists and genuine religious believers interred in the camp to weather intense suffering and evil. Multiple accounts testify to the power of these transformative, millenarian ideologies to place pure, irrational hope against hope in a coming Jerusalem or Soviet victory.[2]

But many others lost their faith, while those without recourse to any kind of faith also endured the death camp. In secular survivor Jean Améry's account, the politically committed total loyalists are shown as better equipped to survive the camp than their more liberal and intellectual counterparts. Meanwhile, secular inmates were forced to look almost enviously at their fellow inmates debating abstruse Marxist theory or observing Orthodox fasts in the midst of starvation, and thus successfully eluding their present suffering.[3] The will to stupidity offered the most successful survival strategy.

Agamben similarly draws together the testimonies of certain sober, intellectual, secular Auschwitz survivors. No comprehensible utterance can emerge from the mouths of the concentration camp's victims, stripped of political life at an extreme of the state of exception. Yet these survivors can offer a maimed, limited perspective into the experience of the camp, in turn illuminating the horror of a now-globalized state of exception.[4] It has become a commonplace to begin Holocaust histories with a disclaimer like the one that opened this chapter, acknowledging the Holocaust's unique, incommensurable nature. But for Agamben, if we relinquish these political testaments as irrelevant to our world, we repeat the violence of the Nazis, who likewise sought to divest Auschwitz's inmates of all political agency.[5]

Agamben argues that a given system can only be understood through the exceptions it relies upon. We can apply this analytic logic to the canon of acceptable Auschwitz literature. The testimonies of two very different Auschwitz survivors and writers, both excluded from Agamben's survey, the pseudonymous writer known as Ka-Tzetnik 135633 and world-famous psychiatrist Viktor Frankl, in a sense represent the limit cases of Auschwitz testimony. Frankl appears to represent pure, feel-good, New Age hope; Ka-Tzetnik, an equally exceptional lunatic despair. Yet, in the context of Auschwitz as absolute state of exception, these absolute limits can prove instructive.

The Holocaust Self-Help Industry

Venerated in his lifetime, Frankl is a controversial figure. He developed a humanistic theory positing that a striving for meaning lay at the center of human experience, as opposed to the drive toward pleasure (and death) posited by Freud, or the drive toward power posited by Frankl's sometime mentor Alfred Adler.[6] This hopeful assessment of human nature, first propounded in 1938, was soon put to the test through the Nazis' attempted extermination of the Jews.

Though Frankl's activities during those years are a matter of some debate, he used his medical qualifications to continue treating Jews as long as possible, saving some from Nazi euthanasia. Frankl would spend years detained in concentration camps, mostly working as a doctor. Very shortly after his release, he wrote (in a reported nine days) a work of auto-biographical psychotherapy called *Man's Search for Meaning*, expounding his theory that humans could save themselves from despair through personal belief in a greater meaning, a theory justified through his observations and experiences in the camps. The book went on to sell over sixteen million copies worldwide, establishing Frankl as the paramount voice adducing a humanistic, uplifting message from the Holocaust.

Holocaust and Jewish historians have since reassessed Frankl's ambiguous activities before and during the war, including prewar associations with a prominent Nazi; controversial, experimental brain surgery performed on suicidal Jewish patients, to the Nazis' benefit; and post-war relationships with and endorsement of Nazi-linked public figures.[7] Notably, it's been shown that Frankl in fact spent "only" (if there can be any such term) three days in a depot near Auschwitz, before being worked close to starvation elsewhere.[8]

Nonetheless, he devotes half his opus to observations of resilience and the quest for "meaning" among inmates in the death camp, where he gives the impression of having spent rather more time. Frankl rapidly and effectively built a global career and devoted following for his claims to have found in himself, and witnessed in others, a will to strive for meaning despite the horrors of Auschwitz.[9]

In themselves, these issues do not necessarily diminish Frankl's role in the theorization of hope after the Holocaust. Whatever his faults, Frankl remained, it's worth repeating, a Jewish victim of the Holo-caust. Those historians who have criticized the eminent psychotherapist therefore typically have done so tentatively, aware they are approaching a "saint," a man who certainly suffered more than any man ought, with every right to find whatever way he could to endure.[10] As argued above, a desire to establish narratives capable of motivating a despairing people is not wicked in itself, even when that narrative might willfully simplify or depart from the truth.

Doubtless, Frankl did indeed improve many of his patients' lives. Doubtless, he believed in his own teachings. There is a poignant des-peration to his attempts to assert that he found cause for optimism in Auschwitz, and his dubious claims to have exhorted fellow inmates with uplifting lectures. If the psychotherapist rewrote history, perhaps he did so for himself, first and foremost.

Frankl critiqued mere "self-actualization."[11] He believed meaning had to be located outside of the self, in a striving for something higher, better, more noble. Like the interred Orthodox Jews and Marxists, he found a humanistic faith through which he could endure great suffering, a "yes to life, in spite of everything."[12] (Sometimes, again, that spite is all we have).

To this end, Frankl retells a Middle Eastern fable of uncertain origin called "Death in Tehran." Death meets a servant who is terrified, leaps on a horse, and bolts off to Tehran, leaving Death bemused: as he tells the servant's master, he was surprised to find the servant at home when he had been planning to meet him that very night in Tehran.[13]

The point of the parable is that though we cannot choose our fate, we can choose how to meet that fate. Frankl believes we can act without a choice as though there were a choice. He was able to survive Auschwitz, he claims, through a determined inner focus on a higher meaning. This enabled him to stare his own death in the eye.

Clearly, there's a ready market for Frankl's reading of the Holocaust as cause for tragic optimism. In one sense, this confirms our general argument thus far. All-too-human, we need to believe hope is possible. Frankl allows the world to think better of itself through his own self-aggrandizing example holding up the ultimate, seemingly inarguable proof that self-aware man is indeed the master of his fate.

But there is also a clear, dangerous dematerialization to Frankl's perspective, a New Age depoliticization that refuses material reality in favor of an individualistic focus on self-improvement, and thus results in mere self-actualization after all.[14] Frankl marched out of the Holocaust into the era of liberal optimism, promising an abstracted hope *for* hope, prefiguring the late-capitalist hope industry's efforts to represent hope as equally available to all. His concept of hope takes no account whatsoever of that hope's evident unattainability for the vast majority of the Holocaust's victims—and whatever the exact details of Frankl's own case, it's clear it sharply diverged from the experience of most of his fellow victims. He refuses the absolute responsibility of Kierkegaard's fear and trembling.

Frankl established a whole school of humanist thought, which he called "logotherapy." In this key precursor to the contemporary hope industry, self-improvement psychobabble and individualist Stoicism are deployed to disciplinary, admonitory ends.

The psychotherapist thereby makes the ugly, inexcusable claim that "the mere knowledge that a man was either a camp guard or a prisoner tells us almost nothing," since there were good guards (who never beat the inmates) and bad inmates (such as the criminal, collaborationist *kapos*— or those who mocked other, weaker inmates).[15] To Frankl, what ultimately matters is one's personal, interior attitude, which can serve to liberate or condemn us, whatever our external circumstances.

But as we hardly need Frankl's leading critic to remind us, "in the inferno of Auschwitz, attitude mattered little to nothing for survival . . . 1.3 million were killed, very few survived."[16] One ultimate lesson of Auschwitz is rather that individual choice, effort, and Stoicism often count for nothing. Formal, material distinctions tell us almost everything, in the end. Hence the need for our hope against hope to be organized and given material form, in the political rather than merely existential realm.

Frankl's philosophy revolves around the maxim, appropriated from Nietzsche, that "he who has a why to live for can bear almost any how."[17] But this appropriation goes too far. As argued above, Nietzsche can indeed be reclaimed for hopeful, transformative ends. But to achieve this reversal, the philosopher should be read as encouraging us to interrogate all those ideologies that condition us to accept our fate, and not merely submit to suffering like a placid Christian. We are not supposed to bear our present existence, though we might, given our recourse to ideologies that shelter us from reality. True Nietzschean hope is messianic, not conciliatory.

It's not uncommon to read, in survivors' accounts, a linkage between the victims of Auschwitz and its perpetrators. But when Frankl claims there are "two races of men in this world, but only these two: the 'race' of the decent man and the 'race' of the indecent man," he denies the superlatively systemic nature of that slaughter, and thus the validity of any more organized resistance.[18] In any circumstance, for Frankl, what matters is simply to be a decent fellow. To describe Frankl's work as Holocaust self-help literature is thus not to dismiss it as an outright scam, but to lay the stress on that "self," the egotism of advocating individual self-improvement on the basis of violence which obliterated the individual as such.

Unsurprisingly, Frankl's repackaging of Auschwitz as an admonitory tale to the weak-willed proved especially popular in the US.[19] His primary audience consisted of bourgeois Americans who knew nothing of the horrors of the camp but were thrilled at this apparent evidence that mere positive thinking could enable a man just like themselves to endure such awful trials.

Frankl follows Schopenhauer's famous representation of the human condition as typified by generalized boredom punctuated by episodes of distress, but he goes on to argue that automation means humanity's future will be defined ever more by boredom than distress. He sets out, in spite of all he endured, to solve bourgeois problems for bourgeois clients.[20]

Little wonder, then, that Frankl has inspired another significant appropriative industry. Despite his stated opposition to mere self-actualization, his musings on Auschwitz have steadily become wholly detached from their context, sent percolating into the world of Instagram-friendly motivational quotes.[21] There is a further quiet tragedy in his lifelong mining of his own grim experience to peddle pop-existentialist logotherapy to disaffected suburban salarymen. The Holocaust comes to be treated as a depoliticized rhetorical source, endlessly mined in the service of the liberal, individualist hope industry, conditioning us to accept our fate.

Ka-Tzetnik: Self-Hate, Self-Denial

In his darkest hour, Frankl sometimes found meaning by imagining the lectures he would one day deliver on "the psychology of the concentration camp" as a world-famous public intellectual.[22] The contrast with the man born Yehiel De-Nur but known as Ka-Tzetnik 135633, after relinquishing his birth name in favor of a Yiddish abbreviation based on his concentration camp number, could not be clearer.[23]

Like Frankl, Ka-Tzetnik wrote his own first work of Holocaust literature very shortly after emerging from Auschwitz and its associated camps.[24] (*Salamandra*, sometimes described as the first-ever Holocaust novel, was reportedly completed in under twenty days.) But though Kat-Tzetnik also made a career as a Holocaust writer, his books are unlike Frankl's and the respectable Holocaust canon. Ka-Tzetnik's work is a bloody cavalcade of pulp fiction full of lurid, crafted-to-shock eyewitness accounts of sex, Nazi ultraviolence, and Jewish terror, helplessness, and betrayal.

Yet Ka-Tzetnik does not trivialize the camp's horrors. On the contrary, his life's work bears urgent testament to their reality. As with Frankl, some biographical details vary in the telling, but there's no sense Ka-Tzetnik is trying to burnish his macabre personal credentials for his audience. Rather, he feels every act of violence as though done to himself, through a profound identification with his fellow inmates. This is the best way the author has to make us understand.

And so he is not comforted, as Frankl is, by the thought there may be good men among the guards, and vice versa. On the contrary, he is tormented by the realization an accident of birth might have made him a camp guard.[25] Like Agamben, he recognizes that the guards and inmates are indeed paradoxically linked—not by the fact of their individual moral stance, but on the converse in a gray zone "behind good and evil," wherein individual morality or activity matters not a jot.[26] In Ka-Tzetnik's writing, no quest for meaning can possibly redeem humankind from the awful lesson of the camps. The violence is absolutely particular and particularly absolute. It denies any possibility of its negation through individual heroism or positive thinking.

For Frankl, flashes of optimism in Auschwitz are evidence that the "size of human suffering is absolutely relative," thus freeing us to draw comfort from the lessons he adduces, applying them to our own day-to-day struggles and concerns.[27] Conversely, when called to give testimony at the 1961 trial of Nazi war criminal Adolf Eichmann, Ka-Tzetnik was famously only able to speak briefly before falling into a swoon. He said, "[Ka-Tzetnik] was not a pen name. I do not regard myself as a writer and a composer of literary material. This is a chronicle of the planet of Auschwitz. I was there for about two years. . . . And the inhabitants of this planet had no names, they had no parents nor did they have children. . . . They did not live—nor did they die—according to the laws of this world. They were human skeletons, and their name was the number 'Ka-Tzetnik.'"[28]

Ka-Tzetnik spent his life trying desperately to make us understand what he saw in Auschwitz, to bear personal witness to the attempted eradication of his nation. And yet he knew he could never truly communicate this message, knew his framework, his name, his pen were all too weak to bear the strain. As he cried out just before collapsing, "Auschwitz stands in opposition to our planet Earth," and therefore it cannot be press-ganged into service as trite moral exemplar.[29] In this radical framing, Auschwitz becomes dramatically unlinked from the rest of reality, rather than standing on a continuum with political, human life.

Hannah Arendt scorned Ka-Tzetnik for this dramatic intervention, which she viewed as a performative fraud distracting from the trial's true function.[30] But regardless of whether it was a performance, the writer's sudden silence nonetheless has a powerful meaning. This dramatic moment of speech-as-silence stages many of the debates over testimony, subjective experience, and meaning that have animated Holocaust historiography ever since.[31] At this extreme limit, the Holocaust's inherent incommunicability collides with the continued necessity of expressing its significance.[32]

For this famous moment of collapse doesn't mean Ka-Tzetnik was unconcerned with the question whether any hope, or moral or political message, could be raked from the ashes of the gas chambers. On the contrary, his whole career was a ceaseless struggle to find and express those truths through any means necessary, however violent, surreal, or ugly.

"Wherever there is humankind, there is Auschwitz," Ka-Tzetnik writes, paradoxically.[33] This violence is so awful as to be in itself an alien planet—and yet it is our own world. We cannot escape it. It is with us today.

It's precisely this paradox that unfolds in *Shivitti: A Vision*. Ka-Tzetnik's masterpiece was first published in 1987, over forty years after Auschwitz, and twenty-five years after Eichmann was sentenced to death. It presents a profound personal journey through fear and trembling. It's here that Ka-Tzetnik writes for the first time in the first person and returns for the first time to reassess his decades-old "planet Auschwitz" metaphor. (In the introduction, Ka-Tzetnik recalls being informed that he had neglected to add his name to the book manuscript. In response, he cries: "The name of the author?! Those who went to the crematorium wrote this book!")[34]

The Hebrew title, derived from the heterodox Jewish tradition, signifies a constant reminder of the presence of God—not, necessarily, of salvation, but of his company with us in our suffering.[35] The text combines feverish psychedelic visions from Auschwitz with an account of the author's participation in experimental LSD trials targeted at enabling Holocaust survivors to overcome their survivors' guilt.

Through his hallucinatory, drug-precipitated journey, the author is able to relive his close brush with the gas chambers, crawling among corpses. It's only once he has "given in and joined their pile of the dead—a human being, dying" that he is able to "re-enter [his] body."[36]

In a sense, this is the same journey undergone by all those who survived the hell of the camps, Frankl included. But Ka-Tzetnik's journey is marked by an awful, absolute identification with the walking skeletons of Auschwitz, rather than dismay at their apparent acquiescence. In the terrible, all-encompassing, liberating blur of his acid trips, he melds wholly into them, and they into him. Like the militant Saint Francis of Assisi, he becomes one with the multitude of the damned.

Identifying with the "Muselmann"

These apathetic, wasted, zombie-like hordes of inmates were known in camp slang by the German word for Muslim, "*Muselmann*."[37] The Muselmann is the lowest form of existence in the camp, the broken prisoner who has given up on life to wait mutely for death, unable to understand "the contrasts good or bad, noble or base, intellectual or unintellectual. He was a staggering corpse, a bundle of physical functions in its last convulsions."[38]

The canon of respectable, moderate Auschwitz literature is thus generally united in treating the Muselmann as effectively beyond theorization due to their utter abjection. Many survivors have felt no choice but to exclude the Muselmann from their testimonies and analyses.[39] They are Agamben's ultimate example of bare life, absolutely excluded from political existence.[40]

The Muselmann has therefore further come to represent the stereotype of the weak and defeated Jew, in contradistinction to the "strong" surviving Jews who went on to found Israel. For his part, Frankl uses the Muselmann's maltreatment by fellow prisoners as evidence that inmates and guards can be equally evil and dehumanized, and he also paradoxically condemns the Muselmann for failing to properly resist the camp's violence.[41] It's clear he viewed himself as a strong Jew, a survivor.

In the hands of Israeli nationalist writers, this infamous metaphor has helped burnish the Israeli state's aggressive self-conception as a homeland for Jewish survivors, paving the way for subsequent dehumanizing violence toward the Palestinian "Muselmann." In the years after the Holocaust, Ka-Tzetnik himself contributed to this process, initially holding the lessons of the alien "planet Auschwitz" at arms' length and thus contributing to Israeli state exceptionalism.

But as the years went by, his views were tempered. And toward the end of his life, in *Shivitti*, he remarkably identifies himself as a Muselmann: "Vowing to be their voice, I lived."[42] He thus becomes the spokesperson and embodiment of the camp's most silenced and dehumanized residents, the most depoliticized people on the planet, coming closer than any other writer to expressing the Muselmann's inexpressible experience.[43]

As a lifelong unredeemed psychiatric patient, Ka-Tzetnik is the direct opposite of Dr. Frankl, who believed all people can be restored to bourgeois wellness. As Bloch suggests with typical verve, "In the consciousness of most doctors the goal itself is a stationary one: namely the restoration of the status quo. . . . This is also why doctors often succumbed much more easily to the fascist slogan of Blood and Soil."[44]

Again, there's a sense in which Ka-Tzetnik's profound maladjustment is politically valid—even necessary. To Adorno, the Holocaust proved once and for all that the good, bourgeois life valorized by Frankl was no longer possible, that the "wrong life cannot be lived rightly"—an aphorism that Kurdish political educators constantly apply to life in capitalist modernity.[45] Rather, only a perpetual political sickness is an appropriate response.

And it's clear that Ka-Tzetnik's own struggle to overcome this maladjustment costs him not less than everything. He was never truly free, and yet it's for that reason that his testimony reaches us through the years. As Ka-Tzetnik reminds us, we need not be or feel free, happy, or well to continue the universal work of freedom.

We need not biographically reconstruct the two men's experiences of the Holocaust, nor imply that one did "better" than the other in circumstances where individual choice and activity counted for almost nothing. But Ka-Tzetnik's experience demonstrates that the struggle to overcome absolute hopelessness need not manifest as a cheap individualism, Adorno's "health unto death," or New Age hope for hope's sake alone. His dreadful, unorthodox course of therapy does not lead him to static peace or bourgeois comfort. But he does attain an enduring, defiant, confused sense of simultaneous individual endurance and dissolution into the whole of suffering humanity (and Jewish humanity in particular). A true poet, he was never supposed to be bound by the constraints of legal testament, as he was at the Eichmann trial, or by bourgeois fulfillment, as Frankl preached.

Ka-Tzetnik's journey through the dark does not lead him to a mere qualified optimism, but onward through a profound, determined, lifelong reckoning with hopelessness. He isn't emancipated from his suffering, nor is he justified through a courageous individual quest for meaning. But he is able to pass through the flames of utter meaninglessness and find, when millions have been turned to ash, there is yet "one last spark" that remains alive.[46]

After the pattern of Bloch's socialist Not Yet, we might call this spark the And Yet. It's that stubborn, absurdist residue, that which remains when life is subtracted from life and yet some form of life still remains. It is not hope in a better future or transcendent external meaning, still less in political organization. This journey costs Ka-Tzetnik not less than everything: and yet. There is something left over.

And indeed, the testimonies from surviving Muselmänner with which Agamben closes his account do not sound wholly voided of political meaning. They are obsessed with hunger, yes, with grasping tricks and survival tactics, with securing a crust of bread at any cost.[47] But to the messianic socialist thinker Ernst Bloch, hunger is the ultimate human drive, implying the political turn toward the socialist Not Yet as its necessary corrective. Is this continued, bare hunger drive wholly apolitical—or does it represent the extreme limit of politics?

Auschwitz as Political Lesson

Despite his initial refusal to draw parallels between Auschwitz and the world beyond its gates, by the time of *Shivitti*, Ka-Tzetnik proves able to imagine the political lessons the Holocaust might imply for the new world that has come in its wake. This occurs particularly with reference to nuclear apocalypse—and Israel's own nuclear weapons program.[48]

In *Shivitti*, Ka-Tzetnik meets a rabbi interred in the camp, who proves unable to tell him "the end product manufactured from the souls of one and one half million burned children." Instead, Ka-Tzetnik must find the answer himself: "Nucleus is the concentrate of the souls of one and a half million living, breathing children . . . I lift my eyes to the skies of Auschwitz and I see nucleus on his throne, under his majestic mushroom dome."[49]

Frankl almost casually references Hiroshima in the final line of an afterword subsequently appended to *Meaning*.[50] It takes Ka-Tzetnik decades of challenging thought and grueling LSD therapy to arrive at the same conclusion. Yet when he gets there, his voice is all the more sincere and compelling for the distance it has had to travel. And it's perhaps at this moment, when Ka-Tzetnik proves able to draw a political lesson from planet Auschwitz and perceive the shadow that industrialized death casts on our own century, that he achieves a degree of freedom from the shade.

The writer remained forever plagued by nightmares of Auschwitz, wearing his camp uniform as he wrote, starving himself anew in an isolated shack. And yet he could, finally, put this continued, lifelong suffering to political use. From his initial post-Holocaust position of right-wing Zionism, decades later he came to recognize the links between historic Jewish and contemporary Arab suffering. He lamented the negative role his own description of Auschwitz as an alien planet, uttered in despair decades prior, had played in contributing to Israeli state exceptionalism.[51] Ultimately, Ka-Tzetnik and his wife proved able to fight against the temptation to visit the violence that haunted their dreams on those now weaker than them, and they even worked to bring Jews and Arabs together in a pioneering peace program.[52]

Ka-Tzetnik's whole life incarnated the grueling, punishing task of memorializing Auschwitz in such a way as to both honor its victims and understand its message today. And he viscerally embodies the tragic, imperfect nature of this process. He reportedly died emaciated, haunted by nightmares, and weighing just thirty kilos. As his obituarist suggests, in this respect he never truly left Auschwitz behind.[53] Here we might also recall fellow survivor Jean Améry's despairing call for Auschwitz to be commemorated through a continued Nietzschean resentment and refusal to accept the postwar rehabilitation of the German state. This is a resentment that need not be justified, that neither forgives nor forgets, but simply remains.[54]

"Like drifting smoke, the lesson of Auschwitz will disappear if man does not learn from it," Ka-Tzetnik warned. "If Auschwitz is forgotten, man will not deserve to exist."[55] The implication being, so long as Auschwitz is remembered, human existence still has a chance.

Bloch's Holocaust

Ka-Tzetnik saw himself as a prophet, issuing grim jeremiads written in blood and thunder. A strange sort of prophet, it might be added. He sought to warn us of a catastrophe that has already happened, like Walter Benjamin's angel gazing back into the maelstrom of history. Ka-Tzetnik therefore lights on politics only indirectly, a self-immolating beacon in the wilderness, warning us away from a precipice.

But among Ka-Tzetnik's contemporaries—Jewish and anti-fascist writers, their lives also profoundly scarred by the Holocaust even if they escaped personal injury—are other thinkers who found a more explicitly political response to twentieth-century catastrophe. In different ways, Bloch and his fellow messianic socialists Adorno and Benjamin recognized (or tragically demonstrated) that no realistic, reasonable hope could survive the killing fields of World War II. Only a total, transcendent socialist transformation could liberate us from humankind's proven inhumanity to humanity.

Bloch has far more in common with Ka-Tzetnik than Frankl. He proves capable of motivating revolutionary organization through a messianic and despairing acceptance of catastrophe, rather than rationalizing it away. In the introduction to his *Principle of Hope*, he describes the challenge the Holocaust years presented to those who still believed in a better world: "Once a man traveled far and wide to learn fear. In the time that has just passed, it came easier and closer, the art was mastered in a terrible fashion. But now that the creators of fear have been dealt with, a feeling that suits us better is overdue. It is a question of *learning* hope."[56]

This is his life's work. For Bloch, hope is not something which merely exists, or can be won through individual, bourgeois fulfillment. Rather, he seeks to prove that hope can be intentionally organized, read into history and even the twentieth-century history of the Jewish people, through active psychic and political struggle. While this wasn't quite Bloch's argument, there's a related sense in which twentieth-century history furthers our claim that hope must be actively, intentionally delivered through political self-delusion. The Holocaust alone demonstrates the foolishness of any liberal hope in innate human goodness.

Bloch was no fool, blindly anticipating global socialist utopia in spite of all evidence. In fact, as early as 1924 he issued an eerily prescient warning against underestimating Hitler.[57] And he was also clear-eyed in identifying individualistic capitalist culture as the successor to fascist dehumanization and violent social atomization. Like Ka-Tzetnik, he treats nuclear warfare as a successor to fascism in annihilating all putative progress toward hope and a future Not Yet.[58] There are no easy ways out, no certain socialist redemption. Indeed, later in life Bloch came to critique the USSR-led state-socialist project. All the hope, endeavor, and struggle he sees mystically prefigured in the universe, human culture, and humankind's endless striving may yet point to nothing—only what might have been.

Bloch's transformative concept of hope can be arrived at only through great suffering. For Bloch, this revolutionary ability stands as a great contribution to the world made by a messianic Judaism.[59] His vision contoured by a profoundly Jewish sense of a future homeland as illuminating our continued suffering, not dismissing it or simplistically justifying it, but remaining present with us in the present moment of hardship. This is *Shivitti* again, with its mystic meaning: "I have set the Lord always before me."[60]

The crucial concept of *Heimat* (homeland), a "still unbecome, still-unachieved homeland," recurs from the opening page of Bloch's trilogy until its final word. For Bloch, the "basic theme of philosophy" is quite simply the task of conceiving and finding this notional homeland, offering utopian deliverance precisely due to its radical, yet-to-be, undetermined nature.[61] As we've seen, the contemporary German Left fears the very word "Heimat" as tainted by its Nazi associations. But Bloch refuses this statist concept of Heimat, whether it's bound up in the German, Israeli, or another state. Instead, he concludes the true homeland for the Jewish people and humanity as a whole can be nothing and nowhere save socialist internationalism. "True Genesis is not at the beginning but at the end, and it starts to begin only when society and existence become radical," he claims.[62] He thus follows a similarly difficult path to the Kurdish movement, which seeks to marshal its own lost, un-reclaimed homeland to utopian, universal ends.

Less than ten years after the liberation of Auschwitz, Bloch therefore boldly locates the true Zion not in the nascent Israeli state but in the anti-Zionist struggle itself. For Bloch, "Zionism flows out into socialism, or it does not flow out at all."[63] The bravery of such a position, at such a juncture, is impossible to overstate.

Indeed, there is perhaps no greater example of hope emerging from utter hopelessness than the proud tradition of Jewish solidarity with the Palestinian people, especially when that solidarity is contextualized and charged by Jewish memories of the Holocaust. This solidarity, which we have witnessed worldwide in brave defiance of the Zionist project following the Israeli state's genocidal war on Gaza, is grounded in bitter lessons like those Bloch derives from his experience of twentieth-century catastrophe.

The Jewish anti-Zionist movement heralded by Bloch is not only a testament to hope's ability to emerge from hopelessness. It further demonstrates how hope can point to that hopelessness as its own justification—a logic the anti-Zionist slogan "never again for anyone" makes profoundly clear. The phrase "never again" is oxymoronic—never, apart from the time which has already happened. But that paradox encodes its power, its ability to locate life in death.

This is how Bloch, too, understood the Holocaust. He uses a famous line from Rilke—"beauty is nothing but the beginning of the terrible"— but inverts the phrase, dwelling rather "wherever terror is the beginning of the beautiful instead of its end."[64]

In passages like these, the philosopher finds a way beyond critical accusations of cheap mysticism, or utopianism blind to the horrors of the world. Instead, he traverses a bitter, terrifying dialectic, which brings as its reward not merely distant and untouchable utopia but the transfiguration of our real world, experiences, and suffering.

Chapter 10

Hope After Death

When peoples face genocidal state violence, moments of solidarity and rebellion will always occur. These moments can even become charged by a messianic sense that absolute suffering precludes any political response short of utopia. At the same time, it's often very hard to imagine or perceive any such absurdist response. Surveying the ruins of the twentieth century or the Middle East's contemporary battlefields, we might well feel we have more in common with Ka-Tzetnik than with Bloch.

For example, the local communes that are the building blocks of Rojava's direct-democratic system are not normally hives of political engagement. But when Turkey's 2019 invasion loomed, attendance was more universal than ever. One felt the palpable urgency, the defiant pride. Old women brandished weapons in packed meeting halls in poor neighborhoods and proudly dared the Turkish Armed Forces to eradicate them, as they surely could have. Comrades raced throughout Rojava, electrified by nervous energy, frantically organizing on a dozen fronts at once. Knowing their various efforts could never prove sufficient to hold back the coming storm, they nonetheless felt bound together in a spirit of defiant comradeship the enemy could never eradicate, could never even really understand.

Yet neither in Syria, nor in the brave, desperate, doomed-to-fail Jewish partisan resistance in the camps and ghettoes, nor in many other twentieth- and twenty-first century conflicts has this spirit of resistance in extremis proven capable of overcoming state might. Hard times will sometimes produce instances of neighborly solidarity, or what has been

231

called "crisis socialism." And existential threats can certainly furnish benefits to a vanguard movement, rejuvenating and motivating a revolutionary people's war.

But in extremis, humans are just as likely to succumb to corruption, self-preservation, or suicide. Civilians flee as best they can, the frontlines eventually buckle under the onslaught, hunger and torture break defiant spirits. As Holocaust survivors have testified, the victims of state violence can naturally find themselves consumed by a wholly negative resentment, which destroys hope without achieving its absurd renewal.[1] If we follow Frankl and only hope in the extent to which we can pick out scattered individual acts of heroism against the dark backdrop of Auschwitz or another human catastrophe, we likely doom ourselves to despair.

In contrast, resistance implies an intractable, pig-headed refusal to give in, pushing back rather than yielding, or indeed breaking through to triumph. Resistance does not deny or justify present suffering but wrestles with it, dwells with it: *Shivitti*. This bitter lesson is present even in Frankl's tragic optimism, while it resides at the very heart of Ka-Tzetnik's dark vision, that stubborn, irreconcilable remnant.

Resistance is not revolt, still less victory. It's closer to what the Palestinians call *sumud*, their steadfast endurance and refusal to yield before state violence. Resistance is ugly, dogged, unreasonable, demanding a pointless commitment we can demand of no one save ourselves, expect of no one save our comrades.

Yet as the Kurdish movement knows, there is a curious alliance between this seemingly wild, irrational resistance and strategic, rational organization. Disciplined organization enables us to resist, trusting in our comrades' ability to endure with us what we cannot endure alone. And in turn, the irrational socialist leap of faith prepares us for the sacrifices that organizing requires. Perhaps, then, our own political culture could do with rather less reason and more organization.

Organizing in a Pandemic

We can usefully explore this relationship between irrational resistance and strategic organization with reference to the Western Left's generally muted, apolitical response to the coronavirus crisis. This latter-day tragedy was conversely marked by chaotic political individualism and its necessary corollary—political despair.

There were brave early efforts at grassroots, community-level organization—a General Electric walkout where workers demanded the right to manufacture ventilators, a fast food restaurant occupied to redistribute food, scattered rent strikes. All point to directions that leftist resistance, or rather the provision of a left alternative, could have taken. There were demands to be made over emergency relief payments, protection for the working class laboring unseen throughout the pandemic, and globally unequal vaccine distribution.[2]

But these rapidly faded away as the state admonished us to stay home, leaving many convinced the sole contribution we could make was to hide in our bedrooms until it was all over. A window of opportunity closed. And indeed, it would have been foolhardy and selfish to defy government orders on an individual basis, absent an organized alternative. Yet a truly organized mass movement could have proven able to offer material support to those who suffered most in the pandemic. In turn, this organized alternative would have fostered a spirit of unreasonable, irrational resistance, of comradeship and compassion.

In such a crisis, no one should seriously dispute the need for social measures aimed at combating the virus's deadly spread, such as quarantine, or top-down, government-led management. But it is nonetheless possible to imagine a Left with the courage and organizational depth to play a vital additional role, to step up where the state failed. Could we have drawn on socialist traditions or an organized present to manage more? To save some of those who died of loneliness? To help workers forced to keep laboring in contaminated warehouses to demand their fundamental rights? And ultimately to force systemic change in response to a self-evidently generational crisis?

The pandemic laid bare the nervous system of contemporary capitalism. It made it easy to identify its pressure points, the clusters of clearly indispensable workers still fundamental to society's operation. But, scattered and divided, we lost the opportunity to exert that crucial pressure.

At some point, most of us made small decisions that deviated from public health orders, knowing that there are values worth considering beyond the R number and recognizing the need to cheer up our own grandmothers or give our struggling neighbor a much-needed break. This wasn't wrong, but how much better it would have been to make those decisions together, as a movement? We could have explored tactics perhaps unjustifiable on the basis of day-to-day statistics but nonetheless ethically right. We could have collectively decided to accept a measure of personal or collective risk, as part of a broader alternative that would justify our personal sacrifice.

Ultimately, therefore, we could have challenged the profoundly ideological claim that average life expectancy is the only possible metric of a life well lived. We might have fallen sick ourselves, while minimizing risks to others, as monks and nuns in the militant Francis of Assisi mold risked their lives tending to lepers, the diseased and unloved for many centuries, knowing there are forms of solidarity that cannot be quantified.

It's not too late for these lessons to be learned. But by the time the next pandemic, financial catastrophe, or climate disaster bursts upon us, we must be ready. Perhaps there's another paradox here. Only existential crisis can push us to the desperate hope without hope needed to underpin committed organization, but by the time that crisis arrives it's already too late for the prior organization that is required to mount a response. If the Kurdish movement's example can help us prepare for a coming revolutionary crisis, perhaps the tragedies of the Arab Spring, the global wave of missing revolutions, and the Left's dereliction of duty during the pandemic can help us imagine how to react as best we can when a potentially revolutionary crisis thrusts itself on a scattered, unprepared, and disorganized Left.

Living with Death

Our revolutionary duties continue long after the revolutionary crisis has passed. Comrades in Rojava often felt prepared for martyrdom and the passage into revolutionary history that would ensue. When the opportunity arose to join a humanitarian convoy into a city almost totally besieged by Turkey, both Kurdish and internationalist comrades argued passionately for the opportunity to participate. Who would want to remain safe and outside?

But for many of these comrades, it proved harder yet to stay alive; to recognize that the long-anticipated airstrike did not in fact have their name on it; to remain motivated through those endless, dreary months after the war when fresh invasion was always threatened but never arrived; or, for the internationalists, to travel back to their own countries, where absolute crisis and absolute redemption seemed even farther away.

For you cannot live in the state of emergency all the time. And conversely, the hardest days were those when the war faded away, when danger seemed distant and previously tight-knit groups of comrades fell back into infighting or depression. I've met veteran comrades who sleep peacefully through barrages yet wake suddenly in the night when there is no shelling, finding the world eerily calm.

This is one reason for the Kurdish movement's political focus on its martyrs. The martyrs serve to bring past crisis into day-to-day civilian life. They make suffering unavoidable, ever-present, animating comrades as though their own lives were already on the line. When individuals join the Kurdish movement and leave their name behind, they assume a martyr's name as a nom de guerre, instigating their struggle for a free life by assuming the mantle of those who never lived to see a free Kurdistan.

In the same spirit, we can seek to restore an urgent sense of crisis to the heart of our own political culture. A sensitive yet profound understanding of doom and catastrophe can productively lead us beyond pessimism or reformism. In particular, the rapidly approaching climate catastrophe is furnishing many of our comrades and movements with just such a sensibility.

This certainly doesn't mean we all need to suffer violence in order to prove our revolutionary worth, or to gain the ability to conceive of a better alternative. That would be an ugly insult to those who have suffered and died. It would delegitimize many ordinary contributions, made by simple people far from the front lines of struggle.

If we seek out suffering or political violence for its own sake, we run the risk of adventurism or voyeurism, and in extreme cases we can even risk becoming anarcho-tourists or conflict tourists. There were some in Rojava, seeking out death and hardship for the thrill of it, rather than accepting these risks as part of a broader internationalist duty.

Similarly, internationalist volunteers (or committed Kurdish revolutionaries) might find cause for absurdist hope in the Kurds' noble resistance, or in their personal experiences of the revolution. But many ordinary Syrians never asked to be on the frontlines of Rojava's existential war, and many would give everything for the chance at a new life in the "hopeless," "individualistic" West. Any personal spirit of justification revolutionaries might feel does not imply ordinary locals' suffering was a price worth paying. On the contrary, the lessons learned from suffering are useful only insofar as they renew political commitment aimed at alleviating that suffering.

In general, we privileged Western comrades should bear in mind that our crisis is never personal but always collective and global. Doomer posturing over the supposedly imminent collapse of our own still-hegemonic capitalist states as a result of runaway climate change can easily become an insult to those on the real front lines of climate catastrophe. Conversely, an understanding of our global struggles as disparate yet linked can help those of us in the West to feel a motivating sense of incipient catastrophe while nonetheless remaining alert to our relative security.

A renewed internationalist sensibility can contribute here. As postcolonial scholars and activists observed long ago, the admonition "there are children starving in Africa" essentializes, Orientalizes, and obscures the structural causes of malnutrition in Africa. In themselves, these critiques are important and logically sound. But the well-meaning criticism of the "starving children in Africa" truism has become a liberal truism in turn. These valid criticisms often serve to exculpate Westerners from caring about Africans at all, when they should impel Westerners toward more thoughtful, structural, or transformative forms of solidarity. Western activists all too happily seize on the opportunity to retreat into individuality and insularity, justifying inactivity as activity, just as we did during the coronavirus crisis. We either hold international struggles at an aestheticized, fetishized distance or simply ignore them altogether. The "think global, act local" rhetoric becomes an excuse to avoid finding ways to stand in meaningful solidarity with people and movements in Africa and throughout the Global South.

It's most often activists based in the West who urge against sharing disturbing images of conflict and famine in Syria, Gaza, and elsewhere.

These admonitions may partially stem from reasonable doubts over the political function served by an endless stream of social media images but also partially from less noble desires to preserve our own equanimity by ignoring the slaughter, frequently citing mental health concerns. As anyone who uses WhatsApp to stay in contact with activists, friends, or comrades on the ground in these sites of global conflict will know, the stream of ghastly images never stops. Even if it's distasteful to us, even if these images don't achieve their perhaps intended effect of influencing Western policy, they are vital because they keep us from looking away. White guilt isn't enough—but that doesn't mean we shouldn't feel bad.

When Turkey used banned phosphorous munitions against Kurdish civilians, the Kurdish movement's media activists rapidly sought to broadcast images of a shrieking, maimed child as widely as possible.[3] They were not only seeking institutional attention but locking eyes with the rest of us in the West, challenging us to turn our shock, horror, and revulsion to political use. These activists do not have the luxury of squeamishness or of a social media detox. They know it's worth being reminded of horror, even if we can do nothing to change it.

Like a nun kissing a leper's sores, we sometimes have a responsibility beyond reason. We're told such images desensitize us to violence; perhaps. But is that the fault of the real victims of the depicted violence? Or is it *our* fault, a fault born of our knowledge we can do nothing to help these victims and which we then seek to cover up by blaming our desensitization on social media?

We don't need to pointlessly defy lockdowns or ogle images of starving children every time we order take-out. But we do need to find ways to bear witness to suffering we cannot change, to remain angry at our own comfort, bitter at our own survival, accepting the ugly and uncomfortable as a fundamental motivating factor in our own struggle.

The Kurdish movement knows full well that triumph is inextricable from agony, despair from hope, that the path to a free life often leads to nothing but martyrdom. As in their parables of prison resistance, salvaging hope from dungeons marred by brutal sexual violence and torture, Kurdish militants have found ways to reckon with the darkest hours their movement has faced.

Alongside the mothers of the martyrs, the war-wounded therefore always lead political demonstrations in Rojava, their maimed limbs and DIY prosthetics displayed as proudly as the rainbow of political flags overhead. The Kurdish movement refers to these walking wounded and disabled comrades as its "living martyrs." They are an incarnate reminder of all that is visceral, catastrophic, and brutal about the movement's struggle.[4] Nothing less than victory can begin to atone for such losses. And even then, we should not consider their suffering automatically, tritely justified. On the contrary, the living martyrs embody the need to remain sick, angry, and dissatisfied, permanently striving toward a revolutionary goal.

Martyrdom: Making Sense of Suicide

Diverse political traditions suggest alternative productive routes to center despair in the pursuit of reform or revolution—AIDS activism, Black nihilism, Fanon's concept of liberatory anti-colonialist violence, the Kurdish movement's veneration of its secular martyrs. Following their example, we can explore ways to acknowledge not only the catastrophes of history but also our personal hardships and communal losses.

As we saw above, activists throughout the political Left are prone to rising rates of depression. At its extreme this tendency can result in suicide, as in the tragic case of Rojava's returning internationalists. (The US's Black Lives Matter and climate movements report similar waves of activist suicides.) We must therefore seek ways to continue onward, despite and through the pain of these losses. This urgent revolutionary duty forms part of what Öcalan broadly defines as "self-defense" (*xweparastin*), an essential right and duty that means we must find ways to fight back against social atomization and suicidal defeatism.

All deaths are political, suicides more so, those committed in the shadow of political violence most of all. As you might expect, Frankl strongly opposed suicide on the basis of his tragic optimism—since "whoever has a why can endure every how." But he also bored holes in the skulls of Jews who had attempted suicide after being seized by the Gestapo, injecting their central nervous system with amphetamines and bringing them artificially back to life for a few dismal hours before they inevitably succumbed—creating a terrible incarnation of Agamben's bare, purely biological life.[5] Again, there is an awful depoliticization here, a refusal to acknowledge that these deaths could register a desperate form of protest against overwhelming Nazi might. Yet as Frankl's biographer notes, suicide as protest has a long pedigree in Jewish history.[6]

The rabbi who speaks to Ka-Tzetnik in Auschwitz warns it would be wrong to resist the camp guards, since resistance would be effective suicide, which is a sin.[7] In different ways, both Frankl's grim attempts to play God and the rabbi's breathtakingly passive stance deny the possibility of death playing a part in resistance.

As the parable of "Death in Tehran" suggests, Frankl wanted us to choose to meet death with our heads held high, yet he stripped that right away from his suicidal subjects. More broadly, none of us are completely free to meet death as we see fit. Whether under the pressure of religious doctrine, economic responsibility, or military occupation, there are many factors prohibiting us from meeting our end as we might choose. But political organization helps us to push back, to prevent that final decision from being made for us.

In contradistinction to squeamish Western culture, which confines death to individual, annual, or funereal rituals of commemoration, life in Rojava is necessarily saturated with death. Each political meeting starts with a minute's silence; photos of the martyrs are as omnipresent as advertisements in the capitalist West; every comrade, commune, and institution bears the name of one of the dead. Internationalist comrades, including those who traveled to Rojava to seek closure and understanding after one of their own friends was killed in a Turkish airstrike, have described the new perspectives on death that they found in the revolutionary context. Mass, formal expressions of grief that at first appeared stiff or morbid were gradually understood to "mean that the pain and sense of loss gets distributed across thousands—even millions—of people, and so does the responsibility to continue the work that our loved ones died for."[8]

Amid these celebrations of sacrifice, it's unsurprising to find many young Kurds are all too ready to throw themselves in front of a bullet. As internationalist comrades serving in frontline medical units have lamented, even carrying basic medical supplies has long been unfashionable among the revolutionary vanguard. On this most sensitive point, the

Kurdish movement's theory and practice are not always entirely clear or consistent, perhaps understandably. These deaths don't entirely fit within the Kurdish movement's secular analysis. Rather, they come at a point of desperation, perhaps serving as a way for the bare body to reclaim its agency from the totalitarian state but also suggesting the dangers inherent to such a radical culture of sacrifice.

In theory at least, as we've seen, the Kurdish movement believes true martyrdom must come unlooked for. To Bloch, the socialist martyr achieves a solidarity which negates the emptiness of death, "precisely because [they do] not want to be a martyr at all."[9] If a revolutionary death is a blessing, it can only ever be bestowed and not taken. Likewise, the secular Kurdish militant who sacrifices their life knows they will not attain Islamic paradise, rather placing their hopes only in the evanescent consolation of elevation to the Kurds' pantheon of martyrs. After Öcalan was captured and scores of Kurds self-immolated in protest, his political movement was repeatedly forced to warn against the practice. These foolhardy actions might be understandable, born out of deep grief. But if so, they cannot ultimately prove transformative.

At the same time, the Kurdish movement celebrates the martyrdom of comrades who self-immolated in Diyarbakir prison or flung themselves at advancing tanks, venerating them as icons of resistance in extremis. Particularly in the Kurdish women's movement, the act of self-sacrifice is reinterpreted as a moment of "resurrection," with individual suicide missions valorized as moments of restoration.

What are we to make of these acts? As a beautiful, sad poem memorializing a famous self-immolation in protest against the Vietnam War suggests, political suicides offer "nothing to quote, nothing to put in quotes."[10] Mohamed Bouazizi, the Tunisian street seller whose self-immolation sparked the 2011 Arab Spring protests, left no note to explain his act. Sometimes, the news reports suggest, these victims do not cry aloud at all. Their act itself is a final shriek of protest when all else is lost. It does not seek glory or a cheap transfer to paradise. Lacking all but the most elementary political meaning, it stands only for itself.

Again, we might carefully critique aspects of the Kurdish movement's relationship to death and martyrdom. It's clear that a Middle Eastern political culture that makes a virtue of death and loss, coupled with a strong revolutionary culture of comradeship superseding the individual self, often does better than our case by case efforts to rescue comrades from depression or suicide. Rojava has many "houses of the wounded," where the living martyrs recuperate, study, and learn new skills. Visiting these inspiring sites of revolutionary self-defense and care, it's impossible not to be moved by the dogged hope against hope that this political culture can inspire, undergirded by broader Kurdish and Islamic cultures of holistic care and mutual responsibility.

Still, comrades in Rojava of course suffer bitter despair and depression. Sometimes, they kill themselves. And in line with both political and Islamic taboos on suicide, these incidents are often brushed under the carpet, with the actual cause of death left undisclosed. A radical conception of the militant personality, and the subsequent prioritization of comradely relationships over individual self-worth, can come at the cost of a more sympathetic, holistic understanding that treats all deaths and all suicides as politicized. The Kurdish movement calls upon its followers to live, to find ways to survive without succumbing to the temptation of self-sacrifice. This responsibility to survive can prove a heavy mantle to bear.

Some internationalist comrades in Rojava have quietly, passionately suggested that even those who committed suicide could properly be considered martyrs. By remembering as martyrs some prominent figures who die young of curable diseases untreatable in the Syrian context or perhaps precipitated by its stresses, the movement has already demonstrated its potential openness to a more holistic approach.

In the same spirit, we ourselves can learn from the Kurdish movement's concept of death by paying more respect to our own martyrs, from the distant and not-so-distant past of our own national liberation, socialist, queer, and ecological struggles. The US has already witnessed the first instances of political self-immolation in response to the climate crisis, with David Buckel (2018) and Wynn Alan Bruce (2022) choosing a form of protest whose imagery has particular relevance to runaway global warming. As I write these words, US soldier Aaron Bushnell has just set himself alight in front of the Israeli embassy in Washington in protest at the war on Gaza.[11] They join Bouazizi, whose despairing, personal act ultimately sparked near-global convulsions. They join the select and desperate ranks of Kurdish militants, monks, refugees, and activists who have put themselves to the torch in a final, silent shriek of protest—indefeasible because it is beyond reason, just like Bloch's bizarre utopian socialism.[12]

Beyond these extreme examples, we all have our own fallen friends and comrades to commemorate. We might think also of the millions of communists, anarchists, and anti-colonial militants slaughtered throughout the twentieth century; of those lost to the opioid epidemic, drowned crossing the Mediterranean, starved in a climate crisis drought, worked to death in a sweatshop; and ultimately everyone who has died too soon, too painfully, or too alone as a result of our extractive capitalist culture.

Enzo Traverso, a theorist of contemporary left melancholy, calls for a left culture that can overcome our self-image as the victims of twentieth-century history. He suggests we rather think of ourselves as a once triumphant but currently vanquished Left, in an alternative self-conception more capable of politicizing and redirecting our melancholy.[13] A renewed, organized martyr culture could directly assist our diverse left movements in answering this call. Rojava's ever-present martyrs are a token of that curious metamorphosis through which death can inspire its opposite. There are those who love life so much they're willing to die for it—and those who love the dead so much they are willing to keep on living.

Out of the Flames

This brings us back to the Holocaust. Agamben suggests the total depoliticization of life in Auschwitz means the dead cannot be counted as martyrs but instead only as mere victims.[14] This is why he uses the Hebrew word "*Shoah*" instead of "Holocaust." The second, more familiar term originally meant "sacrifice by fire" and is refused by Agamben as cheaply implying that we can derive some redemptive message from the slaughter.[15]

But to the Kurdish movement, the martyr concept serves to reanimate their own bare existence, with Kurdish lives liquidated in their own state of exception granted a defiantly repoliticized significance. The term "Holocaust" thus offers a similar potential repoliticization. It need not simplistically justify these deaths but can rather place their unjustifiability in the service of an anti-fascist politics.

Even the Muselmann's bare existence has been seen to encode a perverse form of resistance, surviving each day "invulnerable to hope and therefore to hurt."[16] This does not imply any grand or humanistic redemption, enabling us to consider the Muselmann as happy as Sisyphus. Rather, the grim example of the Muselmann implies a form of hope that does not justify our suffering and does not save us from ourselves. It simply exists, amid the worst of human violence. Broken people may only keep shambling on, unable to think, unable to resist. But yet they keep shambling. This is one meaning of *Shivitti* implied by Ka-Tzetnik: the stubborn residue present in the shell of humanity, enduring even at the extreme limit of dehumanization.

Perhaps Camus and Bloch are right that suicide implies a perverse hope for a better world. But by the same token, the ability of even suicidal people to keep on living day by day implies an innately human ability to hope without rational hope of deliverance. In the shadow of the Holocaust's violence, can we have the courage to follow Ka-Tzetnik, Bloch, and the messianic socialists and strain to identify some desperate hope shambling onward out of that catastrophe?

Any hope we can excavate from the mire may well take the political form of mere survival—of bare life enduring, despite everything. The attempted repoliticization of bare life offers us a way to understand the broader reality of our continued political organization in the globalized state of exception. In one sense, we are all cannon fodder, waiting for the death and defeat we know to be inevitable. And yet we continue, perhaps without quite being able to explain why, neither expecting deliverance nor accepting suicide.

The great Holocaust movie *Son of Saul* seeks to humanize and explore the reality of a group even more vilified in post-Holocaust historiography than the Muselmann—the *Sonderkommando* Jewish prisoner work units charged with operating the ovens. The Sonderkommandos were long seen as complicit in mass murder, though as the film powerfully demonstrates, these Jews were also victims of the Nazis.

The Sonderkommando protagonist shambles on. It's virtually all we see in the film, Saul staggering from site to site, doing what he must to survive, necessarily complicit in awful violence for which he cannot be blamed, engaging in doomed-to-fail resistance, seeking to inter the body of one young victim among all the victims, simply because he must. And at the end, when Saul has done all he can, which amounts practically to no real blow against the Nazi machine, when he knows he is captured, defeated, and about to die, he allows himself one tiny, solitary smile.

Surely, it does not mark a simple redemption, a sense that all this has been made worthwhile. Surely it is marked by willful self-delusion. Surely, Saul smiles to welcome death. And yet—the smile is there.

Chapter 11

Hope in the Climate Apocalypse

Auschwitz is an alien planet, and yet it is our own. Thinking through this paradox means following Ka-Tzetnik, Bloch, and Adorno to grapple with the implications of planet Auschwitz for a post-Holocaust world. There's a striking parallel between the bold, despairing, messianic theorists who, after World War II, argued for renewed socialist struggle toward an evanescent Not Yet and those theorists who have traveled through despair in the face of seemingly runaway climate change to arrive at an equally unexpected, absurdist hope in a future beyond the flames.

We've explored the possibility for hope *after* the Holocaust, following Jewish thinkers who have sought to articulate political responses to that catastrophe. But in the coming crisis, our responsibility is active and personal. Rather than waiting to see what forms of hope prove possible after the world has burned, we must find hope *in* and *through* the climate apocalypse, as we live it unevenly but together.

The Holocaust and Climate Crisis: The State Against the People

Well-meaning ecological activists have often blundered into ill-thought-out comparisons between the Holocaust and climate catastrophe. From former UK archbishop Justin Welby's description of the climate crisis as a genocide on an "infinitely greater scale" through to Extinction Rebellion guru Roger Hallam, who thoughtlessly dismissed the Holocaust as "just another fuckery" among multiple catastrophic violent events driven by human indifference, the supreme example of humankind's inhumanity has often proven an irresistible comparison.[1]

We must seriously consider the entanglement of twentieth-century fascist violence targeting racialized outsiders with contemporary crises, and an incipient wave of state violence against outsider groups, catalyzed by climate catastrophe. By carefully identifying particular modes of state violence as contextualizing both crises, we can avoid any crass, merely rhetorical comparison. Academic Mark Levene, who has studied the complex relationship between these two catastrophes, argues that Hallam's error lies in deploying the Holocaust as mere statistical reference point. For one, prior mass killings like the Belgian colonization of the Congo share more obvious similarities with the coming crisis. Both are specifically defined by resource extraction and the pursuit of material wealth at the cost of human and ecological destruction.

But there are also profound links between the sovereign political order that enabled the Holocaust, the post-WWII consensus which preferred to exceptionalize Nazism while rehabilitating capitalist Germany into the global economy, and the contemporary order set to determine who lives and who dies in the climate crisis. Now, as in the years prior to WWII, statist nationalism violently denies free movement to racialized minorities scapegoated for national crisis.[2] And then as now, this isn't limited to the ugly, in-your-face violence of paranoid, genocidal states and fringe nationalist parties. Rather, self-styled liberal democracies deny shelter to those fleeing certain death, becoming complicit in the production of bare life by pulling up the drawbridge in front of refugees— whether those fleeing Nazi Germany, Assad's Syria, or the coming tidal bore of unnatural climate disasters."[3]

Ever since the Holocaust, liberal elites have smugly repeated the "never again" catchphrase, keeping the horrors of fascist violence safely compartmentalized on Holocaust Awareness Day.[4] Yet these same elites are knowingly complicit in recurrent violence against the stateless, from the population exchanges that marked the immediate post-WWII years through the twenty-first century "refugee crisis" to the first shockwaves of climate displacement. In their hands, the Holocaust has become a "civil religion," deployed to quiet dissent and project the image of a "supranational community built on ethical values."[5] The Holocaust's instrumentalization in justification of Israel's unjustifiable war on Gaza is only the most recent example.

All three crises are interlinked—the Holocaust, wars in the Middle East from 2011 until today (and the consequent "refugee crisis"), and incipient climate catastrophe. They are crises of statelessness, the political production of statelessness, and the denial of humanity to those placed outside state protection. Thus the determined repoliticization of supposedly bare and stateless life must be placed at the heart of our political agenda. Rojava's experience of bitter resource competition, dispossession, and determinedly repoliticized statelessness can provide some direction. As the Kurdish movement has attempted, organized political power must be restored to those excluded from liberal state democracy and targeted by fascist violence.

Though the number of global refugees has doubled in a decade, "refugee" remains a diffuse, diverse political category, and the deadly, steady rise in global temperatures remains slow and hard to organize against. But it will not always be so. The still-shadowy figure of the climate migrant is perhaps our century's true political subject, the organizational fulcrum of the climate revolution that will one day convulse the earth, for better or worse. Some day we will see populist leaders and militant organizations arise with the express goal of channeling the political will of this broad, transnational, and necessarily political class. Is it here that we find our sought-for metanarrative, capable of reanimating a truly universal politics fit for the twenty-first century?

Beyond Climate Despair

These grave political and organizational questions are daunting in their own right. And they're further linked to a more nebulous, more fundamental challenge. In the eerie shadow of a global catastrophe yet to take form, how can we continue to hope? This chapter picks up where Levene ends, following his call for an "alternative current" of post-Holocaust thought and action on the climate crisis, "prophetic, active and purposeful."[6]

Levene seeks new prophets capable of articulating the continuum of our present catastrophe with historic choices made by political elites. In other words, he calls for a new and revolutionary millenarianism, adapted to the twenty-first century. Anti-colonial prophets like Öcalan have long pointed to genocidal state violence as evidence of imminent, divinely mandated, revolutionary transformation. In much the same way, the new climate prophets must use the civilizational threat we face to animate a revolutionary anti-statist politics, capable of organizing resistance along eschatological lines.

In the absence of any such politics, in theory or practice, global fatalism is deepening. This trend is called "climate doom."[7] As the knee-jerk Holocaust comparisons begin to suggest, ecological thought has long been marred by a misanthropic streak tending to ethno-nationalism, even the belief that part or all of humankind must be eradicated to restore Earth's "natural" balance. To the doomer theoreticians, no human or political activity can suffice to save us from the coming catastrophe. Climate change "threatens to render all human projects irrelevant," turning all of us into effective climate change denialists, as we merrily beetle away on the brink of destruction.[8]

Nor is this bleak attitude confined to a radical fringe. As we've seen, opinion polls indicate people worldwide are refusing the liberal, post-1989 claim that the world is inexorably getting better. This turn is partially driven by the climate crisis. Theorists write variously of climate anxiety, climate grief, or "solastalgia"—that is, a bitter homesickness for a world vanishing before our eyes. This disease takes various forms across various cultures and communities.[9] We have already witnessed the first climate suicides.

The point is not necessarily that the science irrevocably proves we're all doomed. But many millions of people worldwide *feel* as though we're doomed, including but not limited to activists on the front lines of global ecological struggles. At its extreme, this attitude can feed into a Western "lifeboat" ethics, with climate doomers promoting a national politics of retreat, which would inevitably leave the Global South to suffer the ravages of displacement and mass death.[10]

But again, there's a curious paradox here. Generations increasingly convinced of their powerlessness in the face of runaway climate change are nonetheless taking an increasingly radical turn in response to that crisis. And on closer inspection, these grim doomer ecological theories have an uncanny habit of transfiguring into their opposite, arriving at the absurd uplands of hope without hope.

Sustainability professor Jem Bendell's 2018 *Deep Adaptation*, an effective manifesto for climate despair, is paradigmatic in this respect. In the most-downloaded climate science paper of all time, Bendell warns that societal collapse is now all but inevitable. He therefore advises we relinquish the idea climate catastrophe can be prevented, in favor of assessing how to conserve some vestiges of our society.[11]

Public figures in the climate community rapidly castigated *Deep Adaptation* as pseudoscientific, alarmist doom-mongering.[12] Though he ultimately dismisses the concern, Bendell himself is alert to the risk of climate alarmism inspiring panic, citing several sources where "the argument made is that to discuss . . . societal collapse due to climate change is irresponsible because it might trigger hopelessness among the general public."[13] Dismissing these concerns, Bendell conversely believes a radical reassessment of our political and social approach to climate change is necessary to free us from despair and begin the process of "deep" social readjustment to climate catastrophe.

On this point, at least, the response to *Deep Adaptation* is proving Bendell right. Extinction Rebellion (XR) is only the most prominent global activist group taking inspiration from Bendell's text, treating his prognosis of doom as a call to arms. Bendell himself has quit academia and relocated to Indonesia, where he's working to establish a farm capable of weathering the impending apocalypse.[14]

We might disagree with either set of tactics in their particulars. Though they deploy some interesting organizational approaches that have encouraged an impressive degree of individual commitment among middle-class Westerners, XR and Just Stop Oil draw on the familiar horizontalist playbook of scattergun disruption of public and cultural events, aimed at winning the attention of the institutional Western media. Once again, it's no substitute for years-long, grassroots mobilization in working-class and migrant communities on the front lines of climate crisis, steadily creating the necessary support and conditions to realize recent calls for more effective strategies including sabotage targeting crucial oil infrastructure and nodes of capitalist exchange.[15] Relatedly, therefore, we might also look for a militant climate politics beyond the survivalist regenerative farming Bendell is attempting in Indonesia.

But the point here is a more general one: climate despair is clearly not a death knell for active or radical political commitment. As Bendell's manifesto claims, it's the liberal reformists who are unable to conceive of the deep adaptations to our social fabric that will be needed if we're to survive. It's not the despairing revolutionaries but these optimistic reformists who are insipid, passive, readily accepting of their fate. If our political pessimism should warn us away from mere reform, by the same token then, only a sense of climate change as apocalypse can inspire truly radical ecological revolution.

Other theorists go further yet along this path, identifying unexpected social, psychological, even spiritual benefits to accepting that our social order faces irrevocable collapse. Working in conversation with Bendell's perspective, the late Michael Dowd sought to invigorate what he called a post-doom political movement, reckoning with and traveling beyond despair. By "post-doom" he means:

> 1. What opens up when we remember who we are and how we got here, accept the inevitable, honor our grief, and prioritize what is pro-future and soul-nourishing.
> 2. A fierce and fearless reverence for life and expansive gratitude—even in the midst of abrupt climate mayhem and the runaway collapse of societal harmony, the health of the biosphere, and business as usual.
> 3. Living meaningfully, compassionately, and courageously, no matter what.[16]

Again, these specific manifesto points do not imply an organized, socialist, or militant response to the coming global transformation. What's significant here is rather is the absurdly freeing quality of despair. The necessary element of messianic mysticism is present here, as it long has been in the climate movement, equipping us to confront apocalypse.

As Dowd's quasi-spiritual language suggests, there's a risk that treating climate collapse as inevitable can lead us to reconcile with catastrophe, retreating into individualistic spiritualism or a hyperlocal communitarianism rather than pursuing a more serious political program aimed at revolutionizing and thus saving human society. He preaches inner peace, not the social dissensus that must characterize true resistance.

Indigenous Voices Against Climate "Genocide"

Self-proclaimed doomer communities certainly skew white and middle-class. Likewise, it's easier to derive comforting spiritual meaning from climate despair from the perspective of a comfortable, sheltered Western vantage point.

But grim prognoses over climate catastrophe are not the preserve of these fringe communities alone. Rather, urgent proclamations of climate doom emerge from Indigenous groups on the frontline of catastrophe. Under Jair Bolsonaro's Right-populist rule, the Articulation of Indigenous Peoples from Brazil (APIB) vocally linked unfettered logging and resource exploitation in the Amazon with the genocide their peoples have suffered.[17] Likewise, a "Red New Deal" penned by Native American activists is located squarely to the left of the mooted Green New Deal, linking their historical genocide to present-day climate apocalypse in order to animate a material and community-based politics.[18] These perspectives suggest paths forward to more productive radical engagements with climate catastrophe. Rather than collapsing in self-pity or self-flagellation, we can learn from communities with firsthand knowledge of what it means to endure the effective end of the world.

In his recent manifesto *How to Blow Up a Pipeline,* Andreas Malm argues the global climate movement must soon reckon with its own left-melancholic attachment to the tried-and-failed arsenal of marches, blockades, climate camps, demands presented to state institutions, and nonviolent resistance, turning instead to (pipeline) sabotage. As Malm notes, this highly effective tactic has already been deployed in diverse circumstances by the PKK, Yemen's Houthis, and the Palestinians' Popular Front for the Liberation of Palestine (PFLP), among others.[19] Again, care must be taken to avoid a voyeuristic fetishization of postcolonial violence, naively treating these acts as a blueprint for Western activists to follow.

Rather than the West's domestic climate movements copying tactics from these experienced militants any time soon, we might particularly expect to see those Indigenous communities and potential climate refugees on the frontlines of global warming deploying drones to strike at oil infrastructure, in a Fanonian response to neo-imperialist climate violence.

Admittedly, these diverse, scattered Indigenous perspectives and acts of resistance currently seem unlikely to unite in an organized response capable of turning the tide against expansionist capitalist logic. Indigenous perspectives more often suggest ways to survive genocide and endure societal collapse, weathering crisis in the cracks between states.

Rojava is another representative example. The Kurdish movement constantly links state fascism, genocide, and ecocide to theorize Turkey's war on Kurdistan, which has deforested mountainsides, drained rivers, drowned Kurdish settlements.[20] This type of eco-warfare will come to define future conflicts, adding further urgency to Öcalan's calls for a total overhaul of humankind's relationship to the natural world.

But in practice, the AANES has struggled to implement any meaningful green reforms in its own right. On the contrary, it is forced to rely on oil revenues from leaking wells to keep its people fed and maintain a modicum of resistance to its genocidal neighbors. Those who visit Rojava expecting a flourishing permaculture oasis will therefore leave disappointed. Comrades must rather busy themselves with urgent efforts to patch up oil pumps repeatedly destroyed in Turkish airstrikes, in order to keep refugees from freezing as winter sets in.

Likewise, Rojava's well-meaning Ecology Committees devote much of their time to repeated tree-planting campaigns. In the context of catastrophic desertification and resource competition over crucial water stations shut off by Turkish-backed militias, these campaigns are once again steeped in a sense of lack, a tragic demonstration of stateless powerlessness in the grip of far greater powers. Their scattered roots can't hold back the droughts and water shortages ravaging the region, killing infants and spreading cancer, all driven by genocidal state politics.

The AANES cannot create a greener Middle East through its own ideology or policies, however noble in intent. The ecological crisis in Rojava underscores the urgent need for climate apocalypse to drive a truly systemic transformation. The Kurdish movement's ecological activists are a voice crying out in the desert, calling for the epochal renewal of what was once the fertile cradle of civilization ("Make Rojava Green Again").

Climate Messiahs: Turning the Tide of History

Indigenous communities who weathered their own apocalypse centuries ago can play a prophetic role in organizing climate doom, harbingers of a politics that must travel through despair to societal renewal. And other prophetic voices will emerge through the climate apocalypse. When Bendell calls for a new politics based on hopelessness, he is effectively proposing a revival of the millenarian vision, which views humankind's suffering amid rising global temperatures as proof that the global order is at the cusp of epochal change. *Deep Adaptation* quotes a climate writer and professor of theology demanding a new "religion of meaning" and "apocalyptic thinking" in response to climate crisis: "In abandoning hope that one way of life will continue, we open up a space for alternative hopes."[21] This is "philosophizing with a hammer" with a twenty-first century ecological twist. A radical critique of (liberal) modernity opens up new and unexpected space—in which both Left and Right can and do operate.

Bendell and his fellow prophets of societal collapse thus find themselves in perhaps unexpected conversation with millenarian religious narratives of redemption through fire and flood. Among others, these utopian-doomer analyses echo Öcalan's vision of an impending civilizational collapse, through which a better world may improbably emerge. This eschatological turn at the despairing limit of climate theory should come as no surprise. There is a growing global interest in eco-theology throughout diverse world faiths and even animist perspectives on the climate crisis. The related concepts of politics-as-faith, infinite resignation, and the revolutionary leap beyond despair can all help structure our response to the climate apocalypse.

Like the Kurdish movement, climate activists have long been mocked by reactionary detractors as a cult. Both could reclaim this pejorative label and wear it with pride. The climate movement cannot rely solely on technocratic appeals to "follow the science" or adapt certain state policies but must rather deploy a science-based approach while simultaneously following the comet's tail of a quasi-religious commitment to total social transformation.

Malm mounts a cold, serious, and considered case for industrial sabotage as an effective next step for the global climate movement. But there's also a vital warm current to *Pipeline* as Malm advocates for an unreasonable, uncalculated response to climate apocalypse. He draws an impassioned comparison with doomed, desperate acts of Jewish resistance during the Holocaust, where "precisely the hopelessness of the situation constituted the nobility of the resistance."[22] It is this absurdist spirit that must animate the revolutionary climate politics of the future.

Surviving the Apocalypse

The psychological strategies offered throughout this book provide further models for reckoning with this apocalypse. For example, the alleged pseudoscience of *Deep Adaptation* offers a productive example of revolutionary simplification and self-narrativization. Even if the manifesto is somewhat exaggerated and alarmist, so what? We lose nothing by sounding the alarm.

Conversely, as a critical pushback against overly doom-laden ecological perspectives suggests, the political practice of self-delusion can help effectively organize this despair. To Dowd, if "[climate] collapse is thus inevitable and unstoppable," then "so is denial, at least to some degree and probably for most people. After all, why would anyone be willing to trade hope for doom, if they are given no opportunity to sense light at the end of the tunnel?"[23]

Indeed, Bendell has revised *Deep Adaptation* since publication, making some edits to justify his dramatic predictions and others to mute the alarmist tone.[24] As it now stands, the text is a curious hybrid document, expressing a kind of qualified despair—the end is nigh, or possibly not so nigh, and so we had better prepare regardless. This new manifesto reads slightly strangely, as though talking itself back from the brink of its own conclusions. But in this way, it recalls the complex, self-deluding, self-motivating psychological strategies explored above.

Indeed, Bendell's own move to sustainable farming demonstrates the liberating political power of self-delusion. Bendell cautioned us against hope in no uncertain terms: "You will become malnourished. You won't know whether to stay or go. You will fear being violently killed before starving to death." Yet he can also be found grinning amid permaculture crops, wearing a t-shirt that reads "Doomsters have more fun."[25] Post-doom, doomer absurdism, cynical idealism, whatever you want to call it—it's clear Bendell has found his own way to leap unexpectedly beyond despair.

The need for a revolutionary act of faith and the need for pragmatic self-delusion go hand in hand. Doomer climate theorists Kingsnorth and Hine urge us to overcome our human subjectivity and individuality, recognizing that we humans are merely "one strand" in a great web of being.[26] This admonition recalls Jineology, the Kurdish movement's "women's science," which requires all of us, but particularly men, to dismantle our privileged subjective position as masters and observers of the world.[27]

But such a total mastery of ego, a true acknowledgment of our inconsequential place in the universe, could only result in insanity or suicide—as horror writer H. P. Lovecraft and sci-fi satirist Douglas Adams have both memorably suggested. It's in our very deepest nature, the very foundation of humankind's survival, to believe we are more than the dust which we are. This was expressed through our primal grunt, our first desperate "NO." To be human is to be distinct from the world.

Even if it were possible, any such radical deconstruction of our unique, human situation would be politically irresponsible. As "dark ecologists" leaning toward survivalist retreat, Kingsnorth and Hine dismiss any and all "technological or political 'solutions'" to the climate crisis as equally hopeless. But there is a world of difference between quick *technological* fixes aimed at maintaining a comfortable Western way of life and organized *political* activity in pursuit of a revolutionary alternative. By dismissing these two possibilities as functionally equivalent, the theorists abdicate themselves from our serious responsibility to explore political solutions that will prevent the mass death Kingsnorth and Hine predict.[28]

Bookchin powerfully warns against this type of misanthropic, anti-social, and anti-socialist ecological thinking. For Bookchin, humans are neither wholly external to the web of creation, nor just another lowly "strand" indistinguishable from any insect or slime mold. Rather, we are the world's "second nature," the privileged, self-aware culmination of evolution. We are not only part of the world but a particular, privileged, and precious part. And just for this reason, we are charged with particular responsibilities.[29] Even obliterating humanity or retreating to isolated compounds and waiting for nature to heal itself, would only mark a final act of egotism. Disappearing into oblivion exculpates us from any responsibility to actually fix this mess—and all the more so when this ultra-despairing radical doomer politics is advanced from a position of Western comfort. There's certainly a place for humbling self-critique of our human egotism and self-perception as masters of the universe. But this infinite resignation must lead us to organize a response to the catastrophe we have wrought. For as we saw with the Pascalian eco-socialist wager, retreat is a political response too. Not making a choice is making a choice.

That's why we need the absurdist or meta-modern psychological flexibility outlined above, feeling the sting of our cosmic insignificance as a goad to political change. We can take a brief, sober glimpse at the scale of the climate catastrophe before clapping our hands over our eyes and charging blindly for perhaps unattainable goals. It's here that radical doomer analyses can prove their worth, by helping reintroduce another unfashionable religious idea to contemporary political practice—penance.

As Kingsnorth and Hine suggest, humankind's role in causing climate catastrophe should make us feel bad. Although we should acknowledge that the burden of guilt rests with the colonizers and capitalists, there is a value in merely bearing witness to our shared human culpability. But unlike mere guilt, penance is an active and political process. We *feel* guilty, but we *do* penance.

The Kurdish movement's practice of self-criticism is again instructive. As well as criticizing comrades in tekmil, comrades are expected to review their own behavior and note the ways in which they've replicated patriarchy and hierarchical power structures. These confessions of guilt, personal shortcomings, and personal imbrication in repressive social systems are not supposed to be an end in themselves. Rather, self-criticism is only meaningful insofar as it results in concrete action for transformative change. If you aren't going to actually try to change your (egotistical, patriarchal, destructive) behavior, Kurdish revolutionaries believe there's no point in apologizing for it in the criticism session. We may well crawl like insects, proclaim our (white) guilt, offer self-flagellating land acknowledgments—but can this guilt open up productive new political perspectives?

Death Again

The climate crisis marks the restoration of death to the center of human existence—to the extent that it ever disappeared, in the mists of liberal post-history and teleologies of triumphal progress.

Not so long ago, Enlightenment science promised us an existence liberated from the burdensome curse of death as a judgment for life. Death and life, we were promised, had been uncoupled from one another: the mystery of death reduced to a puzzle for philosophers, with life simply to be lived as well as rationally possible.

We have therefore been raised in a brief and aberrational historic window, between the collapse of mass religious belief and the coming social collapse driving us to new forms of faith. How few of us, and how briefly, were ever really free from *timor mortis*, the horror of death? Perhaps we were never meant to be so unnaturally free, so unmoored. Perhaps it's time to do penance.

As Bendell suggests, climate change denial is driven by our postmodern repression of the fundamental human fear of death.[30] Across many eras and societies, people have expected to be judged for their life after they die and (in theory at least) moderated their behavior accordingly. As moderns in the secular Western world, we have generally lost this expectation. The climate catastrophe, which threatens an apocalypse directly linked to human activity, means we must all reckon with the potential return of just such a universal expectation of death-as-judgment. In this process, we can learn from those political, national, and Indigenous cultures that have preserved death as an integral part of human existence and political activity—the Kurdish movement included.

This humbling process is politically productive and will remain so even if a predicted climate doomsday never materializes. Representing a present disaster as world-historic can often prove pivotal in motivating effective political change, as we've seen.

In Western contexts, the assumption that our present generation is *the* doomed generation after which all things must necessarily collapse in flames can easily become narcissistic. When we reset the hands on the Doomsday Clock ever closer to midnight, fondly bewailing our generation's particular misfortune, we can easily neglect the fact that many other generations, cultures, and regions have faced or are currently facing their own apocalypse. Any left politics built on an anticipation of worsening global crisis must therefore take care not to devolve into a voyeuristic, anarchistic adventurism, thrilling at the thought of social collapse rippling through Western states.

An internationalist spirit that recognizes we face a diverse and uneven doomsday is once again crucial. As in the distinction we earlier drew between the Kurdish movement and ISIS's varying conceptions of their end times, we can recognize the appalling consequences of climate catastrophe without welcoming these disasters for their own sake. Indeed, we in the West might find ourselves living a peculiar self-aware existence as belonging to the last few generations *prior* to the flood. Even those generations being born today may well not live to see the most dramatic extent of the coming epochal collapse. There is a particular horror to this fate. At such a juncture, not even tasked and privileged with surviving doomsday, it's easy to sink into paralyzed malaise. Over-anxious modern-day Cassandras, we're perhaps fated to foresee disaster—without even believing our own prophecies.

But neither should we forget how rare in human history the experience of living in history is. Most societies and generations have experienced time as circular and unchanging. Only the historically rare experience of revolutionary social change or revolutionary conflict has shown people that one form of civilization can give way to another form altogether, a shocking realization that has often inspired millenarian resistance. In contrast, the climate crisis furnishes us with a particularly modern sense of global transformation. The linear process of global warming, visible before our very eyes, furnishes an excellent impulse to radical political organization. A rate of social transformation now measured by the generation, decade, or fraction of a degree denies any possibility for complacency. Although many generations might fancy themselves particularly cursed, we at least have the statistics to prove it.

The coronavirus crisis suggested a number of ways the coming catastrophe might unfold. The pandemic was marked by state-mandated restrictions on freedom of movement; paramilitary nativist violence; brutal management and expulsion of migrant workers; and jealous government control of essential resources. In all these ways, it prefigured the likely politics of a climate catastrophe, itself anticipated to release fresh plagues into the world.

States will not wither away but accumulate power and legitimacy as global temperatures rise and resources dwindle, doubling down on border securitization, resource accumulation, even the potential ghettoization of minorities within their borders. Right-wing militias, gangs, and paramilitaries will patrol their borders. At the same time, the technocrats who preach "never again" will find ways to massage Western elites into complacency, confining the fires to Kurdistan, Bangladesh, the Horn of Africa, and other conveniently forgettable and out-of-the-way places. As we've seen with the rise of competing visions of post-state power and governance in Syria, both new Rojavas and authoritarian alternatives will flourish and compete in the *terra nullius* left behind by shrinking, jealously protectionist states. Climate catastrophe both opens the possibility for and imperils the hopes of political transformation.

The Climate Dialectic of History

Marx believed technological advances would bring about a clash between exploited workers and those who profited from the ownership of machines and labor. But that does not mean he fatalistically believed this clash would necessarily result in workers' liberation from wage labor, as those machines were placed in the service of humankind. Organization through the revolutionary party remained a prerequisite.

Ernst Bloch frames the same crucial distinction in his own unique way. Arguing Freud's focus on sexuality only helps explain the actions of a particular bourgeois elite, Bloch instead represented the simple hunger drive as the ultimate, primal human drive.[31] (It's this hunger drive which endures, when all else is stripped away, in the testimonies of Auschwitz's utterly dehumanized Muselmänner). In Bloch's drive theory, hunger is dissatisfaction with the present moment, and for that reason inextricable from hope.[32] Hunger demands and expects satisfaction, a satisfaction that (for Bloch) can be universally realized only through the messianic arrival of socialism. Again, Bloch doesn't believe that the universe is mystically pre-destined to arrive at Marxist organization. But in our world, particularly in the mid-twentieth century with the particular set of crises that Bloch witnessed, the drive through hunger to plenty could follow no other course.

With the failure of state socialism, this course became closed off to us. But the climate apocalypse offers a new opening. Newfound, objective drives for water, shade, and survival will reanimate human existence along political contours it remains our subjective task to define.

To Öcalan, "The contradiction between the capitalist social system and its present chaotic state and the catastrophic destruction of the environment . . . is a dialectical relationship. The fundamental contradiction to nature can only be overcome by turning away from the system. It cannot be solved by environmental protection movements alone."[33] In other words, climate catastrophe can reopen the dialectic of history, creating an opposition that must be resolved through some form of revolutionary eco-socialist organization, perhaps built around the climate migrant.

The climate crisis has already created room for a post-Leninist sense of historic revolutionary crisis to creep back into mainstream political discourse. As self-described "apocalyptic optimist" Dana Fisher puts it, "I believe we can save ourselves from the climate crisis that we have caused; I also believe it will only be possible with a mass mobilization driven by the pain and suffering of climate shocks around the world."[34]

This realization is driving climate activists further left, away from a prefigurative politics of retreat and toward the more militant modes of organization and resistance proposed in *How to Blow Up a Pipeline*. Socialism, decolonization, slave emancipation: there are many historic instances of movements that began as peaceful, liberal, and ineffective before making a radical pivot en route to achieving their historic and global victories. Someday soon, the climate movement will have to make its own radical turn. Extinction Rebellion is nothing compared to the extinction revolution that could emerge as howls of protest from the Global South solidify into a truly global movement.

To put it simply: heat is a catalyst.

This isn't to suggest we should all give up on our present causes and rush to join our local climate action group, following a utilitarian assessment that only direct organizing around climate policy is the appropriate response to the statistics. And neither is it meant to imply a Leninist criticism of those communities suffering the brunt of climate catastrophe, admonishing them to adopt a particular organizational approach.

Any emergent, revolutionary subjectivity will not be monolithic. As Malm notes, the US civil rights and South African anti-apartheid movements offer two notable examples where a liberal and rights-based mass movement operated in effective tandem with a radical fringe committed to violent struggle. As we've seen, the Kurdish movement adopts a similar diversity of tactics in its own struggle against extractive and destructive state colonialism. Anarchists might therefore join feminist and postcolonial thinkers in learning from and sustaining those alternative networks of resistance within which the Kurdish movement forms a key node, anticipating that the shock of climate catastrophe will tear apart centers of statist power never yet successfully assailed by anarchist organization.

More broadly, climate catastrophe will invest all our struggles with renewed urgency—from migration to housing to workers' rights. For example, the Euphrates River slaked the thirst of our earliest civilizations, but today this river flows from modern-day Turkey into Rojava, Syria, and Iraq. It has therefore become weaponized, as Turkey reduces the waterflow to make life a misery for millions in AANES territory, creating the conditions for a latter-day cholera epidemic.[35] In the climate crisis, every struggle for fundamental rights will increasingly become a struggle for survival. Öcalan is only one prophetic voice responding to the climate apocalypse. There will be more, accreting around Indigenous, migration, and land struggles, voices crying out in the growing scorched wilderness, demanding militant sacrifices of everyone.

Doom or Apocalypse?

Throughout this chapter, I have spoken not only of climate crisis but also specifically climate apocalypse. This language is deliberate. As we've seen, "apocalypse" is typically used in its biblical sense, referring to a prophesy or description of the end of the world. But the word also implies a disclosure, literally an "uncovering," the *revelation* of a divine secret.

Etymologically, *doom* implies a judgment or condemnation. But a*pocalypse* implies a transformation, a violent catastrophe engendering supernatural change.

The biblical Book of Revelation, a.k.a. the Apocalypse of Saint John, is paradigmatic in this respect. It's a revolutionary text, an allegorical depiction of the total overthrow of the global social and political order. The early Church authorities would have happily excised Revelation from the Bible alongside other now-forgotten apocalypses, but Revelation had already achieved such mass popularity—by offering desperate people a millenarian vision of a world transformed—that it could not be excluded. This is the truly apocalyptic task all political writing must undertake under the new shadow of climate catastrophe.

Out of respect for the victims of Nazi violence, we will refrain from calling the climate crisis a potential Holocaust, or sacrifice by fire. But to properly demonstrate that we've done our penance and learned from the liquidation of so many millions of lives in the twentieth century, we must both reckon with the probability of future mass death and work to derive political meaning from our present catastrophe—even though the signs are ambiguous, pointing to collapse with no promise of renewal. As we rake hope from the ashes of the twentieth century, "apocalypse" is therefore surely an appropriate term.

Manifesto and Revelation

As might be expected given its epochal, world-consuming nature, this climate apocalypse has given birth to a whole range of political manifestos. These new Books of Revelation strive desperately to derive a productive message from the signs and wonders of a world aflame. Green business manifestos; the Green and Red New Deals, plus the Green Nuclear Deal; deep ecological, social ecological, and degrowth manifestos; Indigenous, eco-anarchist, and eco-queer manifestos; the Unabomber's pathetic anti-human ramblings; *Deep Adaptation*; and Öcalan's own *Manifesto for a Democratic Nation*. Each claims to direct a world we all know must soon be remade.

Of course, manifesto-making alone cannot remake history. We're unlikely to see another book with the transformative, world-historical force of Marx and Engels's *Communist Manifesto* emerge any time soon. There is a further paradox to the very act of writing a political manifesto in an era understood as defined by incipient collapse. Political treatises written to herald social transformation through ecological catastrophe issue dire warnings they already anticipate will be ignored.

Indeed, it might seem this book has failed to resist the manifesto-making temptation, issuing a series of stern prescriptions to the contemporary Left. We must take the leap of hope! We must avoid horizontalism, reformism, and melancholy! And so on. But I hope these repeated "musts" will be taken in their intended spirit. They aren't orders but warnings. We simply must—or else.

Perhaps the true manifesto capable of making sense of twentieth-century violence and twenty-first-century collapse is missing, forever to remain unwritten. Adorno dwells in his Cassandric misery, approaching hope only through its absence; Bloch conversely radiates his wild, indefeasible hope without reason. Each expresses half of the equation. Had Walter Benjamin lived to bear witness to capitalist modernity, it is perhaps only his bleak, fragmented, yet messianic voice that could have given true voice to hope without hope in the long shadow of the Holocaust. With typically messianic pessimism, Benjamin conceived of revolution not in Marxian terms as the locomotive of history but conversely an "emergency brake," diverting history from its expected course to disaster.[36] How might he have theorized our current breakneck path toward destruction?

But Benjamin did not survive the war. Instead, broken by the belief he stood no chance of making it across the French-Spanish border, he committed suicide rather than fall into the hands of the Nazis. We must therefore find other ways to pick up the trail of the revolutionary current of hope without hope, which continues thin as a thread yet unbroken through all the trials of the past century, leading us onward into the dark of potential global collapse.

Even Kingsnorth and Hine's seemingly anti-human, apolitical narrative remains open to political redemption. The way these doom-mongers conclude their own fragmented manifesto should by now come as no surprise: "Together, we will find the hope beyond hope."[37]

Conclusion

Utopian Nihilism

The Syrian conflict, it was suggested at the start of this book, is the Spanish Civil War of an incipient global catastrophe. In both cases, regional forces engaged in an anti-fascist struggle for survival found the conflict served a prelude to interstate violence breaking out anew on a grander scale and yet created opportunities to advance a radical democratic socialist alternative through the crisis. The comparison can help us to anticipate the potential ideological, political, and military contours of World War III. We can also explore concepts of internationalism and utopianism, and the possibility of improbable, non-statist leftist alternatives emerging to exploit the breach between quarreling state powers in the contemporary Middle East and beyond.

But the comparison also implies the near inevitability that those left movements will suffer statist repression, manipulation in proxy warfare, defeat, and bloody liquidation. The Kurdish movement has won unexpected victories and embarked on an impressive revolutionary program aimed at remaking Syrian society. But as those who have given their lives to the Rojava Revolution know full well, even these victories are insufficient to demonstrate that democratic, communal organization can successfully counter state power.

Such is the violent opposition the Kurdish movement faces, such is the scale of regional catastrophe, such is the glaring absence of any even nominally leftist state sponsor capable of guaranteeing the Rojava Revolution's long-term survival that any assessment of the revolution's achievements risks rapidly appearing outdated. In this new stage of the Syrian conflict following Assad's deposition by HTS, the democratic confederalist project faces the twin threats of military liquidation and exploitative co-option by state powers. It remains unknown whether the AANES will survive the coming months and years, and if so, in what form. Communism, anarchism, and all prior modes of leftist political organization have ultimately failed to achieve their stated vision of global emancipation. So too will democratic confederalism.

To this end, the Spanish Civil War also offers lessons in memorialization, martyrdom, and noble sacrifice. Whatever fate ultimately befalls northern Syria, we will never forget the sacrifices of its defenders, nor of those ordinary Kurdish, Arab, Christian, and Yazidi civilians who had the misfortune to be born in times of crisis and revolution. And we will never forget the victories either, however small, fleeting, and doomed they might prove to be. Rojava's revolution will stand in history as one concrete utopia, a notional idea that became material, geographic reality, through which all manner of people, movements, and revolutionaries could find cause for hope.

The revolution is not a *tabula rasa* or blank canvas, which we're free to interpret as we please. The Kurdish movement offers a concrete, legitimate, political program, which has proven rugged enough to keep millions alive through a decade of war and is worthy of analytic respect on its own terms. And yet Rojava can simultaneously be a homeland for the Kurds; a safe haven for minorities; a site of extraordinary social transformation benefiting women; part of the blueprint for a future Syria; an instructive exemplar for the world's anarchists, communists, and democratic socialists; and a beacon of hope for all those who need it in their own diverse struggles. Rojava's utopia looks outward, leaps forward.

Anticipating Rojava's Defeat

The poet and playwright Bertolt Brecht always proves able to snatch hope from the jaws of hopelessness. His depictions of doomed struggle in Germany's interwar years well evoke the current mood of embattled revolutionary struggle on the ground in Rojava: "Remember, these are the years/ In which it is not a matter of winning victories but/ Of winning the defeats."[1]

In Rojava, each day's survival is a miracle. Defeat is a permanent possibility. Yet the Kurdish movement does not fear the future, however grim. Its past sacrifices and present militant organization permit it a clear-eyed assessment of the challenges it faces, knowing it can't be thrown off course by any single setback. For this reason, the revolution also deserves serious and comradely criticism in the spirit of tekmil, acknowledging tactical errors and strategic failures as part of the revolutionary process. Let's conclude by following the Kurdish movement's bold example, therefore, and consider Rojava's most likely future defeats.

For example, let Syria's new Islamist rulers demand the liquidation of the multiethnic federation and its armed forces, under the flag of a unitary Islamic state. The Kurdish movement has built something stronger and deeper-rooted: a great network of solidarity built on the basis of Öcalan's ideas, reconciliation committees, women's houses, tentative Kurdish-Arab cooperation. It is in this disjuncture, between how states understand power and how power is experienced in Rojava, that the space for continued resistance may be found. These revolutionary gains will not be wiped away with the changing of a flag, even if they are driven underground.

Or else let Turkey drive Rojava's Kurdish population south into the desert, as Erdoğan has repeatedly threatened. The resistance will only be strengthened. It's true that civilians in Rojava are very tired—tired of war, tired of death, tired of not knowing when the next attack will come. Yet the ceaseless airstrikes endlessly reiterate the message that Turkey will accept nothing less than the eradication of this project and this people in their entirety. No reform, compromise, or resignation is possible. The population has no choice but to remain defiantly and permanently politicized.

Even if Rojava were to suffer a total defeat, this book's core argument would remain true: crisis can dialectically produce an unexpected utopian, democratic politics. Indeed this book's argument would not be disproven even if the Kurdish movement lost sight of its own utopian objectives and devolved into a mere authoritarian statelet, beholden to the US in a bid to preserve itself from ethnic cleansing. Democratic confederalism would only take its place in the history of defeated left movements, part of that dark history through which we fumble toward our negatively defined utopia.

This movement built its original strength in extremis, statelessness, exile; in desert refugee camps and the mountain retreats of Palestinian freedom fighters. It can do so again and again. Each defeat, even an existential defeat, bears within it the possibility of its redemption. The Pandora's box that opened with the 2011 revolutionary crisis will someday be closed. But dangerous, intoxicating hope has already escaped and settled in the hearts of the people, and in the liberated minds of young women being raised to believe they will remake the world in their image.

I went to report and work in Rojava because I was tired of the Western Left's repeated failures, tired of firefighting, tired of taking solace in tiny and temporary victories. I wanted to see if hope remained possible in the twenty-first century and our era of left defeat. But as gradually became apparent, even our generation's paramount revolution is itself a tissue of firefights, partial defeats, and daily struggles, a "mass of contradictions."[2] The Kurdish movement's utopian claims make sense only in dialectical relation to the crises it faces. Indeed, the revolution could not exist in its present form without these hardships. After much critical work and reflection, my own relationship to the Rojava Revolution (and revolutionary commitment in general) is encapsulated by an early Christian dictum: "I believe because it is impossible."

Anticipating Global Defeat

But perhaps even these scenarios of defeat and bloody retribution may prove too optimistic. The Left prefers to keep its twentieth-century defeats at a safe, untheorized distance rather than admit the possibility of socialism's permanent global defeat at the hands of statist capitalism. Even now, there have been few genuine attempts to theorize such a catastrophe.[3]

This book has predicted the return of crisis, urgency, and apocalypse to global politics, bringing about fresh opportunities for transformation. But perhaps we cannot even hope for that much. In Syria, the Middle East, and worldwide, there may ultimately be little to choose between competing strands of state capitalism set to determine global politics throughout our lifetimes.

Similarly, it proved easier to organize militant utopian resistance during open warfare against Turkey than in the long period of frozen conflict that followed. But it is this postwar period that more closely resembles the situation faced by the global Left today—psychological warfare intended to grind down personal and communal resistance, incremental yet irreversible losses, environmental and economic warfare.

Recent years in Rojava have been defined by the drone warfare that Turkey is exporting to battlefields worldwide. Throughout Kurdistan, as on killing fields across the Middle East, Turkey's Bayraktar drones buzz ceaselessly overhead. This dispersed, dehumanized, lethal technology is perfectly suited to an age in which we are all expected to individually produce value minute by minute, even as we rest, socialize, and rely on emergent digital technologies. As we are pursued by faceless, distant, unnamable capital in every corner of our existence, so too the drone pursues its victim across modern-day urban battlefields. The subject of contemporary capitalism is never free, and the drone makes explicit this totalizing logic.

Drone warfare aims to break resistance. It offers no easy target for Fanonian anti-colonial violence, no readily defined battlefield onto which comrades can throw themselves with wild abandon. Dull, ordinary life goes on as it must until the constantly anticipated moment of death arrives all at once, proving that death was always inescapably there. Drone warfare thus demands a particular tactical response on the battlefield: dispersal, scattering, swarming. It is tempting to further view this tactical response as analogous to post-communist theorizations of political organization, of subjectivity and resistance as emerging through the swarm or multitude of contemporary capitalist subjects.

Any such analogy is cause for pessimism. The Kurdish movement has survived worse violence before and may proclaim the occasional shoot-down of a Bayraktar drone, but they are nonetheless struggling to adjust to and survive the latest rounds of alienated, decentralized warfare. Turkey's drones have spent years intentionally targeting and systematically destroying energy, water, medical, and humanitarian infrastructure throughout Rojava. The campaign is intended to break civilian spirits, turn them against the AANES, and drive more locals onto the grim refugee trail to Europe. Friends in Syria describe the inevitable psychic toll: malaise, exhaustion, despair.

And it has proven just as challenging to achieve effective horizontal, decentralized organization against contemporary capitalist hegemony. The Left's broader defeat may rather continue as it has throughout the past decades of missing revolutions and ineffectual horizontalist organization—incremental, atomized, individual, hanging over us like our own individual drones. As we are lost one by one to suicide or other forms of despair, the world may simply pay us no regard.

Toward Utopian Nihilism

Yet even and especially in this grim eventuality, hope against hope remains an organizational and psychological imperative. Some comrades may yet feel able to hope with pure sincerity, firmly convinced that our present modes of organization can prove sufficient to counter omnipotent, state-backed capitalism. Disregarding the psychological survival tactics suggested in this book, they can tap an inner well of simple, genuine hope, sure that we have learned the lessons of the twenty-first century, sure that we are now ready to reckon with climate catastrophe.

Likewise, some comrades in Rojava will doubtless disagree with the postmodern concept of hope presented here. Many find Öcalan's ideology powerful enough in its own right to explain their struggle and the sacrifices they make, needing no absurdist or meta-modern leap beyond reason to motivate their revolutionary commitment. Still, even the idealists must surely sometimes find themselves plagued, like Bakunin, by an inner voice telling them that their hopes are absurd, that too many comrades have sacrificed their lives to make the revolutionary gains worthwhile.

Or perhaps you remain on the other side, unconvinced, with your own hopelessness, skeptical of any revolutionary political commitment in the twenty-first century. You may be critical of the organizational failures of street protest, left populism, defeatist horizontalism, and the pacifist climate movement yet remain unable to imagine any better alternative. Why should we wager our lives on a mere "perhaps"? In the shadow of twenty-first-century movements' failure to hammer a better world out of the raw materials of industrial capitalism, is it reasonable to pursue continued militant organization aimed at regional, national, global revolution? If we feel the need to delude ourselves, to justify our actions with grand talk of a revolution we doubt will ever come, to simplify, pose, and exaggerate, hadn't we better give up? If our resources are limited, shouldn't we confine ourselves to prefigurative organizing inside anarchist safe spaces—or else relinquish politics altogether and focus on improving life for ourselves, our friends, and our families?

We've tried to articulate answers to all these questions, succeeding perhaps only with eye screwed shut, avoiding certain truths. For there is no certain, objective, universal answer. The socialist wager is a wager. The revolutionary leap of faith is a blind leap in the dark.

It is for this reason that this book has not only sought to animate a revolutionary history of defeat but also has looked beyond the political into the realms of existential despair. We met with Bloch's socialist Not Yet, justifying our present struggles and trials in the light of a future socialist dawn perhaps never to arrive. We introduced our socialist And Yet, following Kierkegaard in leaping beyond logic and taking a noble, defiant stance despite the odds stacked against our chosen utopia. To these, we might add a third, tentative concept: the socialist *Why Not?*

At one point, Nietzsche self-deprecatingly suggests that even he remained prone to the folly of Christian mercy, mockingly admitting that "the sight of a small mountain people fighting for its freedom would make me offer my hand and my life."[4] If only he had followed that thought to its conclusion, traveled to the mountains of Kurdistan, and joined the revolution. He wouldn't be the first disillusioned cynic to arrive there, or the last to be transformed.

Where else but in the glorious, absurd, socialist struggle to exceed our flawed human nature should we find the Dionysian pessimism that Nietzsche sought in vain all his life? Where else should we find that ultimate nihilism, which deconstructs even our despairing condition in the true nihilism of capitalist modernity, freeing us at last for a genuine tomorrow?

Through this realization, we arrive at last at a utopian nihilism, the ultimate in absurdism. Utopian nihilism stares the hell of existence squarely in the face. It exults in suffering and its necessary corollary, resistance, determinedly believing these evils will one day be transformed into their opposite.

Revolution and pessimism have always gone hand in hand. The very concept of a historical dialectic implies that only catastrophe and suffering can bring about social and political transformation. The liberal optimists and reformists balk at this profoundly pessimistic idea. Yet it has a proven power to remake the world.

As Walter Benjamin defined it, left melancholy traps us in a defensive relationship to the past, cut off from the history of revolutionary struggle. But there is another tradition of melancholy on the Left, one that does not retreat into defensive self-preservation but has instead recognized, lived with, and dwelled in its despair. Benjamin, Bensaïd, Saint-Just, Rosa Luxemburg, Gramsci, Trotsky, Che Guevara, and the Zapatistas' Subcomandante Marcos have all been inscribed in this genealogy.[5] To this list, we might add Prometheus and Don Quixote, and also Marx, Bakunin, Bloch, Öcalan—all melancholy revolutionaries in their own ways, each fashioning a strange hope from admitted despair.

As one hagiographer of this tradition has suggested, "Not all melancholics are revolutionaries, but every revolutionary is (at least to some extent) melancholic. Dogmatic faith in the revolution can disappear with the first setback. The apparent fragility of revolutionary melancholy can hide the greatest of strengths."[6]

Perhaps there is no guaranteed reason to take socialist revolution as our goal, as the alternative that will necessarily emerge through climate catastrophe. Yet, as Bloch suggests, there is also a sense in which socialism is precisely whatever does not exist in our world. It is our dreams, it is that which we yearn for and have been taught is impossible, it is whatever is denied by the realities of our present murderous order. Socialism necessarily requires an absence, a lack, a despair.

This is not a simple or comforting political philosophy. As socialists, we must never forget the often excised second half of the famous line: "Hope springs eternal in the human breast/*Man never is, but always to be blessed.*"[7] If hope in general, and political hope in particular, is inherently hope for the Not Yet, by definition that hope can never be fulfilled. Even political hope's apparent fulfillment in the successful socialist seizure of state power has only brought fresh despair, as Öcalan has concluded. It is for this reason that socialist organization must always remain in resistance, rebellious and unfulfilled—always *to be* blessed. We must accept this bitter state of affairs as a blessing, welcoming our condition of perpetual and unfulfilled struggle.

Hope without hope may be a narcotic, dulling us to present suffering and unacceptable compromises. It may be an outward sign of inner misery, narcissistic decadence, or fundamental cowardice. It may drive melancholic Western Leftists to seek revolutionary thrills or a metaphysical sense of justification, even at the expense of ordinary people suffering in Syria or other sites of resistance throughout the global state of exception. It may betray a postmodern inability to step into history, place our hope in a better tomorrow, and begin the task of revolutionary organization.

To remain in this position without shrinking before the admitted challenges we face is therefore a great, frightful duty. The Kurdish movement has held its own head up through the darkest days it has faced, not ignorant of the odds it faces but treating them as proof their struggle has the power to remake the world. When Rojava's Kurdish, Arab, and Christian forces defeated ISIS in their onetime capital Raqqa, female fighters hoisted a huge, canary-yellow banner of Öcalan amid the ruins.[8] Their temporary US partners were frustrated, Turkey outraged, geopolitical analysts baffled, and many ordinary locals dismayed. The action simply made no sense. The flag directly undermined US efforts to present the "democratic" Syrian Kurdish forces as ideologically distinct from the "terrorist" PKK, and it perhaps facilitated Turkey's decision to launch its subsequent, punitive military operations against the region, at the very real cost of civilian lives.

But Turkey was always going to launch its invasion, if not tomorrow, then the day after that. In this hopeless context, Rojava's militants concluded, their revolutionary colors may as well fly. More than that, through their reckless action, they demonstrated their fundamental, undeniable freedom. They would not be bought. In victory as in defeat, they would continue to make their choiceless choice as though there were a choice, demonstrating a determined commitment to their revolutionary principles even where that commitment left logic behind.

Or, as a Kurdish militant once told me, "If we offered to pay some- one a thousand dollars, Turkey could offer ten thousand. If we threatened someone with a gun, Turkey would threaten to raze their village. We have nothing to offer but our ideology. And so we can never give that up."

The Kurdish movement has certainly paid the cost of its own absurd- ist commitment, in spilled blood, lost land, and repeated retreat. If crisis can bring with it unexpected opportunity, so too can victory unfold into fresh hardship.

Ernst Bloch has been our constant companion throughout this book, accompanying us through the deepest circles of hopelessness, back toward the light of the socialist Not Yet. But it is here we must leave him behind. The mystic Marxist believed that "every barrier, when it is felt as such, is at the same time crossed. For just coming up against it pre- supposes a movement which goes beyond it."[9] But as we see once again in Rojava, the real-world experience of socialist organization offers no such guarantee of salvation. Politics is marked by defeats that do not have mystic, dialectical transformation but register as mere failures. If any- thing, that distant socialist utopia seems even further away now than it was when Bloch wrote these words.

This is the terrible hollowness at the heart of contemporary political organization, a despair we experience as keenly as the death of God. But whereas Nietzsche hopes the religious faithful will overcome their cow- ardly attachment to their own dream of deliverance, we must find ways to keep striving regardless, in faithless faith, hopeless hope, and the spirit of utopian nihilism.

A Leap in the Dark

When Dante and Virgil cross the threshold into the Inferno, they encoun- ter the legend "All hope abandon, ye who enter here," emblazoned over the gates of Hell. Dante is understandably troubled, but his companion reassures him, continuing: "Here thou must all distrust behind thee leave/ Here be vile fear extinguish'd."[10] It is another famous allusion often stripped of its full meaning.

The point where hope is extinguished is the point where there can be no more fear, since there is nothing more to lose. Dante must traverse hell to fully comprehend and thus reject its horrors, and so finally arrive at Paradise. It is only by abandoning personal, individual hope that we can find it anew, in a belief far greater than ourselves.

Crossing the border into Rojava, you enter a region reputed to be the paradisaical birthplace of human civilization but which has latterly become a "hell on earth."[11] As an internationalist volunteer, you arrive lying flat on your back on a leaky raft, perhaps dodging potshots from Iraqi border guards, as you drift across the River Tigris.

The Garden of Eden is said to lie just downstream at the confluence of the Tigris and the Euphrates, the two rivers that encircled Mesopotamia and now encircle Rojava in their life-giving embrace. In Dante's cosmology, Eden is located atop Mount Purgatory. This earthly paradise represents both our hopes of restoring all that we lost in the fall from Paradise and the long, bitter journey to overcome our fallen condition.

A desperate, hopeless act: to leave your home and travel to Syria to seek out a socialist revolution. You take a small step, the greatest leap of your life, onto the boat and across the border. You put your life in the hands of a revolutionary movement that has improbably claimed to be making a new heaven from Syria's earthly hell. In one sense, it is a step into hopelessness. But if joining the revolution requires you to abandon hope, it also requires you to reject distrust and cast aside fear.

You wonder for a moment about turning back, as you have turned back before from other challenges and crises, retreating into despair or individualism. But not this time; it's too late. You have taken the socialist leap. You stumble ashore. You begin.

All the internationalists who travel to Rojava are ready to die, on some level, for a cause they only very imperfectly understand. As Turkey invades, they make out wills, burn their personal papers, watch the skies for their personal drone-strike. But through that infinite resignation, they are freed.

Rojava's internationalists have been privileged to join the Kurdish movement for a brief spell of its epochal journey, which in turn is just a fragment of a greater socialist journey, measured in millennia and many millions of sacrificed lives, continuing despite all it has suffered. A journey through violence, resignation, frustration, compromise, setbacks, and despair, and on toward their opposite: toward hope.

Acknowledgments

Many of those who contributed the most to this book cannot be named. In the face of Turkish drone strikes and European state repression, there are many who must remain anonymous: from the friend with whom I first walked along the dock at Mytilene discussing Öcalan's library, many years ago; to the countless local and internationalist friends who offered companionship, comradeship, and criticism throughout the years in Rojava; to the diverse Kurdish educators, organizers, and militants quoted in this book. In particular, I would like to thank my dear friends and colleagues at the Rojava Information Center, and especially T, B, and R, for tolerating my variously positivist, pessimistic, and provocative tendencies; sitting late into the night smoking and fiercely debating pretty much every aspect of the revolution as it's discussed in these pages; and always standing together when times were hard. *Hewldanên we u tecrubên me yên hevparî nayin jibîrkirin.* My deep thanks as well to the British caucus (especially H, V, B, and S), who likewise all had their own perspectives on the revolution, its shortcomings, and why it mattered, but nonetheless offered insights, laughter, and support on the journey toward my own cynical-idealist commitment.

In diverse ways, friends, colleagues, and comrades from the Internationalist Commune, Komina Film a Rojava, Zaningeha Rojava, Jineolojî, Jineolojî International, Ragehandina Azad, Kongra Star, Heyva Sor a Kurd, the Autonomous Administration, the Syrian Democratic Council, Kurdistan Solidarity Network, and Tekoşîna Anarşîst have all also supported the development of this book, along with countless other

277

journalists, academics, officials, artists, and families in North and East Syria. It was an extraordinary and unrepeatable privilege to spend those years in Rojava. I would particularly like to thank those friends and comrades who have supported me during the ongoing legal battles I have faced in the UK and Europe as a result of my work in Rojava. They have ensured that I have never felt alone in this small personal struggle.

Earlier versions of passages included in the book were published by, and ideas included in the book were also developed in work published by, the Kurdish Center for Studies; Novara Media; I. B. Tauris/Bloomberg; *Truthdig*; and *UnHerd*; as well as in papers given at the Camp Studies and Kurdish Studies conferences at the Universities of Osnabrück and Sheffield. To this end, I would like to thank Hawzhin Ahmed, Rob Lowe, Zeynep Kaya, and Jeff Miley for their support, comments, and editorial feedback, and Ruby for her timely feedback on a draft of this book. At AK Press, I would particularly like to thank Angelica Sgouros for her thoughtful editorial work and for encouraging me in the quest to find sources of hope in the contemporary Left, as well as Bruno George for a thorough and precise copyedit.

As ever, my sincere thanks to all my friends and family in the UK for their support as I travel, get into scrapes, and return home. Special thanks to Michael, for disagreeing with absolutely everything I say, in the most delightful way imaginable. And most of all I would like to thank R, for providing so many of the perspectives, proposals, pints, and arguments that shaped its course. In so many ways, I couldn't have done it without you.

If the Rojava Revolution inspires diverse perspectives among its critics and observers, it does so all the more among its friends and supporters. While I'm sure many of my friends and comrades will disagree with part or all of the arguments advanced here, in the spirit of *rexnê* and *rexnê-dayîn,* I hope to have advanced arguments worthy of taking their place in a broader comradely, critical discussion in and about the revolution.

The Kurdish movement's partisans understand better than anyone that hope can be found through grief, despair, and suffering. I hope these reflections, in their own small way, will prove a fitting testament to all the losses and hardship endured by the Kurdish people and their revolutionary movement.

Endnotes

Introduction: An Absurd Utopia

1   Asef Bayat, *Revolution Without Revolutionaries: Making Sense of the Arab Spring* (Stanford: Stanford University Press, 2017); Vincent Bevins, *If We Burn: The Mass Protest Decade and the Missing Revolution* (New York: Public Affairs, 2023); Rodrigo Nunes, *Neither Vertical Nor Horizontal: A Theory of Political Organization* (London: Verso, 2021); Arthur Borriello and Anton Jäger, *The Populist Moment: The Left After the Great Recession* (London: Verso, 2023).

2   Mustafa Karasu, "Struggle for Socialism Must Begin Today Starting by Building Sociality and Communal Life," *Academy of Democratic Modernity*, May 2022, https://democraticmodernity.com/wp-content/uploads/2024/06/ADM_Interview_The_struggle_for_socialism_ENG_d95b58aba9.pdf.

3   Mustafa Karasu, "Struggle for Socialism Must Begin Today Starting by Building Sociality and Communal Life."

4   Dilar Dirik, *The Kurdish Women's Movement: History, Theory, Practice* (London: Pluto, 2022), chapter 8.

5   Albert Camus, *The Myth of Sisyphus and Other Essays*, trans. Justin O'Brien (New York: Vintage, 1991), 2.

6   Søren Kierkegaard, *Fear and Trembling*, trans. Walter Lowrie (Princeton, NJ: Princeton University Press, 1941), 7.

7   Kierkegaard, *Fear*, 17.

8   Leyla Güven, "Introduction," *Tevn Magazine*, February 4, 2022, https://capiremov.org/en/culture/kurdish-women-write-in-defense-of-their-language-culture-and-territory.

279

9   "Turkey Refuses to Implement 'Right to Hope' for PKK leader," *Medya News*, October 18, 2022, https://medyanews.net/turkey-refuses-to-implement-right-to-hope-for-pkk-leader.

10 Ali Kemal Özcan, *Turkey's Kurds: A Theoretical Analysis of the PKK and Abdullah Öcalan* (London: Routledge, 2006), 236.

Chapter 1: The Rojava Revolution: Finding Hope in Crisis

1   See, for example: Michael Knapp, Anja Flach, and Ercan Ayboga, *Revolution in Rojava: Democratic Autonomy and Women's Liberation in Syrian Kurdistan*, trans. Janet Biehl (London: Pluto Press, 2016), xxii–xxv, 50.

2   Abdullah Öcalan, *The Third Domain: Reconstructing Liberation*, trans. International Initiative (Stockholm: International Initiative Freedom for Öcalan, 2003).

3   Theodor Adorno, *Problems of Moral Philosophy* (Cambridge: Polity Press, 2000), 175.

4   Azize Aslan, *Anticapitalist Economy in Rojava: The Contradictions of Revolution in the Kurdish Struggles* (Wakefield, QC: Daraja Press, 2023), 39–67.

5   Joost Jongerden, "Learning from Defeat: Development and Contestation of the 'New Paradigm' within Kurdistan Workers' Party (PKK)," *Kurdish Studies* 7, no. 1 (2019): 72–92; Knapp, Flach, Ayboga, *Revolution*, 36–47.

6   Jongerden, "Learning."

7   Abdullah Öcalan, *Beyond State, Power, and Violence*, trans. Michael Schiffman and Havin Guneser (Oakland: PM Press/Kairos, 2022).

8   Abdullah Öcalan, *War and Peace in Kurdistan*, trans. International Initiative (Stockholm: International Initiative Freedom for Öcalan, 2009), 30–31.

9   Aslan, *Anticapitalist*, 67–124.

10 Leila Al-Shami and Robin Yassin-Kassab, *Burning Country: Syrians in Revolution and War* (London: Pluto, 2016).

11 Eva Savelsberg, "The Kurdish PYD and the Syrian Civil War," in *The Routledge Handbook on the Kurds* (London: Routledge, 2018), 357–65.

12 Giorgio Agamben, *Homo Sacer: Sovereign Power and Bare Life*, trans. Daniel Heller-Roazen (Stanford: Stanford University Press, 1995), 18.

13 Thomas McGee, "The Stateless Kurds of Syria: Ethnic Identity and National ID," *Tilburg Law Review* 19, no. 1–2 (2014): 171–81.

14 Thomas Schmidinger, *Rojava: Revolution, War and the Future of Syria's Kurds* (London: Pluto, 2016), 5–6.

15 Lukas Slothuus, "Antonio Gramsci and the Problem of Fatalism," in *Revolutionary Hope in a Time of Crisis*, eds. Maša Mrovlje and Alex Zamalin (New York: Routledge, 2024), 31–48.

16 Abdullah Öcalan, *The Sociology of Freedom: Manifesto of the Democratic Civilization, Vol. III*, trans. Havin Guneser (Oakland: PM Press, 2020).

17 Schmidinger, *Rojava*, 86–101.

18 See the various charters, declarations, and social contracts at Rojava Information Centre, Political System: Documents, https://rojavainformationcenter.org/background/political-system-documents.

19   Knapp, Flach, and Ayboga, *Revolution*, 232.

20   Giorgio Agamben, *State of Exception*, trans. Kevin Attell (Chicago: University of Chicago Press), 1–32.

21   Wladimir van Wilgenberg and Michael Knights, *Accidental Allies: The US–SDF Partnership against the Islamic State* (London: I. B. Tauris, 2021), 227–30.

22   Cemil Bayik, quoted in Knapp, Flach, Ayboga, *Revolution*, 252.

23   Amberin Zaman and Fabrice Balanche, "As Syrian Constitution Talks Kick Off, Is Kurdish Administration 'Finished'?," *Al Monitor*, https://www.al-monitor.com/originals/2019/10/syria-constitution-talks-kick-off-kurdish-administratio.html, October 30, 2019.

24   Agamben, *Homo Sacer*, 39.

25   Wilgenberg and Knights, *Accidental*, 128–85.

26   Rojava Information Center, *Beyond Rojava: North and East Syria's Arab Regions*, https://rojavainformationcenter.org/storage/2021/06/RIC-Dossier-Arab-regions.pdf, June 8, 2021.

27   Rojava Information Center, "Explainer—Cooperatives in North and East Syria," November 8, 2020 https://rojavainformationcenter.com/2020/11/explainer-cooperatives-in-north-and-east-syria-developing-a-new-economy.

28   Rojava Information Center, "Criticisms and Proposals from Syrian Democratic Council Consultation in Raqqa," October 3, 2020, https://rojavainformationcenter.org/2020/10/translation-criticism-and-proposals-from-syrian-democratic-council-consultation-raqqa.

29   Aslan, 193–215.

30   Salih Muslim, "We Didn't Call Them, We're Not Sending Them Away," *ANF*, December 21, 2018, https://anfenglish.com/news/muslim-we-didn-t-call-them-we-re-not-sending-them-away-31568.

31   Claudia Aradau, "Law Transformed: Guantánamo and the 'Other' Exception," *Third World Quarterly* 28, no. 3 (2007): 489–501.

32   Agamben, *Homo Sacer*, 103.

33   Agamben, *Auschwitz*, 133.

34   Syrian community mediator, private interview, November 20, 2023.

Chapter 2: ISIS, Rojava, and the Non-State Alternative

1   Harriet Allsop and Wladimir van Wilgenburg, *The Kurds of Northern Syria: Governance, Diversity and Conflicts* (London: Bloomsbury, 2019), chapter 6.

2   Ghayath Naisse, "The 'Islamic State' and the Counter-Revolution," *International Socialism* (2015), 147.

3   Giorgio Agamben, *Homo Sacer: Sovereign Power and Bare Life*, trans. Daniel Heller-Roazen (Stanford: Stanford University Press, 1995), 72–73.

4   Gordon Lubold and Michael Gordon, "A Ticking Time Bomb: In Syrian Camps, Fears of an Islamic State Revival," *Wall Street Journal*, March 25, 2024, https://www.wsj.com/world/middle-east/a-ticking-time-bomb-in-syrian-camps-fears-of-an-islamic-state-revival-a89f2ac3.

5   Human Rights Watch, *Revictimizing the Victims: Children Unlawfully Detained in Northeast Syria*, January 27, 2023, https://www.hrw.org/news/2023/01/27/revictimizing-victims-children-unlawfully-detained-northeast-syria.

6   Khaled Issa, interview, July 2024.

7   For an overview of the hypocritical media circus over Begum, see Matt Broomfield, "In the UK, Pity for Begum, None for the Kurds," *Medya News*, September 1, 2022, https://medyanews.net/in-the-uk-pity-for-begum-none-for-the-kurds.

8   Leila Al-Shami and Robin Yassin-Kassab, *Burning Country: Syrians in Revolution and War* (London: Pluto, 2016).

9   Michel Foucault, *Discipline and Punish: The Birth of the Prison*, trans. Alan Sheridan (New York: Random House, 1995), 150.

10 See Kathy Durkin, "From Coast to Coast: Hands off Syria!," *Workers World*, April 17, 2018, https://www.workers.org/2018/04/36593.

11 Al-Shami and Yassin-Kassab, *Burning*.

12 Dilar Dirik, "Radical Democracy: The First Line against Fascism," *Roar Magazine*, April 2, 2017, https://roarmag.org/magazine/dilar-dirik-kurdish-anti-fascism.

13 Foucault, *Discipline*, 226.

14 Foucault, *Discipline*, 201–209.

15 Christian Vianna de Azevedo, "ISIS Resurgence in Al Hawl Camp and Human Smuggling Enterprises in Syria: Crime and Terror Convergence?" *Perspectives on Terrorism* 14, no. 4 (2020): 43–63.

16 Nur Azman, "Islamic State's Narratives of Resilience and Endurance," *Counter Terrorist Trends and Analyses* 12, no. 1 (2020): 82–86.

17 Agamben, *Homo Sacer*, 23.

18 Foucault, *Discipline*, 251–56.

19 Abdullah Öcalan, *The Sociology of Freedom: Manifesto for a Democratic Civilization, Vol. III*, trans. Havin Guneser (Oakland: PM Press, 2020), 82–87.

20 Rojava Information Center, "Hidden Battlefields: Rehabilitating ISIS Affiliates and Building a Democratic Culture in Their Former Territories," December 2020, https://www.icct.nl/sites/default/files/import/publication/RIC_Hidden Battlefields_-DEC2020.pdf.

21 Onur Sultan et al., "Reintegration of ISIS Returnees: A Myth or Reality," *Horizon Insights* 3, no. 3 (2020): 1–16.

22 Quentin Somerville and Riam Dalatai, "Raqqa's Dirty Secret," BBC, November 13, 2017, https://www.bbc.co.uk/news/resources/idt-sh/raqqas_dirty_secret.

23 Rojava Information Center, "Battlefields."

Chapter 3: Reorganizing and Revitalizing the Left

1   Viyan Qerecox, "The New Paradigm," *Social Ecology and the Rojava Revolution*, ed. Internationalist Commune of Rojava (London: Dog Section Press, 2022), 109–22.

2   Abdullah Öcalan, *The Sociology of Freedom: Manifesto for a Democratic Civilization, Vol. III*, trans. Havin Guneser (Oakland: PM Press, 2020), 293–94.

3   Enzo Traverso, *Left-Wing Melancholia: Marxism, History, and Memory* (New York: Columbia University Press, 2016).

4   Vincent Bevins, *If We Burn: The Mass Protest Decade and the Missing Revolution* (New York: Public Affairs, 2023), 264–74.

5   Freddier DeBoer, *How Elites Ate the Social Justice Movement* (New York: Simon and Schuster, 2023).

6   Bevins, *If We Burn*, 12.

7   Asef Bayat, *Revolution Without Revolutionaries: Making Sense of the Arab Spring* (Stanford: Stanford University Press, 2017).

8   Arthur Borriello and Anton Jäger, *The Populist Moment: The Left After the Great Recession* (London: Verso, 2023).

9   Jodi Dean, *The Communist Horizon* (London: Verso, 2012).

10   Ipsos, *Ipsos Global Trends 2017*, May 5, 2017, https://www.ipsos.com/en-uk/ipsos-global-trends-2017-biggest-survey-its-kind; Ipsos, *Ipsos Global Trends 2023*, April 13, 2023, https://www.ipsos.com/sites/default/files/2023-Ipsos-Global-Trends-Report.pdf.

11   National Education Association, "Gen Z: The Most Pro-Union Generation," April 7, 2023, https://www.nea.org/nea-today/all-news-articles/gen-z-most-pro-union-generation.

12   A. J. Willingham, "How the Iconic 'Whose Streets? Our Streets!' Chant Has Been Co-Opted," September 20, 2017, https://edition.cnn.com/2017/09/19/us/whose-streets-our-streets-chant-trnd/index.html.

13   Walter Benjamin, "The Author as Producer," trans. John Heckman, *New Left Review* 1, no. 62 (July–August 1970).

14   Wendy Brown, "Resisting Left Melancholia," in *Loss: The Politics of Mourning* (California: University of California Press, 2003), 458–66; Jodi Dean, "Communist Desire," in *The Ends of History* (London: Routledge, 2013), 5–22; Rodrigo Nunes, *Neither Vertical Nor Horizontal: A Theory of Political Organization* (London: Verso, 2021), 56–78.

15   Nunes, *Neither*, 245; Borriello and Jäger, *Populist*.

16   Bevins, *If We Burn*, 283–99; Nick Srnicek and Alex Williams, *Inventing the Future: Postcapitalism and a World Without Work* (London: Verso, 2015), 14.

17   Lukas Slothuus, "Antonio Gramsci and the Problem of Fatalism," in *Revolutionary Hope in a Time of Crisis*, eds. Maša Mrovlje and Alex Zamalin (New York: Routledge, 2024), 31–48.

18   T. J. Clark, "For a Left with No Future," *New Left Review* 1, no. 74 (Mar/April 2012), https://newleftreview.org/issues/ii74/articles/t-j-clark-for-a-left-with-no-future.

19   Traverso, *Left-Wing*, 9–10.

20   Mark Fisher, *Capitalist Realism* (London: Zero Books, 2009).

21   Yousef Khalil, "Neoliberalism and the Failure of the Arab Spring," *New Politics* 15, no. 3 (2015); Bayat, *Revolution*, 69–91.

22   Mansour Hussein, "From Freelance Jihad to Crony Capitalism: Al-Julani's Monopolists in Northwestern Syria," trans. Anas Al Horani, *al-Jumhuriya*,

May 24 2024, https://aljumhuriya.net/en/2024/05/24/from-freelance-jihad
-to-crony-capitalism.

23   See, for example: Shane Lopez, *Making Hope Happen: Create the Future You Want
for Yourself* (New York: Atria, 2013).

24   Rebecca Reichard, James Avey, Shane Lopez, and Maren Dollwet, "Having the
Will and Finding the Way: A Review and Meta-Analysis of Hope at Work," *Journal of Positive Psychology* 8, no. 4 (2013): 292–304.

25   Chingching Chang, "Being Inspired by Media Content: Psychological Processes
Leading to Inspiration," *Media Psychology* 26, no. 1 (2023): 72–87.

26   Mark Athitakis, "Stoicism Is More Popular Than Ever. Too Bad It's Incoherent
Now," *Washington Post*, March 28, 2024, https://www.washingtonpost.com/
books/2024/03/28/stoicism-ryan-holiday-mark-tuitert.

27   Staci M. Zavattaro, "Brand Obama: The Implications of a Branded President,"
Administrative Theory and Praxis 32, no. 1 (March 2010), 123–28.

28   Barack Obama, *The Audacity of Hope: Thoughts on Reclaiming the American Dream*
(New York: Crown Publishing, 2016).

29   Obama, *Audacity*, 27.

30   Angela Nagle, *Kill All Normies: Online Culture Wars from 4Chan and Tumblr to Trump
and the Alt-Right* (London: Zero Books, 2017).

31   Srnicek and Williams, *Inventing*, 25.

32   Francis Fukuyama, *The End of History and the Last Man* (New York: Penguin
Books, 2012).

33   Andrea Wolf Institute of Jineoloji Academy, *Killing and Transforming the Dominant
Man*, January 2021, https://jineoloji.eu/en/wp-content/uploads/2021/02/
Killing-and-Transforming-the-dominant-man-booklet-en-compressed_
compressed-1.pdf.

34   Bevins, *If We Burn*, 297.

35   Nunes, *Neither*, 148.

36   Nunes, *Neither*, 23.

37   Nunes, *Neither*, 167.

38   Vladimir Lenin, *What Is To Be Done?* trans. Tim Delaney, Marxist Internet
Archive, https://www.marxists.org/archive/lenin/works/download/what-itd
.pdf, 85.

39   Internationalist Commune of Rojava, "Resistance Is Life: Welcome to the
Commune," *It's Going Down*, September 19, 2018, https://itsgoingdown.org/
welcome-to-the-commune.

40   "About Us," Internationalist Commune, https://internationalistcommune
.com/about-us.

41   For an excellent further overview of this concept and its potential application
in anarchist organizing, see "Tekmil: A Tool for Collective Reflection," *Anarchist Struggle*, April 28, 2022, https://avtonom.org/en/freenews/tekmil-tool
-collective-reflection.

42   Nunes, *Neither*, 183.

Chapter 4: "Could It Be?": The Myth of History

1   Saul Newman, "Post-Anarchism and Radical Politics Today," in *Post-Anarchism: A Reader*, eds. Duane Rousselle and Süreyyya Evren (London: Pluto, 2011), 46–68.

2   Thomas Miley, *Self-Determination Struggles: In Pursuit of the Democratic-Confederalist Ideal* (Toronto: Black Rose Books, 2023), 152–79.

3   Abdullah Öcalan, *Civilization: The Age of Masked Gods and Disguised Kings*, trans. Havin Guneser (Norway: New Compass Press, 2015); Murray Bookchin, *The Ecology of Freedom: The Emergence and Dissolution of Hierarchy* (Palo Alto: Cheshire Books, 1982).

4   Abdullah Öcalan, *The Sociology of Freedom: Manifesto for a Democratic Civilization, Vol. III*, trans. Havin Guneser (Oakland: PM Press, 2020), 293–94.

5   David Graeber, "Öcalan as Thinker: On the Unity of Theory and Practice as Form of Writing." In *Building Free Life: Dialogues with Öcalan*, ed. International Initiative (Oakland: PM Press, 2020), 167–90.

6   Graeber, "Öcalan as Thinker," 183.

7   Graeber, *Civilisation*, 10.

8   Bookchin, *Ecology*, 11.

9   Dilar Dirik, *The Kurdish Women's Movement: History, Theory, Practice* (London: Pluto, 2022).

10   Giorgio Agamben, *Homo Sacer: Sovereign Power and Bare Life*, trans. Daniel Heller-Roazen (Standford: Stanford University Press, 1995), 27.

11   Jean-Jacques Rousseau, *Discourse on the Origin of Inequality*, trans. G. Cole (Zurich: ISN, 2008), 8.

12   Bookchin, *Ecology*, 58.

13   Graeber, "Thinker."

14   Theodor Adorno and Max Horkheimer, *Dialectic of Enlightenment* (London: Verso, 2016), 1–35.

15   Abdullah Öcalan, *Liberating Life: Woman's Revolution*, trans. International Initiative (Cologne: International Initiative, 2013), 43.

16   Dirik, *Movement*, 80.

17   Nadje al-Ali and Isabel Kaser, "Beyond Feminism?: Jineolojî and the Kurdish Women's Movement," *Politics and Gender* 18, no. 1 (2022): 212–43.

18   Dirik, *Kurdish*, 95.

19   Aliza Marcus, *Blood and Belief: The PKK and the Kurdish Fight for Independence* (New York: NYU Press, 2007), 44.

20   Friedrich Nietzsche, *Beyond Good and Evil*, trans. Helen Zimmern (New York: Modern Library, 1919), 65.

21   Paolo Freire, *Pedagogy of the Oppressed*, trans. Myra Bergman Ramos (New York: Continuum, 2000).

22   As Stephen Knight and Jenny Schultz demonstrated at the Kurdish Studies Conference 2024.

23   Öcalan, *Capitalism*, 276.

24   Murray Bookchin, *Social Anarchism or Lifestyle Anarchism* (San Francisco: AK Press, 1995), 36.

25   Murray Bookchin, *Listen, Marxist!* trans. Jonas Holmgren, Marxist Internet Archive, https://www.marxists.org/archive/bookchin/1969/listen-marxist.htm, June 9, 2010; Bookchin, *Ecology*, 20.

26   Bookchin, *Ecology*, 141.

27   Nietzsche, *Beyond*, 9–10.

28   Murray Bookchin, "What Is Social Ecology?" in *Social Ecology and the Rojava Revolution*, ed. Internationalist Commune of Rojava (London: Dog Section Press, 2022), 25.

29   Harriet Allsop and Wladimir van Wilgenburg, *The Kurds of Northern Syria: Governance, Diversity and Conflicts* (London: Bloomsbury, 2019), chapter 4.

30   Richard Rorty, *Contingency, Irony and Solidarity* (Cambridge: Cambridge University Press, 1993), 3–43.

31   Bookchin, *Ecology*, 359.

32   Frans de Waal, *The Bonobo and the Atheist: In Search of Humanism among the Primates* (New York: W. W. Norton, 2014).

33   David Graeber and David Wengrow, *The Dawn of Everything: A New History of Humanity* (New York: Picador, 2023).

34   Jenni Keasden and Natalia Szarek, *Worth Fighting For: Bringing the Rojava Revolution Home* (London: Active Distribution, 2024).

35   Öcalan, *Civilization*, 88.

36   Howard Williams, "The End of History in Hegel and Marx," in *The Hegel-Marx Connection*, eds. Tony Burns and Ian Fraser (London: Palgrave Macmillan, 2000), 198–216.

37   Daniel Gaido, "The July Days," *Jacobin*, July 27, 2017, https://jacobin.com/2017/07/russian-revolution-bolshevik-party-july-days.

38   Ernst Bloch, *The Principle of Hope*, trans. Neville Plaice, Stephen Place, and Paul Knight (Cambridge, MA: MIT Press, 1986), 3: 1355–56.

39   John Holloway, "Zapatismo and the Social Sciences," *Capital and Class* 26, no. 3 (2002): 153–60.

40   Bloch, *Hope*, 3: 1175.

41   Bloch, *Hope*, 1: 205–10.

42   Bloch, *Hope*, 1: 114–78.

43   Bloch, *Hope*, 1: 87; Karl Marx, *Capital Volume 1*, trans. Samuel Moore and Edward Aveling, available at https://www.marxists.org/archive/marx/works/download/pdf/Capital-Volume-I.pdf, 127.

44   Bloch, *Hope*, 1: 4.

45   Bloch, *Hope*, 3: 1026.

46   Walter Benjamin, "Surrealism: The Last Snapshot of the European Intelligentsia," *New Left Review* 1, no. 108 (1972): 47–56.

47   Bloch, *Hope*, 1: 56.

48   Bloch, *Hope*, 1: 131; 11.

49   Bloch, *Hope*, 1: 310.

50   Steven Pinker, *The Better Angels of our Nature* (New York: Penguin Books, 2021), 292–93, 550–52.

51   Bloch, *Hope*, 1: 195.

52   Öcalan, *Sociology*, 3: 178.

53   Terry Eagleton, *Hope Without Optimism* (Charlottesville: University of Virginia Press, 2015), 95.

54   Bloch, *Hope*, 1: 367, 1371.

55   Theodor Adorno, *Minima Moralia*, trans. E. F. N. Jephcott (London: Verso, 2005), 85.

56   Rousseau, *Inequality*, 29.

57   Rousseau, *Inequality*, 49; Adorno and Horkheimer, *Dialectic*, 1–35; James Scott, *Against the Grain: A Deep History of the Earliest States* (New Haven: Yale University Press, 2017).

58   Rousseau, *Inequality*, 47.

59   Rousseau, *Inequality*, 17.

60   Josep Maria Antentas, "Daniel Bensaïd, Melancholic Strategist," *Historical Materialism* 24, no. 4 (2016): 51–106.

61   Gilles Deleuze and Felix Guattari, *Anti-Oedipus: Capitalism and Schizophrenia*, trans. Robert Hurley, Mark Seem, and Helen Lane (Minneapolis: University of Minnesota Press, 1972), 236.

62   Öcalan, *Liberating*, 31.

63   Öcalan, *Liberating*, 56.

64   Dirik, *Kurdish*, 308–319.

65   Friedrich Nietzsche, *Human, All Too Human*, trans. Alexander Harvey (Chicago: Charles Kerr and Company, 1908), 141.

Chapter 5: Apocalypse as Revelation

1   James Crossley and Alastair Lockhart, "Millenarianism," *Critical Dictionary of Apocalyptic and Millenarian Movements*, January 15, 2021, www.cdamm.org/articles/millenarianism.

2   Richard Landes, "Apocalyptic Millennialism: The Most Powerful, Volatile, Imaginary Force in Human History," in *The End(s) of Time(s)*, ed. Hans-Christian Lehner (Leiden: Brill, 2021), 358–92.

3   Richard Landes, editor, *Encyclopedia of Millennialism and Millennial Movements* (London: Routledge, 2000).

4   Abdullah Öcalan, *War and Peace in Kurdistan*, trans. International Initiative (Cologne: International Initiative, 2009), 11–15.

5   Norman Cohn, *The Pursuit of the Millennium: Revolutionary Millenarians and Mystical Anarchists of the Middle Ages* (Oxford: Oxford University Press, 1969), 74.

6   Cohn, *Pursuit*, 194.

7   Cohn, *Pursuit*, 7.

8   Margaret Owen, "The Miracle of Rojava," *UNA-UK*, March 20, 2017, https://una.org.uk/magazine/1-2017/miracle-rojava.

9   Abdullah Öcalan, "May Day Message," updated October 1, 2021, https://www.kjkonline.net/en/nivis/134.

10   "Aldar Xelîl: Şerê Efrînê şerê hebûn û nebûnê ye," *Hawar News*, March 17, 2018, https://hawarnews.com/kr/1521322380205; "Genocide in Afrin," *ANF News*, March 18, 2018, https://anfenglishmobile.com/rojava/genocide-in-afrin-25568.

11   "Crimes in Syria: The Neglected Atrocities of Afrin," ECCHR, January 18, 2024, https://www.ecchr.eu/en/case/crimes-in-syria-the-neglected-atrocities-of-afrin.

12   Rachel Hagan, "How Syria's Afrin Became Hell for Kurds," *Open Democracy*, November 11, 2020, https://www.opendemocracy.net/en/north-africa-west -asia/how-syrias-afrin-became-hell-for-kurds.

13   Cohn, *Pursuit*, 35–40.

14   Cohn, *Pursuit*, 38, 59.

15   Armenak Tokmajdan and Kheder Khaddour, "Border Nation: The Reshaping of the Syrian-Turkish Borderlands," *Carnegie Middle East Center*, March 30, 2022, https://carnegie-mec.org/2022/03/30/border-nation-reshaping-of-syrian -turkish-borderlands-pub-86758.

16   Luther Blissett, *Q*, trans. Shuan Whiteside (London: Heinemann, 2003).

17   Blissett, *Q*, 132.

18   Mark Perry, "ISIS and the Thirty Years' War," Strategy Bridge, May 10, 2016, https://thestrategybridge.org/the-bridge/2016/5/10/isis-and-the-thirty-years -war.

19   Blissett, *Q*, 225.

20   Robert Whalen, "Doomsday," *Encyclopedia*, 232.

21   Landes, "Peace of God," *Encyclopedia*, 529–30.

22   Eric Hobsbawm, *Social Bandits and Primitive Rebels* (Glencoe, IL: Free Press, 1960).

23   Cohn, *Pursuit*, 74.

24   Peter Thompson, "Ernst Bloch on Thomas Muntzer," *Spiked*, October 27, 2017, https://www.spiked-online.com/2017/10/27/ernst-bloch-on-thomas -muntzer/#.Wuwvm8gh3YJ.

25   Abdullah Öcalan, *Capitalism: The Age of Unmasked Gods and Naked Kings*, trans. Havin Guneser (Oslo: New Compass, 2009), 289.

26   Öcalan, *Capitalism*, 115.

27   Öcalan, *Capitalism*.

28   Nick Danforth, "Notes on a Turkish Conspiracy," *Foreign Policy*, October 2, 2014, https://foreignpolicy.com/2014/10/02/notes-on-a-turkish-conspiracy.

29   Michael Lazich, "Asia," *Encyclopedia*, 70.

30   Catherine Keller, "Columbus/Colon," *Encyclopedia*, 175–78.

31   Javier Villa-Flores, "Religion, Politics, and Salvation: Latin American Millenarian Movements," *Radical History Review* no. 99 (2007): 242–51.

32   Mike Davis, *Late Victorian Holocaust: El Niño Famines and the Making of the Third World* (London: Verso, 2021), 189–95.

33   Holger Jebens, ed., *Cargo, Cult and Culture Critique* (Honolulu: University of Hawaii, 2004).

34   Rojava Information Center, "Hidden Battlefields: Rehabilitating ISIS Affiliates and Building a Democratic Culture in Their Former Territories,"

December 2020, https://rojavainformationcenter.org/2020/12/hidden
-battlefields-rehabilitating-isis-affiliates-and-building-a-democratic-culture
-in-their-former-territories.

35   Friedrich Engels, "A Review of 'Past and Present' by Thomas Carlyle," trans.
Christopher Upward, Marxists.org, February 6, 1996, https://www.marxists
.org/archive/marx/works/1844/df-jahrbucher/carlyle.htm.

36   Friedrich Nietzsche, *The Antichrist*, trans. H. L. Mencken (New York: Knopf,
1921).

37   Murray Bookchin, *The Ecology of Freedom: The Emergence and Dissolution of Hierarchy* (Palo Alto: Cheshire Books, 1982), 129.

38   See, for example, Sema Gabar, "YJA Star Guerrilla Roj Argeş: Xakurkê Is a Paradise for Us," *ANF News*, May 8, 2021, https://anfenglishmobile.com/kurdistan/
yja-star-guerrilla-roj-arges-xakurke-is-a-paradise-for-us-51897.

39   Bronn Taylor, "Environmentalism," *Encyclopedia*, 251–57.

40   Graham Macklin, "The Extreme Right, Climate Change and Terrorism," *Terrorism and Political Violence* 34, no. 5 (2022): 979–96.

41   Jeff Diamant, "About Four-in-Ten US Adults Believe Humanity Is 'Living in
the End Times,'" Pew Research Center, December 8, 2022, https://www.pew
research.org/short-reads/2022/12/08/about-four-in-ten-u-s-adults-believe
-humanity-is-living-in-the-end-times.

42   Julie Ingersoll, "The Christian Reconstruction Movement in US Politics," *Oxford
Handbook Topics in Religion*, available at https://academic.oup.com/edited
-volume/41330/chapter/352334811.

43   Bookchin, *Ecology*, 72.

44   David Redles, "Holocaust," *Encyclopedia*, 322–28.

45   Michael Rubin, "It's Time to Acknowledge the PKK's Evolution," *The National
Interest*, January 25, 2019, https://www.aei.org/articles/its-time-to-acknowledge
-the-pkks-evolution.

46   Aliza Marcus, *Blood and Belief: The PKK and the Kurdish Fight for Independence* (New
York: NYU Press, 2007), 44.

47   Ali Kemal Özcan, *Turkey's Kurds: A Theoretical Analysis of the PKK and Abdullah
Öcalan* (London: Routledge, 2006), 246.

48   Sakine Cansız, *Sara: Prison Memoir of a Kurdish Revolutionary*, trans. Janet Biehl
(London: Pluto Press, 2018).

49   Rojin Mukriyan, "Women, Life, Freedom from Rojava to Rojhelat," Kurdish
Peace Institute, December 5, 2022, https://www.kurdishpeace.org/research/
womens-liberation-and-leadership/woman-life-freedom-from-rojava-to
-rojhelat-connections-and-solidarities.

50   Rubin, *Acknowledge*; Dirik, *Movement*, 72–75; Joost Jongerden, "Learning from
Defeat: Development and Contestation of the 'New Paradigm' within Kurdistan
Workers' Party (PKK)," *Kurdish Studies* 7, no. 1 (2019): 72–92.

51   Stephen Kinzer, "Rebel Kurds Back Leader in Peace Offer," *New York Times*,
June 2, 1999, https://archive.nytimes.com/www.nytimes.com/library/world/
europe/060399turkey-ocalan.html.

52 Alex Zamalin and Maša Mrovlje, *Revolutionary Hope in a Time of Crisis* (New York: Routledge, 2024), 18.

53 Rodrigo Nunes, *Neither Vertical Nor Horizontal: A Theory of Political Organization* (London: Verso, 2021), 127–58.

54 Hassan Hassan and Omar Abu Leyla, "Assad's Hidden Hand in the Uprising against the Kurds in Eastern Syria," *New Lines Magazine*, September 4, 2023, https://newlinesmag.com/argument/assads-hidden-hand-in-the-uprising -against-the-kurds-in-eastern-syria.

55 Jessica Stern and J. M. Berger, *ISIS: The State of Terror* (New York: Harper Collins, 2017), 219–31.

56 Wes Enzinna, "A Dream of Secular Utopia in ISIS's Backyard," *New York Times*, November 24, 2015, https://www.nytimes.com/2015/11/29/magazine/a-dream -of-utopia-in-hell.html; Chris den Hond, "Rojava, Utopia in the Heart of Syria's Chaos," *Orient XXI*, November 2, 2017, https://orientxxi.info/magazine/ rojava-utopia-in-the-heart-of-syria-s-chaos,2098.

57 Cohn, *Pursuit*, 146.

58 Si Shepperd, "What the Syrian Kurds Have Wrought," *The Atlantic*, October 25, 2016, https://www.theatlantic.com/international/archive/2016/10/kurds -rojava-syria-isis-iraq-assad/505037; Jan Yasin Sunca, "Growing Utopian Crack: Ten Years of the Rojava Revolution," *Jadaliya*, November 14, 2022, https://www .jadaliyya.com/Details/44581.

Chapter 6: Copium Strategies: Cynicism and Naivety

1 Bob Clampett, "What's Up Doc?" in *Draw the Looney Tunes: The Warner Bros. Character Design Manual* (San Francisco: Chronicle Books, 2005), 166.

2 Joshua Foa Dienstag, *Pessimism: Philosophy, Ethic, Spirit* (Princeton, NJ: Princeton University Press, 2006), 201–26.

3 Thomas Ligotti, *The Conspiracy Against the Human Race: A Contrivance of Horror* (New York: Hippocampus Press, 2010), 43.

4 Sigmund Freud, "Screen Memories," *The Standard Edition of the Complete Psychological Works of Sigmund Freud*, trans. James Strachey (London: Penguin Vintage Classics, 2001), 3: 299–322.

5 Friedrich Nietzsche, *Thus Spake Zarathustra*, trans. Thomas Common (New York: Modern Library, 1917), 153.

6 Richard Rorty, *Contingency, Irony, and Solidarity* (Cambridge: Cambridge University Press, 1993), 3–43.

7 Sigmund Freud, "Humor," *The Penguin Freud Reader* (London: Penguin, 2006), 563.

8 Sa'ed Atshan, "Why 'Queers for Palestine' Is Not 'Chickens for KFC,'" *Them*, December 2023, https://www.them.us/story/lgbtq-solidarity-palestine-saed -atshan.

9 Miguel Cervantes, *Don Quixote*, trans. Edith Grossman (London: Vintage, 2005), 939.

10   Ernst Bloch, *The Principle of Hope*, trans. Neville Plaice, Stephen Place, and Paul Knight (Cambridge, MA: MIT Press, 1995), 2:473.

11   Bloch, *Hope*, 3: 1355.

12   Mikhail Bakunin, *The Confession of Mikhail Bakunin: With the Marginal Comments of Tsar Nicholas I*, trans. Robert Howes (Ithaca: Cornell University Press, 1977).

13   Albert Camus, *The Rebel*, trans. Anthony Bower (London: Penguin Classics, 1951), 174.

14   Bakunin, *Confession*, 57, 88, 107.

15   Bakunin, *Confession*, 37.

16   Bakunin, *Confession*, 121.

17   Bakunin, *Confession*, 80.

18   See, for example: Cher Weixia Chen and Paul C. Gorski, "Burnout in Social Justice and Human Rights Activists: Symptoms, Causes and Implications," *Journal of Human Rights Practice* 7, no. 3 (2015): 366–90.

19   Paolo Freire, *Pedagogy of Hope*, trans. Robert Barr (New York: Continuum, 1994), 24–28.

20   Freire, *Pedagogy*, 26.

21   Arthur Borriello and Anton Jäger, *The Populist Moment: The Left After the Great Recession* (London: Verso, 2023), chapter 4.

22   John Holloway, "Zapatismo and the Social Sciences," *Capital and Class* 26, no. 3 (2002): 153–60.

23   Kariane Westrheim, "Education in a Political Context: A Study of Knowledge Processes and Learning Sites in the PKK" (PhD diss., University of Bergen, 2009).

24   Freire, *Pedagogy*.

Chapter 7: More Copium Strategies: Toward the Doomer Revolutionary

1   "The Tragedy of Afrin," Washington Kurdish Institute, August 13, 2018, https://dckurd.org/2018/08/13/the-tragedy-of-afrin.

2   Peter Zapffe, "The Last Messiah," trans. Gisle R. Tangenes, *Philosophy Now* 45 (2004): 5.

3   Ernst Bloch, *The Principle of Hope* (Cambridge, MA: MIT Press, 1995), 1: 24.

4   Leo Tolstoy, *Confession*, trans. David Patterson (New York: W. W. Norton, 1983), 54.

5   Emil Cioran, *A Short History of Decay*, trans. Richard Howard (New York: Viking Press, 1975), 83–84.

6   To be precise, these are "non-specific therapies": not sugar pills but treatments without any specific benefit to the condition in question. See Klaus Linde et al., "How Often Do General Practitioners Use Placebos and Non-Specific Interventions? Systematic Review and Meta-Analysis of Surveys," *PloS ONE* 13, no. 8 (2018).

7   Mallika Marshall, "A Placebo Can Work Even When You Know It's a Placebo," *Harvard Health Blog*, July 7, 2016, https://www.health.harvard.edu/blog/placebo-can-work-even-know-placebo-201607079926.

8   Friedrich Nietzsche, *Beyond Good and Evil*, trans. Helen Zimmern (New York: The Modern Library, 1919), 107.

9   Nietzsche, *Beyond*, 1–2.

10   Friedrich Nietzsche, *The Will to Power*, trans. Walter Kaufmann and R. J. Hollingdale (New York: Random House, 1968), 227.

11   Joshua Foa Dienstag, *Pessimism: Philosophy, Ethic, Spirit* (Princeton, NJ: Princeton University Press, 2006), 226–44.

12   Friedrich Nietzsche, *Thus Spake Zarathustra*, trans. Thomas Common (New York: Modern Library, 1917), 325.

13   Jonas Ceika, *How to Philosophize with a Hammer and Sickle: Nietzsche and Marx for the Twenty-First-Century Left* (London: Repeater, 2021), 50–67.

14   Nietzsche, *Beyond*, 9–10.

15   Nietzsche, *Beyond*, 284–85.

16   John Gray, *Straw Dogs: Thoughts on Humans and Other Animals* (London: Granta, 2002), 44–48.

17   Friedrich Nietzsche, *Ecce Homo*, trans. Anthony Ludovici (New York: MacMillan, 1911), 50.

18   Friedrich Nietzsche, *The Antichrist*, trans. H. L. Mencken (New York: Knopf, 1921), 37–38.

19   Timotheus Vermeulen and Robin Van Den Akker, "Notes on Metamodernism," *Journal of Aesthetics and Culture* 2, no. 1 (2010): 5677.

20   Rodrigo Nunes, *Neither Vertical Nor Horizontal: A Theory of Political Organization* (London: Verso, 2021), 222.

21   Richard Rorty, *Contingency, Irony and Solidarity* (Cambridge: Cambridge University Press, 1993), 61–73.

22   Paolo Freire, *Pedagogy of Hope*, trans. Robert Barr (New York: Continuum, 1994), 45.

23   Friedrich Nietzsche, *Human, All Too Human*, trans. Alexander Harvey (Chicago: Charles Kerr and Company, 1908), 169.

24   "Jineoloji and Ethics-Aesthetics," Jineolojî, January 2, 2021, https://jineoloji .eu/en/2020/04/27/jineoloji-and-ethics-aesthetics.

25   Nietzsche, *Human*, 88.

26   Søren Kierkegaard, *Either/Or*, trans. David and Lillian Swenson (Princeton, NJ: Princeton University Press), 241.

27   Jack Halberstam, *The Queer Art of Failure* (Durham, NC: Duke University, 2011).

28   Nadje al-Ali and Isabel Kaser, "Beyond Feminism? Jineolojî and the Kurdish Women's Movement," *Politics and Gender* 18, no. 1 (2022): 212–43.

29   Jineology Europe, "Open Letter to the Public About the Article 'Beyond Feminism? Jineoloji and the Kurdish Women's Freedom Movement,'" *Jadaliyya*, May 24, 2021, https://www.jadaliyya.com/Details/42819.

30   Jenni Keasden and Natalia Szarek, *Worth Fighting For: Bringing the Rojava Revolution Home* (London: Active Distribution, 2024), 92–93.

31   Halberstam, *Queer*, 9.

32   Keasden and Szarek, *Worth*, 92.

33   Kierkegaard, *Either/Or*, 2: 163.

34   Kierkegaard, *Either/Or*, 2: 143.

35   Kierkegaard, *Either/Or*.

36   Søren Kierkegaard, *Fear and Trembling*, trans. Walter Lowrie (Princeton, NJ: Princeton University Press, 1941), 12.

37   Abdullah Öcalan, quoted in Havin Guneser, *The Art of Freedom: A Brief History of the Kurdish Liberation Struggle* (Oakland: PM Press, 2021), 64.

38   Albert Camus, *Myth of Sisyphus and Other Essays*, trans. Justin O'Brien (New York: Vintage, 1991), 52.

Chapter 8: The Revolutionary Leap of Faith

1   Kierkegaard, *Either/Or*, 2:70–71.

2   Søren Kierkegaard, *Fear and Trembling*, trans. Walter Lowrie (Princeton, NJ: Princeton University Press, 1941), 17.

3   Ernst Bloch, *The Principle of Hope*, trans. Neville Plaice, Stephen Place, and Paul Knight (Cambridge, MA: MIT Press, 1995) 3:1195–204.

4   Lukas Slothuus, "Antonio Gramsci and the Problem of Fatalism," in *Revolutionary Hope in a Time of Crisis*, eds. Maša Mrovlje and Alex Zamalin (New York: Routledge, 2024), 39.

5   Kierkegaard, *Either/Or*, 2: 133–41.

6   Kirkegaard, *Either/Or*, 2: 230.

7   Søren Kierkegaard, *The Sickness unto Death*, trans. Walter Lowrie (Princeton, NJ: Princeton University Press, 1941), 20.

8   "Profile: Öcalan Inspires Loyalty, Hate," *CNN*, February 16, 1999, http://www.cnn.com/WORLD/europe/9902/16/ocalan.profile/index.html.

9   Kierkegaard, *Fear*, 62.

10   Matt Broomfield, "How a Revolution Really Feels: Rojava 8 Years On," Novara Media, July 17, 2020, https://novaramedia.com/2020/07/17/how-a-revolution-really-feels-rojava-8-years-on.

11   Sigmund Freud, *Beyond the Pleasure Principle*, trans. James Strachey (New York: W. W. Norton, 1961), 7.

12   Rebecca Solnit, *Hope in the Dark* (Chicago: Haymarket, 2016).

13   John Holloway, *Hope in Hopeless Times* (London: Pluto Press, 2012); Terry Eagleton, *Hope Without Optimism* (Charlottesville: University of Virginia Press, 2015); Saladdin Ahmed, *Revolutionary Hope After Nihilism: Marginalized Voices and Dissent* (New York: Bloomsbury, 2022).

14   Joshua Foa Dienstag, *Pessimism: Philosophy, Ethic, Spirit* (Princeton, NJ: Princeton University Press, 2006).

15   Dienstag, *Pessimism*, 261–63.

16   Thomas Ligotti, *The Conspiracy against the Human Race: A Contrivance of Horror* (New York: Hippocampus Press, 2010), 76.

17   Holloway, *Hope*, 45.

18 Ernst Bloch, *The Principle of Hope,* trans. Neville Plaice, Stephen Plaice, and Paul Knight (Cambridge, MA: MIT Press, 1995), 1: 333–35.

19 Dienstag, *Pessimism,* 221.

20 Bloch, *Hope,* 3: 1212.

21 Abdullah Öcalan, *Capitalism: The Age of Unmasked Gods and Naked Kings,* trans. Havin Guneser (Oslo: New Compass, 2009), 24.

22 Ernst Bloch, *The Spirit of Utopia,* trans. Anthony Nassar (Stanford: Stanford University Press, 2000), 168; Josep Maria Antentas, "Daniel Bensaïd, Melancholic Strategist," *Historical Materialism* 24, no. 4 (2016): 51–106.

23 Jem Bendell, "Deep Adaptation: A Map for Navigating Climate Tragedy," *IFLAS,* July 27, 2020, https://lifeworth.com/deepadaptation.pdf, 21.

24 Fyodor Dostoyevsky, *Devils,* trans. Constance Garnett (London: Wordsworth Classics, 2010).

25 Albert Camus, *The Rebel,* trans. Anthony Bower (London: Penguin Classics, 1951), 228.

26 Camus, *Sisyphus,* 22.

27 Camus, *Sisyphus,* 37.

28 Camus, *Rebel.*

29 Jean-Paul Sartre, Philippe Gavi, Pierre Victor, *Is It Right to Rebel?* trans. Adrian van den Hoven and Basil Kingstone (London: Routledge, 2019).

30 Sigmund Freud, "The Economic Problem of Masochism," *The Standard Edition of the Complete Psychological Works of Sigmund Freud,* trans. James Strachey (London: Penguin Vintage Classics, 2001), 6:157–70.

31 Azize Aslan, *Anticapitalist Economy in Rojava: The Contradictions of Revolution in the Kurdish Struggles* (Wakefield, QC: Daraja Press, 2023), 36.

32 Kierkegaard, *Either/Or,* 2: 133.

33 Mikhail Bakunin, *The Confession of Mikhail Bakunin: With the Marginal Comments of Tsar Nicholas I,* trans. Robert Howes (Ithaca: Cornell University Press, 1977), 129.

34 Friedrich Nietzsche, *Beyond Good and Evil,* trans. Helen Zimmern (New York: The Modern Library, 1919), 224.

35 Michael Hardt and Antonio Negri, *Empire* (Cambridge, MA: Harvard University Press, 2000), 413.

36 Kierkegaard, *Either/Or,* 2: 201.

37 Friedrich Nietzsche, *Human, All Too Human,* trans. Alexander Harvey (Chicago: Charles Kerr and Company, 1908), 73.

38 Nietzsche, *Human,* 92–93.

39 Karl Marx and Friedrich Engels, *Manifesto of the Communist Party,* trans. Samuel Moore, available at https://www.marxists.org/archive/marx/works/download /pdf/Manifesto.pdf, 27.

40 Ernst Bloch, *The Principle of Hope,* trans. Neville Plaice, Stephen Plaice, and Paul Knight (Cambridge, MA: MIT Press, 1986), 3: 982–84.

41 Fyodor Dostoyevsky, *The Brothers Karamazov,* trans. Constance Garnett (New York: Random House, 1900), 26.

Chapter 9: Hope After the Holocaust

1   "Hope," Wikipedia, last modified April 25, 2024, https://en.wikipedia.org/wiki/Hope.

2   Enzo Traverso, *Left-Wing Melancholia: Marxism, History, and Memory* (New York: Columbia University Press, 2016), 51–52.

3   Jean Améry, *At the Mind's Limits: Contemplations by a Survivor on Auschwitz*, trans. Sidney and Stella Rosenfeld (Bloomington: Indiana University Press, 2009), 12–20.

4   Giorgio Agamben, *Remnants of Auschwitz: The Witness and the Archive* (New York: Zone Books, 1999), 15–41.

5   Agamben, *Auschwitz*, 157.

6   David Mikics, "The Lie of Viktor Frankl," *Tablet Magazine*, September 10, 2020, https://www.tabletmag.com/sections/arts-letters/articles/viktor-frankl.

7   Timothy Pytell, "Is It OK to Criticize a Saint: On Humanizing Viktor Frankl," *Psychology Today*, https://www.psychologytoday.com/us/blog/authoritarian-therapy/201703/is-it-ok-criticize-saint-humanizing-viktor-frankl, March 31, 2017.

8   Pytell, "OK."

9   Viktor Frankl, *Man's Search for Meaning* (New York: Washington Square, 1984).

10 Pytell, "OK."

11 Frankl, *Meaning*, 133.

12 Frankl, *Meaning*, 161–79.

13 Frankl, *Meaning*, 76–77.

14 Mikics, "Lie."

15 Frankl, *Meaning*, 107.

16 Pytell, "OK."

17 Frankl, *Meaning*, 97.

18 Frankl, *Meaning*, 108.

19 Mikics, "Lie."

20 Frankl, *Meaning*, 130.

21 Mattie Kahn, "How Instagram Turned a Holocaust Memoir into a Self-Help Manifesto," *Vox*, November 28, 2022, https://www.vox.com/the-goods/23467058/mans-search-for-meaning-frankl-holocaust-memoir-wellness-instagram.

22 Frankl, *Meaning*, 94–95.

23 Annette Timm, ed., *Holocaust History and the Readings of Ka-Tzetnik* (London: Bloomsbury, 2019).

24 Dina Porat, "An Author as His Own Biographer—Ka-Tzetnik: A Man and a Tattooed Number," in *Holocaust History*, 13–37.

25 Ka-Tzetnik 135633, *Shivitti: A Vision*, trans. Eliyah Nike De-Nur and Lisa Herman (Nevada: Gateways, 1999), 13.

26 Agamben, *Auschwitz*, 20–21.

27 Frankl, *Meaning*, 64.

28 Ka-Tzetnik, quoted in *Holocaust History*, 15.

29 Uri Cohen, "Ka-Tzetnik, Primo Levi, and the Muslims," in *Holocaust History*, 153–69.

30 David Mikics, "Holocaust Pulp Fiction," *Tablet Magazine*, April 19, 2012, https://www.tabletmag.com/sections/arts-letters/articles/ka-tzetnik.

31 Annette Timm, "Testimony in Holocaust Historiography," in *Holocaust History*, 37–67; Agamben, *Auschwitz*, 12.

32 Timm, "Testimony," 44.

33 Mikics, "Pulp."

34 Ka-Tzetnik, *Shivitti*, 18.

35 Iris Roebling-Grau, "How to Understand *Shivitti*?" in *Holocaust History*, 167.

36 Ka-Tzetnik, *Shivitti*, 107.

37 Ka-Tzetnik, *Shivitti*, 106.

38 Améry, *Limits*, 9.

39 Améry, *Limits*, 9.

40 Agamben, *Auschwitz*, 41–45; Cohen, "Ka-Tzetnik," 155–56.

41 Frankl, *Meaning*, 95.

42 Cohen, "Ka-Tzetnik," 159–60; Ka-Tzetnik, *Shivitti*, 106.

43 Agamben, *Auschwitz*, 111–33.

44 Ernst Bloch, *The Principle of Hope*, trans. Neville Plaice, Stephen Plaice, and Paul Knight (Cambridge, MA: MIT Press, 1995), 2: 463.

45 Theodor Adorno, *Minima Moralia*, trans. E. F. N. Jephcott (London: Verso, 2005), 38–39.

46 Ka-Tzetnik, *Shivitti*, 15.

47 Agamben, *Auschwitz*, 169–70.

48 Roebling-Grau, "Understand *Shivitti*," 172.

49 Ka-Tzetnik, *Shivitti*, 41–43.

50 Frankl, *Meaning*, 179.

51 Porat, "Biographer," 15–31.

52 Anthony Rudolf, "Obituary: Ka-Tzetnik 135633," *Independent*, July 26, 2001, https://www.independent.co.uk/news/obituaries/katzetnik-135633-9234518.html.

53 Rudolf, "Obituary: Ka-Tzetnik 135633."

54 Améry, *Limits*, 62–73.

55 Rudolf, "Obituary: Ka-Tzetnik 135633."

56 Bloch, *Hope* (Cambridge, MA: MIT Press, 1995), 1: 3.

57 Ernst Bloch, "Hitler's Force," April 1924, GHDI, https://ghdi.ghi-dc.org/sub_document.cfm?document_id=3914.

58 Bloch, *Hope*, 2: 660–69.

59 Bloch, *Hope*, 2: 610.

60 Psalms 16: 8 (King James Version).

61 Bloch, *Hope*, 1: 9.

62 Bloch, *Hope*, 3: 1375–76.

63 Bloch, *Hope*, 2: 598–611.

64 Bloch, *Hope*, 3: 990.

Chapter 10: Hope After Death

1   Jean Améry, *At the Mind's Limits: Contemplations by a Survivor on Auschwitz*, trans. Sidney and Stella Rosenfeld (Bloomington: Indiana University Press), 100.

2   Kim Moody, "How 'Just-in-Time' Capitalism Spread Covid-19," *Spectre Journal*, April 8, 2020, https://spectrejournal.com/how-just-in-time-capitalism-spread -covid-19.

3   Zana Sidi, "Though He Escaped ISIS, Mohammed Was Burnt by Turkish Occu- pation's White Phosphorus," *ANHA*, November 26, 2019, https://hawarnews .com/en/157474650012920.

4   Anna Davies and Revan Kobane, "Injured but Not out of Action: Rojava's Mala Birîndara," Kurdish Institute of Brussels, https://www.kurdishinstitute.be/en/ injured-but-not-out-of-action-rojavas-mala-birindara.

5   David Mikics, "The Lie of Viktor Frankl," *Tablet*, September 10, 2020, https:// www.tabletmag.com/sections/arts-letters/articles/viktor-frankl.

6   Mikics, "Lie."

7   Ka-Tzetnik 135633, *Shivitti: A Vision*, trans. Eliyah Nike De-Nur and Lisa Her- man (Nevada: Gateways, 1999), xix.

8   Jenni Keasden and Natalia Szarek, *Worth Fighting For: Bringing the Rojava Revo- lution Home* (London: Active Distribution, 2024), 134.

9   Ernst Bloch, *The Principle of Hope*, trans. Neville Plaice, Stephen Place, and Paul Knight (Cambridge, MA: MIT Press, 1986), 3:1174.

10 George Starbuck, "Of Late," *Poetry Magazine*, https://www.poetryfoundation .org/poetrymagazine/poems/30436/of-late.

11 Solcyre Burga and Simmone Shah, "The History of Self-Immolation as Politi- cal Protest," *Time*, March 6, 2024, https://time.com/6835364/self-immolation -history-israel-hamas-war.

12 Terry Eagleton, *Hope Without Optimism* (Charlottesville: University of Virginia Press, 2015), 95.

13 Enzo Traverso, *Left-Wing Melancholia: Marxism, History, and Memory* (New York: Columbia University Press, 2016), xv.

14 Giorgio Agamben, *Remnants of Auschwitz: The Witness and the Archive* (New York: Zone Books, 1999), 25.

15 Agamben, *Auschwitz*, 28.

16 Eagleton, *Hope Without Optimism*, 123.

Chapter 11: Hope in the Climate Apocalypse

1   Damian Carrington, "Justin Welby Apologises for Likening Climate Threat to Nazis," *Guardian*, November 1, 2021, https://www.theguardian .com/uk-news/2021/nov/01/justin-welby-apologises-for-likening-climate -threat-to-nazis. "Extinction Rebellion: Co-founder Apologises for Holocaust Remarks," *BBC*, November 21, 2019, https://www.bbc.com/news/world-europe -50501941.

2   Mark Levene, "The Holocaust Paradigm as Paradoxical Imperative in the Century of Anthropogenic Omnicide," *Genocide Studies and Prevention: An International Journal* 16, no. 1 (2022): 76–92.

3   Levene, "Holocaust," 84.

4   Levene, "Holocaust," 80.

5   Traverso, *Left-Wing*, 15.

6   Levene, "Holocaust," 80.

7   Jeremy Brecher, *Against Doom: A Climate Insurgency Manual* (Oakland: PM Press, 2017).

8   Paul Kingsnorth and Dougald Hine, *Uncivilisation: The Dark Mountain Manifesto*, 2009, https://library.uniteddiversity.coop/Media_and_Free_Culture/Uncivilisation-The_Dark_Mountain_Manifesto.pdf, 6.

9   Maria Ojala et al., "Anxiety, Worry, and Grief in a Time of Environmental and Climate Crisis: A Narrative Review," *Annual Review of Environment and Resources* 46 (2021): 35–58.

10 Janet Fiskio, "Apocalypse and Ecotopia: Narratives in Global Climate Change Discourse," *Race, Gender and Class* 19, no. 1/2 (2012), 12–36.

11 Jem Bendell, "Deep Adaptation: A Map for Navigating Climate Tragedy," *IFLAS*, https://lifeworth.com/deepadaptation.pdf, July 27, 2020.

12 Thomas Nicholas, Galen Hall, and Colleen Schmidt, "The Faulty Science, Doomism, and Flawed Conclusions of 'Deep Adaptation,'" *Open Democracy*, July 4, 2020, https://www.opendemocracy.net/en/oureconomy/faulty-science-doomism-and-flawed-conclusions-deep-adaptation.

13 Bendell, *Adaptation*, 14.

14 Jem Bendell, "Regenerative Farming—It's Time," jembendell.com, August 11, 2023, https://jembendell.com/2023/08/11/regenerative-farming-its-time.

15 Andreas Malm, *How to Blow Up a Pipeline: Learning to Fight in a World on Fire* (London: Verso, 2020).

16 Michael Dowd, "Post-Doom," https://postdoom.com.

17 "UNPRECEDENTED: APIB Denounces Bolsonaro before the ICC, in The Hague, for Indigenous Genocide," APIB, August 9, 2021, https://apiboficial.org/2021/08/09/unprecedented-apib-denounces-bolsonaro-before-the-icc-in-the-hague-for-indigenous-genocide.

18 The Red Nation, *The Red New Deal: Indigenous Action to Save our Earth* (Philadelphia: Common Notions, 2021), 14–20.

19 Malm, *Pipeline*.

20 Internationalist Commune of Rojava, *Make Rojava Green Again* (London: Dog Section Press, 2018).

21 Bendell, *Adaptation*, 15; Tommy Lynch, "Why Hope Is Dangerous When It Comes to Climate Change," *Slate*, July 25, 2017, https://slate.com/technology/2017/07/why-climate-change-discussions-need-apocalyptic-thinking.html.

22 Malm, *Pipeline*, chapter 3.

23 Michael Dowd, "Collapse and Denial: Inevitable and Unstoppable," *The New Ecozoic Reader* no. 7, June (2023): 22–27.

24   Bendell, *Adaptation*.

25   Bendell, *Adaptation*, 13; Jem Bendell, instagram, https://www.instagram .com/p/CtdxGZnsSPV.

26   Kingsnorth and Hine, *Uncivilisation*, 13.

27   Andrea Wolf Institute of Jineoloji Academy, *Killing and Transforming the Dominant Man*, January 2021, https://jineoloji.eu/en/wp-content/uploads/2021/02/ Killing-and-Transforming-the-dominant-man-booklet-en-compressed_ compressed-1.pdf.

28   Kingsnorth and Hine, *Uncivilisation*, 19.

29   Murray Bookchin, "Social Ecology versus Deep Ecology: A Challenge for the Ecology Movement," *Green Perspectives: Newsletter of the Green Program Project* 4–5 (1987), available at http://www.naturaepsiche.it/fileadmin/img/M._Book- chin_Social_Ecology_versus_Deep_Ecology_A_Challenge_for_the_Ecology_ Movement.pdf, 7.

30   Bendell, *Adaptation*, 17.

31   Bloch, *Hope*, 1: 67–70.

32   Bloch, *Hope*, 1: 11.

33   Abdullah Öcalan, *Social Ecology and Democratic Confederalism*, trans. Michael Schiffman and Havin Guneser (Rojava, Syria: Make Rojava Green Again, 2020), 3–6.

34   Dana Fisher, "Apocalyptic Optimism Could be the Antidote for Climate Fatal- ism," *Time*, January 24, 2024, https://time.com/6565499/apocalyptic-optimism -climate-change.

35   Water for Rojava, *A Report from the International Water Forum held in Hasakah, North and East Syria*, November 30, 2021, https://mesopotamia.coop/wp-content /uploads/2021/11/NES_Water_Forum_Report_2021.pdf.

36   Neil Davidson, "Walter Benjamin and the Classical Marxist Tradition," *Interna- tional Socialism* 2, no. 121 (2009).

37   Kingsnorth and Hine, *Uncivilisation*, 19.

Conclusion: Utopian Nihilism

1   Bertolt Brecht, *Collected Poems*, trans. Tom Kuhn and David Constantine (New York: Liveright, 2018), 316.

2   "A Real Revolution Is a Mass of Contradictions," Libcom, March 2017, https://libcom.org/article/real-revolution-mass-contradictions-interview -plan-c-member-rojava.

3   Traverso, *Left-Wing Melancholia: Marxism, History, and Memory* (New York: Columbia University Press, 2016), 32.

4   Friedrich Nietzsche, *The Gay Science*, trans. Josephine Nauckhoff (Cambridge: Cambridge University Press, 2008), 192.

5   Traverso, *Left-Wing*, 233; Josep Maria Antenas, "Daniel Bensaïd, Melancholic Strategist," *Historical Materialism* 24, no. 4 (2016).

6   Antenas, "Bensaïd," 96.

7   Alexander Pope, *An Essay on Man: Epistle 1* (emphasis added), available at https://www.poetryfoundation.org/poems/44899/an-essay-on-man-epistle-i.

8   "Terrorists Raise Flag of PKK Leader Öcalan in Newly Liberated Raqqa," *Daily Sabah*, October 20, 2017, https://www.dailysabah.com/war-on-terror/2017/10/20/terrorists-raise-flag-of-pkk-leader-Öcalan-in-newly-liberated-raqqa.

9   Ernst Bloch, *The Principle of Hope*, trans. Neville Plaice, Stephen Place, and Paul Knight (Cambridge, MA: MIT Press, 1986), 1: 444.

10   Dante Alighieri, *Dante's Inferno*, trans. Henry Francis Cary (Chicago: Charles C. Thompson, 1901), 16.

11   *Hell on Earth: The Fall of Syria and the Rise of ISIS*, dir. Sebastian Junger and Nick Quested (US: NGC Networks, 2017).

Index

AK PRESS is small, in terms of staff and resources, but we also manage to be one of the world's most productive anarchist publishing houses. We publish close to twenty books every year, and distribute thousands of other titles published by like-minded independent presses and projects from around the globe. We're entirely worker run and democratically managed. We operate without a corporate structure—no boss, no managers, no bullshit.

The **FRIENDS OF AK PRESS** program is a way you can directly contribute to the continued existence of AK Press, and ensure that we're able to keep publishing books like this one! Friends pay $25 a month directly into our publishing account ($30 for Canada, $35 for international), and receive a copy of every book AK Press publishes for the duration of their membership! Friends also receive a discount on anything they order from our website or buy at a table: 50% on AK titles, and 30% on everything else. We have a Friends of AK ebook program as well: $15 a month gets you an electronic copy of every book we publish for the duration of your membership. *You can even sponsor a very discounted membership for someone in prison.*

Email **friendsofak@akpress.org** for more info, or visit the website: **https://www.akpress.org/friends.html**.

There are always great book projects in the works—so sign up now to become a Friend of AK Press, and let the presses roll!